THE EAST SIDE OF ADDICTION

D0815828

James DiReda, Henry Grosse, and Jack Maroney

ISBN: 0692565574
ISBN 13: 9780692565575

Indeed, I believe, if we take habitual drunkards as a class, their heads and their hearts will bear an advantageous comparison with those of any other class. There seems ever to have been a proneness in the brilliant and warm-blooded to fall into this vice. The demon of intemperance ever seems to have delighted in sucking the blood of genius and of generosity. What one of us but can call to mind some dear relative, more promising in youth than all his fellows, who has fallen a sacrifice to his rapacity? He ever seems to have gone forth, like the Egyptian angel of death, commissioned to slay if not the first, the fairest born of every family.
—Abraham Lincoln

PREFACE

If you live in America, you are likely aware of the opioid drug epidemic that is ending the lives of many of our youth and contributes to many accidental deaths, which is now the third leading cause of death in the United States. Deaths from drug overdose have been rising steadily over the past two decades and have become the leading cause of injury death in the United States. According to the Centers for Disease Control and Prevention (CDC), every day in the United States, 113 people die from drug overdose, and another 6,748 are treated in emergency departments (ED) for the misuse or abuse of drugs. Nearly nine out of ten poisoning deaths are caused by drugs. This epidemic has prompted a long-overdue national awareness of the disease of addiction, its cost to society, its treatment, and our attitudes toward this chronic and debilitating disease. Thanks in part to people and grassroots movements such as Joanne Petersen's Learn2Cope, the parents' support group organization; the Mark Wahlberg Youth Foundation awareness film *If Only*, produced by Jim Wahlberg, Chris Herren and the Herren Project; and documentaries such as Greg Williams's *Anonymous People,* and Bess O'Brien's *The Hungry Heart,* the conversation has shifted to a more meaningful dialogue focused on finding solutions instead of assigning blame.

During the 1980s, the nation witnessed the crack cocaine epidemic and the introduction one of the more potent and deadly designer drugs, the morphine derivative fentanyl, then called China White. This "new" drug caused many overdose deaths and resulted in entire neighborhoods falling to the scourge called drug addiction. But you'd be mistaken if you thought this had never happened in America before. In the 1960s, a tidal wave of illicit and dangerous drugs swept through neighborhoods across the country, striking communities little prepared to defend themselves. One of those neighborhoods was the one we grew up in: Shrewsbury Street, a blue-collar neighborhood on the East Side of Worcester, Massachusetts.

At the start of the 1960s, the Street, as most of us called it, was a close-knit neighborhood of triple-decker houses occupied by first-generation immigrants, their children, and their grandchildren. Tradition still held sway over the largely conservative enclave. But with the arrival of drugs, tradition would be upended, and a neighborhood largely destroyed. *The East Side of Addiction* tells the story of the Street and of a group of friends swept up in the storm of addiction. Some were lost forever. But those who survived have a story to tell—and we believe it's one worth hearing.

Telling such a story isn't easy. After all, it's been in the making for over half a century with uncountable characters, plots, and subplots. And for us personally, there's an element of risk in publicly identifying ourselves as addicts and writing about things we are not proud of. But for us, there is only one way to share our story: to tell the truth, simply, powerfully, and without holding back. To tell as much of it as we can—the sad parts, the funny parts, the brutal, the bitter, the sweet, and the tragic parts. In sharing our story, we hope other people can learn from it—the families of those suffering from addiction, the people suffering it themselves, and those in recovery, who are trying to change or who have already changed their lives.

In some ways, the story of the Street and its inhabitants is not unique. We all know that drugs create problems in our society. We all know that addicts exist. We all know that some get clean and some don't, that some recover from their illness and some die. But it is only through the stories of particular individuals that we can begin to see those suffering from the disease of addiction not just as "those people" but fully as human beings in need of help. Only then can we begin to heal the shame and drive away the stigma that for so many stands in the way of recovery.

The East Side of Addiction is a story filled with ordinary people, people who, in the beginning, wanted the same things from life that everyone wants—a home, a good job, happiness, and love. Unfortunately, the environment they grew up in and their particular human frailties or genetic disposition combined to push those multiple desires aside in favor of one desire: to blot out the pain and insecurity of life with drugs.

That story of survival is one of culture, love, relationships, friends, families, tradition, and destruction. It's a story of sadness and laughter as well as heartache, success, losses, and gains. Most of all, it's a story of lifelong relationships and how friendship, mutual support, hope, faith, and the power of the spirit can help rebuild shattered lives. Not all of the characters in this story survived. Those who did suffered all the losses that go hand in hand with addiction: the loss of jobs, careers, friends, and loved ones; the loss of opportunity and potential; and, most devastating of all, the loss of self. As you read this book, please remember that its central message is not one of suffering but one of endurance and redemption. In the book, we have inserted what we hope to be thought provoking passages on our understanding of addiction, some alternative viewpoints and a few interesting correlations based on new findings in science and our collective experience. It is our sincere hope that this book will help people with addiction—and their families and friends—to make that kind of change.

—James DiReda, Henry Grosse, and Jack Maroney

CHAPTER ONE

And then there was darkness. Spiraling downward was no longer just a metaphor for Jack's life when he felt the chill of cold steel pressed against his temple. Seemingly from far away, an angry voice echoed in his ear, "Stop or I'll blow your head off!" Suddenly, Jack's descent was interrupted, but only for a brief moment, before the fall began again.

As a kid growing up on Shrewsbury Street in Worcester, Massachusetts, Jack built a reputation for being fleet of foot—perhaps it was nature's way of compensating for his diminutive stature, which had frustrated him during his early years. He had often relied on this quickness to get him out of precarious situations, but this time, the stakes were higher.

In his haste to escape the clutches of the fast-closing-in Massachusetts state police trooper and oblivious to the gunshots being fired behind him, Jack had unwittingly catapulted himself into what appeared to be safety—thick woods and their enveloping blackness. But the dark held its own dangers—a steep, cliff-like embankment that Jack couldn't see. At full speed, he'd launched himself into the air and onto a tree, nearly thirty feet above the ground. Implausibly, the trooper had managed to jump right along with him, grasp him in a bear hug, and press the gun against his head. Together, they clung to the groaning branches. He heard— or imagined he heard—a terse, furious voice.

"Go ahead. Make my day, punk."

A terrifying, drug-induced psychosis raged inside Jack's skull, and he wondered if he was hallucinating. Was this for real, or was it the coke? Was this a *Dirty Harry* movie character or a real cop crushing him in his arms? A figment of his imagination or a real gun barrel pressed against his temple? Throughout most of Jack's drug-addicted adult life, there'd been no clear demarcation between fact and fiction, but this part was fact. Jack was perched in a tree, thirty feet up in the air, in the arms of a state trooper who was pressing a revolver against his head. It was almost funny enough to laugh about, had it not been for his terror. And then there was an ominous crack of a breaking branch, and the bottom dropped out.

Like pinballs in a machine from the I&T Vending Company on Worcester's East Side, Jack and the trooper fell, descending magically, almost comically, in starts and stops. They hit one branch, changed direction, and bounced to another, turning, pausing, and falling again. Jack grunted as a branch slammed into his ribs; he tried to cover his face, but the trooper held his arms down. They met the earth with a tooth-jarring slam, and Jack heard the breath pop out of the trooper's lungs with a sharp huff. He no longer felt the pressure of the gun barrel pressed against his head or the iron-hard grasp he'd been wrapped in during their drop. The trooper had absorbed the full impact of the fall, with Jack's weight providing the necessary energy to stun him into temporary unconsciousness.

Instinctively, as if Jack had been trained in paratrooper school, he rolled off the motionless trooper and ran deep into the woods.

His chest was heaving, and his heart raced to the limits of its capacity. His head hammered as if it were going to explode.

Just minutes ago, Jack had been blissfully stoned, dreamily anticipating a night of eroticism while sitting in his car waiting for one of the dancers from Pudgy's, a gentlemen's nightclub, to finish her show or, as she preferred to call it, her performance. Jack had stayed in the car while his friend, Joey, went into the club to tell Crystal, if that was even her real name, that Jack was waiting outside.

Jack had been awake the usual three or four days snorting (or sniffing—the terminology depended on how refined present company was) cocaine. The coke brought euphoria but other effects, too: an uncomfortable edginess and paranoia that Jack usually ameliorated with periodic infusions of methadone and/or Percodan.

Tonight, it seemed, would be a good night—one with drugs in hand and a party in the offing. And when Crystal arrived, it would only get better. But suddenly, Jack's thoughts of partying were interrupted by intense high beams searing through the rear window of his mother's 1986 Chevrolet, a car he borrowed whenever he sneaked back into Worcester to visit his old haunts.

A state police cruiser had pulled up behind him; in the rearview mirror, Jack saw the trooper get out of the car and walk slowly and cautiously toward him. Jack's heart sank, and he struggled to hold back the conditioned fear that accompanied any interaction with the law. There were plenty of reasons for that fear. Most drug addicts are always at odds with the police, their lives constantly controlled by finding the ways and the means to get more drugs; virtually all of those means are illegal. Jack's anxiety was magnified by the knowledge that there were warrants out for his arrest and that directly underneath his seat was a loaded Smith & Wesson .38, a handgun that, until that night, had only been fired at tin cans.

"License and registration" was the state trooper's way of saying hello. Jack handed the cop his mother's registration and his fake driver's license. Not really the best thought-out deception but good enough for a coked-out drug addict.

"Get out of the car," ordered the trooper, and the evening's prospects rapidly dimmed.

Slowly, Jack backed away from the car, trying to put some distance between the trooper and himself. Jack watched as the trooper reached under the Chevrolet's front seat, and then he bolted. Almost instantly, the trooper followed in hot pursuit, waving Jack's Smith and Wesson in his hand. Streaking toward the woods at full speed, Jack heard a gunshot rip the night open. His heart surged with fear; he waited for a bullet to slam into his back, and when one didn't, he ran even faster.

⊶⊷

Aching from his fall from the tree, Jack stumbled through the woods. At least for now, the trooper was far behind him. But leaning against a tree, unable to catch his breath or put together a rational thought, Jack remained paralyzed in a world that had little connection to reality. Lights resembling the aurora borealis flashed in the distance; they were barely discernible through the dark thicket. As the fog in his mind began to lift, Jack realized that the eerie shimmers belonged to a small army of state police cars. Physically and mentally, Jack was exhausted, a deer trapped in the headlights of an oncoming car. His mind racing, he desperately searched for a way to escape. His first thought was to bury himself under a pile of leaves. That had worked in that *Rambo* movie, or something. *Please*, he prayed, pulling the damp leaves over him. *Just please. This one time.* He buried his legs first, then his trunk, and finally his face. The scent of leaves brought back a flash of his childhood: Jack and his friends running to leap into the tall piles of colored leaves in the yards of Merrifield Street. The image calmed him; slowly, Jack began to catch his breath and regain his senses. But calm soon became a double-edged sword, as the gravity of his situation became undeniable.

Still, there was hope. For the first time he could remember, Jack listened to total silence. There was no thumping party music, no revving car motors or coke-induced braggadocio, no sound of his own voice wrapped in a tangle of lies. It was peaceful, if only for the moment. But the peace wouldn't last. Little did Jack know that the state police had developed and refined extensive tactics in the art of search and rescue. Even less did he realize how voracious the brotherhood in blue could be once gunfire has been exchanged. No one but Jack and the trooper who pulled the trigger knew who'd fired that shot. Later, Jack would be charged with attempted murder to save the trooper the embarrassment of admitting to firing at an unarmed junkie who was fleeing in terror, an act that could have had repercussions of its own.

Quietly and in blackness, Jack's pursuers came on. First, he heard the rustling in the brush and the crunching of twigs under foot. His heart picked up speed again and with it came fear and the voice of self-loathing. So *how about it, Mr. Big Shot? Look at what you made of yourself. A fucking idiot, that's what, buried in a pile of leaves like a scared little kid.* And then he heard the steps coming closer, the whine of a search dog. He prayed, but it was for nothing; the dog's panting grew deafening in his ear. The last flicker of hope disappeared when he felt the dog's foul breath warm against his cheek, the dog's nose and large canine incisors a mere inch from his face. The next sensation was even more unsettling, as once again the steel barrel of a larger-than-life handgun was pressed hard against his skull. Two things were certain: Jack was no Rambo, and this incident was not going to have a Hollywood ending.

In one of his psychology courses, Jack had heard it explained that the brain operates much like a computer, and that a brain under the influence of drugs, especially for extended periods, is like a computer taken over by bad software. Once you take away the drugs, most of the aberrant behavior goes away, but data is lost. In this experience, that analogy would be both accurate and fortuitous. Jack was about to experience inordinate amounts of pain and suffering, including things he would need to forget in order to survive and stay sane.

What Jack remembers today is not pleasant: being unceremoniously handcuffed, dragged from the woods rather briskly, and slammed roughly into the backseat of a state police cruiser, where the interrogation began immediately. Jack knew how the good cop/bad cop thing worked, but apparently, the good cop had called in sick.

"How dare you fuckin' shoot at a trooper!" A voice emphatically shouted from the front of the car.

"What? How could I shoot a trooper? I don't even have a gun!" Jack sniffled a reply.

"Don't lie to me, you scumbag! Wait till we get you back to the barracks."

At the Grafton State Police Barracks, things went from bad to worse. Jack's pleas of innocence went unheard. He was escorted into the basement, stripped, and cuffed to the leg of a steel table that was bolted into the cement floor. Deleting both the expletives and the gory details, Jack was warmly greeted by a procession of well-wishers who all seemed to take great pleasure in acquainting his rib cage with their long-handled flashlights while reminding him that shooting at a state trooper was not a good idea. It wasn't long before Jack both felt and understood their meaning. After the first few rounds, Jack gave up professing his innocence: no one was buying. Not that he blamed them.

At the end of that seemingly endless receiving line, there was silence. Jack lay on the floor panting, pain shooting through his rib cage with every shallow breath. To make matters worse, he began to dread the arrival of a new day, which he knew would usher in the pangs of drug withdrawal.

Jack was still naked when he was finally led into a cell and advised of his right to one phone call. Temporary bail had been set at $1,000. With that, a glimmer of hope began to resurface. A thousand bucks wasn't that much. Jack would have called his lawyer, except no lawyer was going to come down in the middle of the night with a thousand dollars, and truthfully, he really didn't have a lawyer to call. Jack desperately needed someone to come down with the cash to bail him out before the first flu-like symptoms of withdrawal began—and just as importantly, before he appeared before a judge who would likely be informed of his outstanding federal parole violation, thereby eliminating any chance of a reasonable bail and quick release and consigning him to another cold-turkey withdrawal.

There is an old adage that talks about "counting all your true friends on one hand," but at this stage of his addiction, Jack couldn't count them on one finger; he had scammed everybody he knew until they had all cut him off cold. There was only one person who would make the sacrifice of getting out of bed in the middle of the night, answering the telephone, scraping up a thousand dollars in cash, and coming to the barracks in the predawn hours.

Jack dialed the number he knew all too well; he could picture the phone on the wall in the kitchen of their three-decker on Merrifield Street. "Ma," he said when his mother answered, "don't ask any questions. Just get Patrick, a thousand dollars, and come down to the state police barracks."

Jack's father had been dead for many years, and trouble was no stranger to his mother when it came to her eldest son. His mother and his brother, Patrick, were all that was left of his immediate family, and there was no need or time to answer a lot of questions.

"Where are you, Jackie?" his mother whispered back uneasily.

"Grafton, Ma. Hurry." Jack could not see beyond his immediate need for release. So wrapped up in the circumstances of the situation, he was unable to sense the fear and dread in his mother's voice during their brief, middle-of-the-night phone conversation, and he was just as oblivious to the pain his addiction was causing her. He had reached the point where everything was about himself and his addiction.

"Look under the dresser in the bedroom," Jack said in hushed tones, not wanting to be heard. "There's five thousand dollars taped underneath the bottom drawer."

⊨+ +⊨

Back in the cold, damp cell, Jack shivered and anxiously awaited the arrival of his mother. He knew that despite the innumerable heartaches he had caused her, she could only see him as the baby she once held in her arms, the son who had once had so much promise.

As he waited, the severity of the situation began to sink in, and Jack's thoughts raced through a myriad of scenarios. He started to dread the inevitable disappearance of the darkness and the lightening of the sky. It was sure to be a miserable morning, made even worse without the fortification of his daily dose of narcotics. He sat naked, bruised, and beaten on a sliver of a mattress covering a cold slab of steel. He faced God knows how many serious felony charges. Yet, he couldn't concentrate on anything except how he was going to get that next fix.

In the world of self-help, hitting an addiction bottom often is described as "the state of having things get worse faster than you can lower your standards." Jack was up against that moment, yet obsession still ruled. The drugs were the key, and Jack had to get them.

Time dragged unmercifully. Dawn's first glimmers of light only served to increase Jack's uneasiness. That anxiety would melt away

8

if he could only get a few more lines of coke or another one hundred milligrams of methadone, but he needed to get out of jail first. His despair was reinforced by the words from a Cat Stevens song, but instead of "morning has broken," this morning *was* broken. Little did Jack know just how broken it was.

In a strange sort of inverse proportionality, as the light inside his cell grew brighter, Jack's hopes grew dimmer. Where was Ma? He needed to get out of here and now. Something was terribly wrong.

Already, Jack had planned a few moves ahead. Once he made bail, he would default on his court appearance, get high, and scurry back to New York City, where he had been hiding for the last several months, trying to avoid arrest on his federal warrant. This temporary roadblock was just another unfortunate instance of being in the wrong place at the wrong time, something that seemed to happen with great frequency. But if Ma didn't bring the money, and Jack went to court, he knew that no bail would be set. Or, if one was set, it would be too high for him to make quickly, and he would be remanded into federal custody immediately.

As sunlight streamed in through the opaque window, Jack's despair grew deeper. It is no coincidence that the father of modern psychology, Carl Jung, coined the term "hopelessness" when giving a prognosis to the prominent industrialist Rowland Hazard during his yearlong treatment and subsequent relapse for alcoholism. No one has the uncanny capacity for swinging between raging optimism and utter hopelessness like an addict does. Jack was in a perfect storm, and he knew it. If Ma didn't arrive, he would be forever lost at sea.

Suddenly, without warning, the cell door opened. In flew a single deck shoe, now caked in mud, Jack's torn, dirt-stained trousers, and a tattered yellow polo shirt. Whatever jewelry Jack was wearing had mysteriously—or not so mysteriously—disappeared. He had left his rented hotel room the day before dressed like a high roller from *Miami Vice*, complete with the usual gold accompaniments that a typical drug dealer might display. The camouflage sometimes worked; looking at Jack, others would see a man who had it made. They would not see the feelings Jack kept hidden: his complete lack of self-identity and self-esteem. Jack tried to muster a sliver of dignity, but he couldn't hide the truth from himself. Ma wasn't coming, and he was alone. And although he couldn't see it in the clear morning light, his life, as he had lived it, was about to end. Thank God.

CHAPTER TWO

"How did a sharp guy like me end up in a place like this?" JD thought, sitting in a stiff, hard-back steel chair and staring out the windows of the Worcester State Hospital dayroom. He had been there a few days, and the fog was starting to lift, but he still felt woozy from the methadone they were giving him to detox. This was his first attempt at any kind of treatment for his heroin addiction, and it was a completely new world.

Through the bars, he saw the grounds of the hospital, a massive gothic complex of quarried stone and slate shingles surrounded by breathtakingly beautiful forests and fields. Opened in 1833 as Massachusetts's first hospital for the mentally ill, it had been known by various names over the years, including Bloomingdale Asylum, Worcester Insane Hospital, and Worcester Lunatic Asylum, but the profile of the facility's residents had changed little over time. Simply put, they were people whom society chose to shut away, those who, for one reason or another, had been deemed unfit for the company of others. JD was only the latest in the procession.

Locked in with a sad and lost group of fellow addicts trying to find their way, he felt suffocated by despair and defeat, a feeling magnified by the drab and sterile building with its chipping, institutional-green walls; its antiquated light fixtures, plumbing, and bathroom tiles; and its ancient, drafty window sashes. A sagging mattress atop squeaky steel springs was the only furniture in his shabby room. The place reeked of bodily fluids, antiseptics, cigarette smoke, and vanquished hope. It was anybody's definition of hell, and despite the presence of scores of other residents, JD faced it alone.

His head throbbing, he stared out at the grassy fields and beautiful old trees, watching the mentally ill patients aimlessly wander the grounds and the parking lots and congregate below the windows, near the entrance, chain-smoking and bumming butts from anyone who passed by.

Life was funny. As a child, JD had joined his friends when they left the confines of Worcester's East Side neighborhood to roam the grounds of this very place, climbing the trees and collecting wild chestnuts, which they called horse cobblers, or ice skating on the tiny pond behind the building in which he was now imprisoned. And now? This was crazy; it was someone's idea of a cruel joke. Or maybe it was payback for all those times that he and his childhood friends had made fun of the mental patients living here. He vividly recalled joining Joe A. and Stevie in taunting one very large and scary patient, getting him to chase them, running to safety, laughing, and desperately trying to catch their breath, without thinking about what it might be like to live here or to be that poor tortured soul.

Still, the memory gave JD pause. This was a place for crazy people—but not for him. He liked to get high and drunk, but didn't everyone? There was nothing wrong with his brain, was there? Most times, he thought he was quite normal, whatever that meant for an addict. However, when the beast called to be fed, he fed it. When it was hungry, he lied, cheated, stole, and sold anything of any value, including his soul, to satisfy it. Was that crazy? His thoughts raced. He was overwhelmed by his current life situation and the increasing fear of what was happening to him. But there he sat, waiting. Waiting for the next dose of methadone to help take the edge off, and then what? Wait some more? For what?

As JD waited, one thought returned again and again. *What went wrong? This wasn't what I planned for my life. I'm smarter than this, and I had it more together than this. How could this be* me *sitting here?*

But the sad reality was that it was JD, and this train wreck of a life was his. It was March 1985, and he was thirty-three years old. He had been back in Worcester for the past year trying to shake his opiate habit and get a handle on his life, which had proved to be far easier said than done. He had been living and working in Las Vegas since 1975, sparring with his addiction, which had started in his early adolescence. He managed to stay on his feet, though, and not totally succumb to it; although at times, he came close.

During his early years in Vegas, JD had been able to stay afloat. He could always find work, and in turn, he always had the means to drink and drug. He was able to avoid the "serious" drugs like cocaine and heroin, relying on alcohol, marijuana, or hash and an assortment of pills to get his buzz. It seemed that as long as he stayed away from certain drugs, he did all right. But this last time, opiates and heroin had taken him down hard. He fled Vegas after playing his last trump card and blowing what little he had, returning home to nurse his wounds and try to recover.

Once, JD had dreamed of an easy life, the big score that would make everything easy. By the time he came back from Vegas, only a sliver of that dream remained. What happened to it? he wondered. And what happened to me, that sharp guy who thought he could shake and move with the best of them?

What had happened was that the beast had gotten hungry again, and he'd had no choice but to feed it. Not a lot at first, but like any addict, the progression of his disease dictated the amount he used and how frequently. He tried to maintain some semblance of control, but it was like trying to stop the tide; it rose to his neck and then beyond.

He had managed to con his way into the family business (again), probably because his family members were the only ones who would tolerate his antics. But he was unable to work without his daily dose of alcohol, heroin, and any other type of opiate he could get his hands on. In order to support that daily habit, he needed a source of heavy cash, and the money Dad paid him wasn't enough. As usual, he'd resorted to stealing, borrowing, and lying to his family to get the money. They'd tolerated it for as long as they could, but the end had come. Soon, he was unemployed, living at his mom's, paying no rent, and sponging off anyone he could.

What a pathetic existence, he thought, as he sat there replaying his life, one horrible scene after another. It was a terrifying feeling to know that he was at the end of the line, and he had no cards left to play. If only he had another ace in the hole, he'd get his ass out of there and back down to Florida, he desperately told himself. But the sad reality was that he had no aces left, and he had nothing in Florida, either, other than memories. He flashed back to living there, working on the beach parking cars or as a bellman at one of the resort hotels. Things were good, he remembered. He'd partied like a madman but not with heroin or opiates. He could survive as long as he steered clear of those.

What JD couldn't see in Florida, in Vegas, or in a locked psych unit was that everything—even what he considered the good times—was all part of his progressive condition, and everything—even the alcohol and marijuana—played a role in his eventual decline. What he couldn't recognize yet was that he merely substituted drugs, changing his preference based on availability, finances, and his living conditions. He was always using something. He was never totally abstinent, something he hadn't been since his adolescent days back on the East Side. Short periods of sobriety came when he was in boot camp as part of his military training or in jail, but he had never willingly stopped using on his own.

Worst of all, every time he started up again, things got worse. He had been losing control of his drug and alcohol use since adolescence, and he was now at the end of his rope. He was totally out of control. He could no longer pick and choose when he would use, or what he would use, or how much. And he definitely had lost control over the outcome of his partying. He'd ended up blacked out or in emergency rooms or jail.

JD's life was like a runaway train, heading for a crash, but he just couldn't see it. Others could, though, and they tried to help him. But he couldn't see through his denial, which was a major part of his illness. He tap-danced, made excuses, rationalized, and justified his behavior as long as he could, until all of his supporters walked away, and the bottom fell out. Here, locked in, and completely alone, he was done. He had nowhere to go and no means to get there if he did. He was utterly beaten. And he was empty, by every definition of the term: financially, emotionally, physically, and spiritually.

CHAPTER THREE

A melancholy hit song from the 1970s, "He Ain't Heavy, He's My Brother," was playing softly on the car radio, but this time the line, "The road is long, with many a winding turn," and the song's timeless message of perseverance reminded Hank of his own heavy load. Hank was exhausted and still had a few more miles to go on his journey home after a perilous day's work of hustling drugs at a couple of the many New York City methadone clinics. "How could I do this again?" Hank thought.

He was late, very late. He knew that his mother would be quietly suffering the uncertainty of his arrival. It was December 24, 1984, Christmas Eve, an important event for Hank and his family. He had promised to drive his mother, Toni (short for Antoinette), to Jane's house in Rockport, a two-hour drive from his mother's Shrewsbury Street apartment. It was now close to 8:00 p.m., and Hank was still an hour away from home. Christmas Eve at his sister's house was definitely out of the question for him. Toni, running out of time and hope, reluctantly got into her car and drove to Rockport accompanied only by her heartache.

What happened next, as best as Hank could recall in his drug-influenced state, was that he stumbled into his relatives' Christmas Eve party on the floor directly above his mother's apartment. There were plenty of questioning stares and a few perfunctory welcoming gestures. Hank, even in his impaired state, recognized that he was barely tolerated or, more accurately, simply ignored.

The nights often turn into days in the life of a drug addict, and it wasn't long before Hank found himself alone and freezing on a Massachusetts interstate highway, waiting for his sister, Jane, to pick him up. Hank's car had failed to start that morning so he asked his cousin Paul who was heading toward New Hampshire to drop him off on the way. After what seemed like an eternity, his sister finally arrived. Hank slid into the passenger seat and immediately saw the cold look of disgust on his sister's face. The following admonition made the freezing temperature outside feel tropical. "Do you think I have nothing better to do on this Christmas morning?" Jane said. "I have three small kids at home, a husband, our whole family, his whole family."

Hank knew that she was right.

Jane continued to pour out her hurt. "I just drove an hour to pick you up. Do you realize what you're doing to our family?"

The pain of the moment did not escape Hank. Even in his somewhat disoriented state, he felt a deep emptiness inside. Hank knew that he was the cause of a great deal of unhappiness and humiliation. "Do you think I want to be like this?" Hank said, tears flowing. This was the first time Hank had ever cried in front of his sister.

There was nothing left to say. The ride to Rockport was quiet. The family had heard Hank's apologies many times before, and although no one was willing to excommunicate Hank from the family, his sister and mother both suggested that he go upstairs and not disrupt the occasion any further.

Exiled to a remote section of the house had its advantages; there, Hank could continue his descent into oblivion pretty much uninterrupted. The trip to New York had fortified Hank with plenty of methadone, and he'd used some of that stash to barter for enough cocaine to put him in a state of semi consciousness, which helped negate the pain of exclusion from the family.

At six the next morning, Hank's brother-in-law, Freddie, swung open the door and exclaimed, "Get ready. I'm taking you to the bus station in Boston."

The ride to Boston was inexplicably silent, which was remarkable because both Freddie and Hank loved to talk. Perhaps it was simple resignation on both their parts or Hank's learned helplessness. Regardless of the reason, this was another relationship that addiction had torn apart. Hank thought—no, he actually *knew*—that Freddie had had enough. The past October, Freddie had said to his wife, "Jane, I don't want Hank to be alone with the kids." That remark had followed Hank's last attempt at being a good uncle, a well-intentioned trip to the movies with his young niece.

Hank stared out the window, unable to face Freddie or the shame of his existence. The words, "How could you?" echoed in his ear as he recalled the telling of their trip to the movies from the perspective of a little girl.

"Uncle Hankie stopped at the liquor store on the way to the movies, and he was drinking something out of a brown-paper bag during the movie." She continued, "He was always going to the bathroom, and he left me alone all the time."

Hank was lost in his thoughts when they pulled into the South Station bus terminal around eight. He heard Freddie say, "We're here. Have a Merry Christmas," making it sound like, "Get out."

He solemnly slid out of the car at the nearly deserted depot and found himself among a few desperate individuals, each searching for a semblance of normalcy. "Get away from me," he heard himself say, but when he looked around, no one was there. "What do you want from me?"

Words were coming out of his mouth that he didn't mean to say. He was incoherent, suffering from a drug-induced psychosis after three days of methadone, cocaine, and no sleep. Hank could not control his mumbling, and he was starting to scare himself. Feeling alone, he thought back to Worcester State Hospital's mentally ill, aimlessly roaming Shrewsbury Street and talking to themselves. He now realized that he was one of them.

Later that morning he somberly rode the bus back to his mother's second-floor apartment on Shrewsbury Street, and for the next few weeks, Hank temporarily stopped mumbling but could not recall the New Year's celebration or his activities for the entire month of January. His last recollection was of another trip to New York City for more methadone and another week of nonstop partying.

Hank was in a car with some friends when the mumbling started again.

"What did you say? That didn't make any sense," said a pretty young blonde, from the backseat. That pretty blonde, who happened to be Hank's best friend's sister, was as innocent and sweet as one could imagine and was soon destined to be as adversely affected from substance misuse as the rest of the gang.

Hank, still clinging to a thread of reality, caught himself and quickly changed the subject. Somewhere in the back of his mind, Hank realized that he needed to stop using drugs and that he needed help to do so. The drugs soon ran out, and with their departure came the unwelcome pains of withdrawal. For two horrifying weeks, Hank lay on his mother's couch, the discomfort of opiate withdrawal gnawing at his very being. Those two weeks echoed Hank's last two years as an addict. Utter loneliness and horrific periods of withdrawal were his constant companions. Despite that, he continued to use. He didn't want to stop or didn't know how.

Salvation came in the form of his sister. Jane, whom he had so disappointed just a few weeks earlier, spearheaded the search for treatment. Was it her undying devotion to her brother or her desire to ease her mother's suffering? Hank really didn't know. What he did know was that Jane didn't desert him, and for that, he remains eternally grateful.

On a cold February morning, Hank managed to crawl into his brother's car. He was still weak from yet another prolonged methadone withdrawal—an excruciating withdrawal mitigated only by some blood pressure pills that Hank had secreted from his mother's medicine cabinet and a hundred milligrams of methadone that he foolishly swallowed all at once instead of slowly titrating himself down as planned.

The ride to Dorchester Detoxification Unit, or DDU, in some ways reminded Hank of the post-Christmas ride to South Station. Addiction had so strained the relationship that Hank and John barely talked or even looked at each other. To complicate matters, neither knew exactly where they were headed. Neither had any clue where DDU was or what to expect when they got there. Hank recalled hearing a distinctly inner-city voice over the phone telling him that a bed would be waiting for him on Friday, and now here they were in Dorchester, driving past several burned-out buildings, looking for the place he wasn't sure he wanted to go to.

In a dank, dreary waiting area, Hank was unceremoniously given a bottle of Kwell, an insecticidal shampoo, instructed to "wash the bugs off," and escorted to his room. His first impulse was to run, and during the intake process, Gilbert, a diminutive African American counselor, said, "Hank, you won't make it here till Monday," pretty much confirming that he really didn't belong there. But somehow, he stayed—primarily because his brother, John, had already left, and he was stuck in Dorchester with nowhere else to go.

Later that afternoon, Hank went to his first meeting, a group of about thirty people. They were mostly black, and two-thirds were men. DDU was a state-funded detoxification center, and its inhabitants did not have many options for treatment. It was in that group that Hank's resolve was sealed.

During the meeting, Hank was telling his version of his life as an addict—that he viewed himself as a good kid, despite the fact that he sold and used drugs daily. Without warning, Gilbert interrupted his soliloquy and flatly stated, "Hank, you're a maggot piece of shit and a chump to boot."

Hank was mad, but being the only white person in the room, he refrained from telling Gilbert exactly what he was thinking, which was a lot more colorful than a simple, "Go fuck yourself." Instead, he thought, "I'll show you, you little fuck! I will be here on Monday." It was fear disguised as anger that changed Hank's life.

For the next three weeks at DDU, Hank became close not only to Gilbert, Edris, Paula, and the rest of the counseling staff, but to Johnnie F., T-Baby Marshall, Eddie C., Electra, and the rest of the patients, who looked so different on the outside but were so similar on the inside. It was T-Baby who convinced Hank not to leave after the first week.

During the second week, Gilbert told the group, "You should all be like Hank and stop taking methadone," holding him up as a shining example of what successful recovery could look like. For the first time in a long time, Hank felt good about himself. When his time at DDU ended, Hank reluctantly waved good-bye to the people who had loved him back to life. Friends he had never met before had taught him life's most valuable lessons. On the way out, he read the slogan on the wall, "To be aware is to be alive," and he knew he had a chance.

The first step towards getting somewhere is to decide that you are not going to stay where you are

−Unknown

Why do some people become addicted and others do not? This is an interesting and important question. In our stories, you may find some possible explanation.

One of the commonly accepted explanations is that somehow, some people's brains are just different, and that people who become addicted have a predisposition to addiction. Certainly, there is some evidence for this. Even so, it does not seem to explain fully why some people get addicted but others don't. We also know from twin studies that even when the genes are the same, one twin may become addicted, and the other may not.

Addiction is now defined by the American Society of Addiction Medicine (ASAM) as a chronic disease of the reward, motivation, memory, and related circuitry in the brain. Dysfunction in these circuits leads to characteristic biological, psychological, social, and spiritual manifestations. For substance-abuse professionals and the families of addicts alike, it can be difficult to understand why some people are more vulnerable to addiction than others are. Often referred to as "the disease that has no boundaries," addiction doesn't discriminate based on color, ethnicity, height, weight, or social status. Attempting to identify the cause of addiction usually yields a complex answer. There are numerous risk factors that may predispose a person to addictive behavior, regardless of an individual's upbringing or moral code. Many individual, social, and biological variables (epigenetics) combine to increase the chances that there will be onset and progression of addiction if an individual is exposed to a substance or behavior. In no way are we attempting to provide the answer to such a complex issue in this book. Yet, our stories, despite their anecdotal nature, underscore the validity of genetics and environment as two primary risk factors for the disease of addiction.

CHAPTER FOUR

J ack was born in Worcester, Massachusetts, in 1949, the year that Harry S. Truman was sworn in as the thirty-third president in the first televised inauguration and two years after an Italian American named Frank Fiorillo opened Worcester's first pizza place. Prior to World War II, pizza had been known only to Worcester's Italian families, but GIs serving in Italy during the war had sampled the dish and brought a taste for it home. Fiorillo, who would later sell America's first home pizza mix, was among the earliest Americans to profit from what would become an American culinary staple.

Joining Jack as part of the continuing postwar baby boom in 1949 were Jeff Bridges, Meryl Streep, Richard Gere, John Belushi, Lionel Richie, and the Boss, Bruce Springsteen. Unfortunately, all similarities end there, except maybe for John Belushi, who perhaps came within one or two degrees of separation in the course of Jack's story.

In 1949, a Coke and a coffee each cost a nickel, and the Boston Red Sox signed Ted Williams for $100,000, making him the highest-paid player in baseball. That did not, however, prevent the hated Yankees from beating the Red Sox to win the American League pennant and then go on to defeat the Brooklyn Dodgers to win their twelfth World Series. *Dragnet, Father Knows Best,* and *Women's Roller Derby* appeared for the first time on TV, and Gene Autry recorded "Rudolph the Red Nosed Reindeer."

During World War II, Jack's father had served as an air force bomber mechanic in England; Jack's uncle Eugene gave his life for his country, and Jack's mother worked at Worcester Pressed Steel, fabricating parts for the military. Jack's parents married a few years after the war ended, and Jack's life began less than a year later in what was known then as Doctor's Hospital, a neighborhood health-care facility that his grandmother's doctor helped to incorporate. Later, this same hospital would become a nationally known center for substance-abuse treatment. It would provide Jack with his first real job and, in a way, became the genesis of this book.

Today, Jack often jokes that if the doctor who delivered him had really been at the top of his game, he would have taken Jack's ass downstairs to an AA meeting instead of slapping it. That would have saved him twenty years of hard luck. Still, in retrospect, the doctor's slap seemed to predict that life would contain an abundance of pain and suffering. "Here," the slap seemed to say. "Get used to it. You'll be kicking *yourself* in the ass soon enough."

Jack lived on the Upper East Side in the city of Worcester, which was then near its peak population of two hundred thousand and the second-largest city in Massachusetts. The affectionate, self-invented designation of Upper East Side differentiated those living on Belmont Hill, one of Worcester's Seven Hills, from the valley dwellers of Shrewsbury Street, the main drag and the hub of commercial activity on the East Side, which was where the action was.

On Shrewsbury Street, you could grab a stack of pancakes with a side of bacon and a cup of joe at the Parkway Diner—or across the street at the Boulevard Diner, which was built by the

Worcester Lunch Car company in the southwest part of the city. You could pick up fresh cod, ground chuck, or a tub of ricotta at Turo's Market or settle in for a haircut and some baseball chatter at Manuel's Barber Shop. If you were feeling a little less industrious, you could settle on a street-side bench in East Park, watching shiny, postwar Chevys, Fords, and Buicks cruise by, or listen to the rumble and slam of coupling railcars at the switchyards, just a couple of blocks southeast. The big wire and footwear factories that had made Worcester a commercial center had long since shut down, but the city still felt prosperous, although the East Side was distinctly working class. The Blackstone Canal, which linked Worcester to Providence, Rhode Island, and Narragansett Bay, had helped to foster America's Industrial Revolution. Closed in 1848 and largely covered over, the canal still flowed beneath the city, powerful but unseen.

The neighborhood in which Jack grew up was primarily first- and second-generation Italian; US Census data for 1950 shows more than eight thousand Italian-born residents living in Worcester County, and a good number of them made their homes on the East Side. At the time, this clannishness likely owed as much to protective instinct as it did to familiarity. Jack's maternal grandparents had come to this country when Walter Wyckoff, a Princeton scholar and social scientist, neatly summarized the prevailing sentiment in *The Workers: The West.* "There should be a law to give a job to every decent man that's out there and another law to keep all them I-talians from comin' and takin' the bread out of the mouths of honest people."

In Worcester, the Irish had moved a step higher on the immigrant ladder, and they wouldn't let the Italians move up without a fight. Although now a minority, the Irish remained a significant part of the East Side: if you weren't lucky enough to be Italian, then you had to be Irish. The newborn Jack split the difference: his mother's parents were from Italy, and his father's parents were from Ireland.

This played out negatively for Jack almost from the start. Worcester was a city where the Italians despised the "Irish bastards" who ran city hall and patrolled the streets in police uniforms, and the Irish despised the "Wops" and "Guineas" who controlled most of the city's organized crime. Jack was, depending upon the situation, the target of ethnic slurs directed at either group. Time and again, depending upon whom he was with, he longed to be fully Italian or fully Irish, rather than fifty-fifty.

To underscore the dynamics of this cultural division, Jack's father was an only child and his mother was one of seven, maybe eight and possibly nine, Italian children. Jack knew that one of his mother's brothers had died in action during World War II. There was also a step-uncle who was occasionally talked about, and then there were the whispers about another uncle who died mysteriously, possibly at the hands of Jack's grandfather.

What the composition of his parents' families meant in practical terms was that every big family gathering and holiday celebration involved his mother's side, and that Jack developed his closest to ties the Italian side of the family. Of even greater influence was that Jack grew up in his Italian grandparents' house, a three-family housing unit that was emblematic of the blue-collar city known as the "Land of the Three-Decker." Filled with aunts and uncles, Jack's grandparents' house in many ways seemed like something out of a storybook. But like the streets of Worcester, dark currents ran beneath the surface.

CHAPTER FIVE

When JD moved to the East Side in the mid-1960s, he was twelve—old enough to see the neighborhood as a step up. Thus far, he'd spent his life in Worcester's poorest neighborhoods, while his mother waited tables and counted pennies to keep her daughter, her oldest son, and JD, the baby, sheltered and fed. JD had visited the neighborhood on a number of occasions, usually to stop by his father's place of business, where JD waited as his mother employed vigorous verbal shaming and pure moxie in an attempt to force his dad to do his duty and contribute a few dollars to his children's upbringing.

JD saw the East Side as unique and alluring. As he rambled its streets, he felt a buzz he had never experienced before. The East Side featured not just businesses but a huge park where kids and adult teams played ball, cooled off in the wading pool during the heat of summer, and watched the July Fourth fireworks. Fairly close to Worcester's downtown, it offered easy access by foot to school, to his classmates' homes, and to Lake Quinsigamond, a slender jewel that ran north–south along much of the East Side. JD's family, his dad's business—though it held negative connotations—and even the Worcester police seemed to radiate excitement.

JD's Dad, Muggsy, was a colorful character in a neighborhood full of them. He was born and raised on "the Street," as Shrewsbury Street was universally known. He made his living running a "restaurant" that fronted for his real business, a neighborhood bookmaking operation. Garrulous and handsome, he bore a striking resemblance to the actor Victor Mature, who'd played virile lead roles in Hollywood pictures like *Samson and Delilah* and *The Glory Brigade.*

In fact, the East Side of the 1960s looked like the set for a movie expressing the American dream—shoppers mingling on the Street, kids playing on the sidewalks and in the park, friends calling to each other from the windows of their cars and the porches of their triple-deckers. The familiarity and the insularity felt comfortable. But behind the doors of those triple-deckers, the atmosphere might be anything but cozy.

JD recalled the Easter that he was seven, waiting for his dad to come to his mother's apartment on Sigourney Street to take the three children to dinner at a relative's house. JD was wearing his Easter Sunday best—black slacks a little too short, a worn Oxford shirt, and an inexpertly tied plaid necktie—and sitting on the worn sofa, reading the *Worcester Telegram* Sunday comics. That morning, JD had the usual mixed emotions he often felt about his father, emotions that frequently confused him. It would be great to see Dad. But would he show up? If he did show up, would he be drunk or sober? Even if he was sober, how long would it be before he did get drunk? What would happen when he did? To further complicate his distress, JD always had the awful feeling that he was unwanted or in the way.

The son of a bookie, JD knew the best odds of any of these scenarios were that his dad wouldn't show at all, and as he sat waiting on the sofa, those odds seemed to be improving. Dad was scheduled to pick them up at noon, and it was already one thirty. JD focused on the adventures of Pogo the Possum and Albert the Alligator as he tried to make the familiar fears disappear: Dad didn't care about him, didn't love him, and didn't want him. Already, JD knew many of the East Side characters, including those who frequented his dad's place to lay down bets, but he scarcely knew his dad at all. Although Muggsy surfaced every now and again, his visits were short and his interactions with JD were brief and shallow; no real hugs or "I love you's" were ever exchanged. Muggsy just didn't seem to be that kind of guy.

But if JD lacked a nurturing father figure, so did many of his friends. In many families, the dad was missing and the mom worked like hell to provide for everyone. JD knew that from listening in on his mother's gossip sessions with the women who'd chosen these men for better or worse—and gotten worse. They would smoke their Viceroys or Parliaments and drink their Tom Collinses or red wine and rag on their men. This one had been caught in bed with that woman from over Plum Street; that one drank before work in the morning, during work, and when he came home, if he ever did come home; this one was a good, honest guy, but he just wasn't a family man. JD's ignorance truly was bliss, and as a child, he never suspected that anything was wrong with his family, especially when compared with the other families he knew.

On that Easter Sunday, as the clock on the chipped plaster wall ticked, JD looked at the *Telegram*'s puzzle page, compared two pictures, and tried to figure out what was missing in one of them They look so similar, almost identical, in fact, and yet…In a way, he was starting to realize, his life was like that. Important things were missing, but they weren't apparent. What, exactly, was wrong? Why did all the mothers choose to marry these guys if they were such poor husbands and fathers? Why did the kids have to deal with the mess those choices made? JD never knew. He didn't think to ask or know how to ask. And besides, who could tell him? It wasn't as if he had great mentors and caregivers who taught him how to express his emotions.

In JD's family, most feelings were tamped down—except, of course, anger, rage, or frustration, which were expressed with abandon, even if it meant using physical violence. Although Muggsy did not live with JD and his family, JD's mother did not hesitate to call on her ex-husband to mete out the punishment for JD's increasingly frequent episodes of misbehavior. Punishments, usually a strong verbal reprimand or, when absolutely necessary, an ass kicking, were something that JD endured but rarely learned anything from. It seemed ridiculous to JD that a guy he rarely saw and who didn't seem to care about him was called in to teach him lessons about life. What a joke.

To make matters worse, by then JD's mom had met and married Tony, another deadbeat. This one, however, was physically violent and pretty scary, even to a tough kid like JD. But this, too, was something JD did not express. It was all part of learning about the neighborhood's classification of "acceptable" and "unacceptable" emotions, and he adapted quickly. When he felt the unacceptable feelings of fear, hurt, loneliness, or not being wanted, he suppressed them or made believe they didn't exist. JD survived using whatever means were available to him, which sometimes meant simple endurance.

There were other possibilities, however. Early on, JD discovered the transitory power of the lie. At school, he never talked about Muggsy's absence. He did everything he could to avoid the humiliation of the truth, that his stepfather, Tony, had made the newspapers after being arrested for stealing or physically assaulting his mother. Instead, JD fabricated stories that portrayed his father as a legitimate businessman and upstanding member of the community, and he kept quiet about his stepdad's violence. Of course, high financial status played a part in the fantasy. When teachers innocently polled students as to what they'd eaten for dinner the night before, JD responded with tales of elaborate dinners of steak and lobster. He knew full well that his family could never afford those expensive foods, but the stories held back the shame that accompanied the bald truth: the family often dined on welfare surplus food that they'd waited in line for like beggars.

For JD, it was easier to make up stories than to face the truth about how horrifying it was to lie awake at night, crying and helpless, while Mom and Tony argued, their voices escalating to a scary pitch. Lying to himself was easier than admitting to being scared while his mom was being beaten within earshot of his bedroom.

One night when he was eight or nine years old, JD couldn't stand it any longer and went after his stepdad with a kitchen knife to stop a beating. His efforts were effective, and the beating stopped, but it was only for that night. He never told anyone about what happened. Instead, he just lived with it for the next ten years until his stepdad was sent to Walpole State Prison for a fifteen-to-twenty-five-year sentence following a career of crime. JD was too ashamed to admit what his life was really like, but then, so were all of his friends. They made up lies of their own. Lying and its codependent activity, denial, helped to keep the shame and rage at bay. The anger, the confusion, and the feeling of being lost in life overwhelmed JD emotionally. Playing make-believe helped him survive, but the feelings never disappeared. As he grew up, so did they.

By 2:00 p.m. on that Easter Sunday, it was late enough for JD to realize that Dad wasn't going to show. JD turned the newspaper page and desperately tried to focus on the comics to read the words through his tears.

Mom was in the kitchen that afternoon, smoking cigarettes, drinking coffee, and bad-mouthing Dad. "Yeah, and do you think that lousy bastard could show up on Easter for his fucking kids? I just called over to the bar, and they said he's not there, but I know goddamn well he is."

Quietly, so his mother wouldn't notice, JD folded the newspaper, tiptoed into the tiny bathroom, closed the door, and turned on the light. He slid the footstool over to the chipped porcelain sink, hiked himself up, and quietly swung open the medicine cabinet door. His heart was pounding with anger for Muggsy and fear of getting caught. Fingers trembling, JD pulled out the bottles one by one. Aspirin. Pepto. Penicillin from when he'd had the flu. And in a brown, screw-top bottle, he found what he was looking for: terpin hydrate, the sticky, purple syrup his mom had given him for his cough. One of the kids had said it contained codeine, a drug that could "give you a good lift." Slowly and deliberately, JD unscrewed the cap and tipped the bottle to his lips.

As the smooth liquid flowed down his throat, he felt warmth, then something better. It was like warm honey washing over his body and carrying away all the anger, all the fear, all the feelings of shame and abandonment. And with that, his imagination took over. Instead of being a tiny, scrappy kid full of shame, he could become John Wayne or anyone else he chose to be and forget his troubles for a while. Just by ingesting an intoxicating substance, he could change his life, at least in his mind. It was a revelation, a miracle drug that fixed everything.

The bottle empty, JD stuffed it in the bottom of the bathroom wastebasket and went to his room to lie on his sagging twin mattress and enjoy his waking dreams. He never told anyone about his discovery, but that seed began to grow inside him, never letting him forget the dream-like state that awaited him the next time he could get his hands on that magic substance. For JD, a new life had begun.

CHAPTER SIX

I n a Worcester City Hospital delivery room, Antoinette labored without protest during the birth of her first child, a son she named Henry. Unbeknownst to her, the pain of delivery was a harbinger of what was to follow. The date was December 16, 1950. In five days, Toni and her newborn boy would return to 244 Shrewsbury Street, and for the next thirty-four years, Hank would refer to his home as "the Street," announced as succinctly and as proudly as if he was a starting offensive lineman proclaiming that he was a graduate of the newly crowned national champs "the Ohio State University" prior to the start of the Sunday night football game.

The Street was a mile-long thoroughfare where the Italian community that occupied the side streets could find all the necessities of life. D'Errico's, Manzi's, Turo's, Abascia's, and Balsamo's markets all provided the staples of traditional Mediterranean cuisine, and the many small coffee shops, candy stores, bars, diners, and restaurants provided venues for socializing. There was even a chicken farm on the East Side gateway. At the downtown end were the neighborhood Catholic church and its adjacent recreation center.

Hank lived in a three-decker and was surrounded by friends and family. A great-uncle named Frank Galantino and his wife, Aunt Grace, lived on the third floor; the Collaros lived on the first. On either side of Hank's three-decker were six-decker dwellings, which created a small enclave that was occupied by about fifteen families on a hundred feet of Shrewsbury Street. Hank's cousins, Franny and Chickie, lived in 242 Shrewsbury Street, and his best friends, Johnny and Stevie, lived in 246. Hank considered himself fortunate to grow up in a place where "everyone knows your name." Hank credits his sagacity to this early exposure to an environment that felt safe and secure. Before the age of five, Hank was comfortable talking to adults. He learned the importance of being respectful. He loved walking to school—not so much the final destination but the independence he experienced roaming the neighborhood.

It was at Adams Street School that Hank met most of his early childhood friends, many of whom would play important roles in later life. Chickie, the kid who lived next door, was two years older than Hank and often walked to school with him. Even at an early age, Chickie was athletic, good-looking, and extremely popular among the neighborhood kids. He introduced Hank to many of the older kids, such as Frankie Gut, Harbie, and Nicky Nap. He also provided that "older brother" protection that Hank thoroughly enjoyed. Other kids, such as Joe Arts, Stevie the Sailor, Tony "One-eye" Balsamo, Leo the Crusher, Denis Desobar, Cubba, Kid Curry, and JD and his brother, Tommie, all lived nearby. There was also Eileen, Hank's first crush. They sat next to each other in kindergarten. She was his first communion partner in second grade, and the two had a mock marriage ceremony in third grade, after which Eileen and her family moved out of the neighborhood and into a new school. It would be twenty years before they would see each other again.

Hank's recollections of his childhood before the age of nine lack clarity, but he did know that his mother, Antoinette, was a warm, caring, loving, strong, honest, intelligent woman who was ahead of her time. Antoinette lost her mother at age eleven and her father at sixteen. She managed to attend nursing school and graduated from college when most of her contemporaries were lucky to finish high school. She went off to war in 1942 and was stationed in London as an army lieutenant. After the war, she met Hank's father, and in 1947, Antoinette and Minnie (Henry senior) were married. Minnie was half Italian and half English, but he considered himself Irish, which was odd in a predominantly Italian neighborhood, where people viewed the Irish as their oppressors. Hank knew his dad to be honest, hardworking, and carefree; he was a man who loved to have a good time. As a kid, Minnie graduated from Sacred Heart Academy grammar school but never had the opportunity to finish high school as he opted to join the war effort in 1940 and toured with the Fighting Sea Bees in 1942. When he was drinking, which, as Hank recalled, was just about every day, except for the forty days of Lent, he often talked about repairing the naval station in Pago Pago or the retaking of the Philippines.

One of Hank's few memories of his early years was the 1954 flood on Shrewsbury Street. The water was three feet deep, nearly rising to the first-floor doorstep, and boats traveled up and down the Street. The cast of characters from Hank's childhood was a menagerie of misfits and dysfunctional types who greatly shaped Hank's view of the world. Two of those characters, both related by blood, were Raymond and Uncle Tony. Raymond was as close to normal as one could find on Shrewsbury Street, but Uncle Tony, who really was Hank's older cousin, took the term "dysfunctional" to another level. Uncle Tony was larger than life, figuratively and literally. Uncle Tony had huge hands. Hank's hand looked dwarfed whenever he reached for a piece of candy, which Uncle

Tony seemed always to have. Tony was Hank's idol. He often took Hank to places that were very exciting to a young boy, but Uncle Tony was a pathological liar who was incapable of telling the truth. The innate ability to embellish without a hint of embarrassment would serve him well in his quest to become the top car salesman in New England. Uncle Tony once told Hank, who was four, to wave at airplanes because he was going to join the air force and he would be flying them overhead. "Hankie," Uncle Tony would say, "see those planes up there? That's going to be me flying that plane. Make sure to wave so I can see you."

Every day on the way to school, the kids made fun of Hank because he waved at every plane that flew overhead, yelling, "Uncle Tony, Uncle Tony! I'm here!" One day, Chickie finally said, "Hank, your Uncle Tony is a mechanic. He's afraid to fly."

Uncle Tony would continue to bullshit Hank for the rest of his life—a life that was shortened dramatically by a drug overdose.

Aside from the Shrewsbury Street friendships, sports played an important yet somewhat misguided role in Hank's life. At six, Hank remembers watching his twelve-year-old cousin Anthony play baseball at East Park on Shrewsbury Street. Anthony was an All Star player and had just made the play of the game. Hank heard a thousand people cheering, or at least that was how he felt. One of the fans bought Hank a hot dog and an ice cream. Hank said to himself, "Life doesn't get any better than this."

Hank was surrounded by talented athletes. Everyone played sports: his cousins and his next-door neighbor, Chickie, made the All Star teams, and Hank enjoyed cheering for them. When the Joe DiMaggio Little League decided to move from East Park to Mount Carmel field near the downtown end of Shrewsbury Street two years later, Hank felt as though it was the Brooklyn Dodgers moving to California. The baseball field was new and beautiful. It had dugouts, a real fence with local companies advertising on it, a scoreboard, and, best of all, a press box. Only the pros had that, but now the kids from the Joe DiMaggio Little League had it, and to put the icing on the cake, Joltin' Joe DiMaggio, himself, was scheduled to appear on opening day. Everyone wanted to be like Joe forty years before the "everyone wanted to be like Mike" era. Opening day would be especially exciting because Hank's family was integral in creating the new field. Hank's father, a mason, helped build the dugouts. His uncle Joe was on the board of directors. Hank's mother and aunt raised money for the field, and his next-door neighbor was the president of the Little League. This was going to be the Super Bowl of Hank's early life. The big day came, but Joe DiMaggio did not. His brother Dominic showed up in his place. Dominic was a good baseball player, a member of the Boston Red Sox even, but he was no Joltin' Joe.

For the next three years, that field and that game provided Hank with "the thrill of victory and the agony of defeat." It really shaped his competitive nature, which would give him great joy and cause him great pain. It also was a platform for meeting many of the neighborhood's great athletes. Antoine, Joe Cap, Tinker Bell, Joe B., Emil, and Paul T. were all accomplished baseball players. Paul went on to build a career as a pitcher and eventually was head of scouting for the world-champion San Francisco Giants. Tinker Bell, who was perhaps the neighborhood's most gifted athlete, got into drugs and never recovered. His was the typical unspoken tragedy.

Some of the great mentors in the area coached Hank. Among them were Frank Giannitti, who ran the basketball program at Mount Carmel Recreation Center, and Mel Poti, Hank's Local 1885 baseball coach, whose son, Emil, was in Jack's class at Sacred Heart Academy and whose grandson would later become an all-star defenseman for the NHL's New York Rangers. They instilled in Hank a love for the game, but somehow that love for the game transmuted into betting on the game more than actually playing.

Baseball was not the only sport in Hank's life. Basketball at the Mount Carmel Recreation Center allowed him to participate in team sports almost year-round and gave him the opportunity to meet kids from outside the neighborhood. Hank thought he was a natural athlete and fashioned his style of play after the great Bob Cousy, Worcester's resident hero, who played on the local Holy Cross College NCAA team and later guided the Boston Celtics to six straight NBA championships. When Hank was not passing the ball behind his back, he was running to Jimmy's East Central Street Market to buy twenty-five-cent club sandwiches for the older kids. Hank loved being in the action and hearing the older kids tell their lurid stories of sexual conquests, commonly known as "getting to first base" or "copping a feel" and staying out late. Sports were great equalizers. Regardless of players' ethnicity, skin color, or age, the vernacular of the game brought people together.

The zenith of Hank's love of sports and the start of his eventual descent into the world of sports betting and bookmaking took place at the Worcester Academy Summer Camp. Hank spent his tenth, eleventh, and twelfth summers participating in every sport imaginable from 9:00 a.m. until 4:00 p.m. every day. Many soon-to-be legends in their fields taught baseball, basketball, track, swimming, diving, wrestling, tennis, and even arts and crafts. Dee Rowe, then head basketball coach and athletic director at Worcester Academy, ran the camp. He would later become head basketball coach at the University of Connecticut, where he is known as the father of UConn basketball. The camp counselors and coaches were a Who's Who in athletics. Buster Sheary, Dee Rowe's third-grade gym teacher, once coached at Holy Cross College and led the small Jesuit college to a National Invitational Tournament championship. Among his players were All-Americans Bob Cousy, Togo Palazzi, and Tommie Heinsohn. Buster was in his sixties at the time and was one of the best Irish storytellers of all time. Dave Gavitt, then a twenty-something camp counselor, eventually became the head basketball coach and athletic director at Providence College in Providence, Rhode Island. He was also the first commissioner of the Big East Conference and sat on the committee that created the 1992 Olympic Basketball "Dream Team." Paige Rowden and Andy Laska, both legendary local head coaches, rounded out the exemplary camp staff. Even at twelve, Hank knew he was lucky to have some of the greatest mentors in sports.

At the end of summer camp each year, there was an awards ceremony. Hank liked playing sports and received a few awards for his skills and proficiency, but the "Best Camper Award" surprised him. The award was given to an athlete who possessed not only superior skills and abilities but who displayed exceptional sportsmanship and sacrifice for his fellow campers. Hank rolled his eyes as Dee Rowe said, "Now, for the award we have all been waiting for..." He never imagined that he was a candidate for the camp's biggest honor, but when Dee Rowe announced, "That camper is Hank," and then described how kind Hank had been to a camper from Italy who struggled with the language and customs of another country. Hank beamed with pride. He was smiling from ear to ear when he accepted the trophy and the congratulatory handshake. Hank knew then that sports and the lessons he learned at Worcester Academy Summer Camp were written indelibly on his heart.

There is no learning without remembering.

—Socrates

In addition to the predisposition to addiction hypothesis, a second explanation for why some people become addicted and others do not is that people may use drugs to self-medicate other conditions. Edward Khantzian, MD, explored this idea and proposes that people become addicted because they have underlying psychological and psychiatric conditions. This is an attractive theory, as there is a large correlation between psychiatric disorders and drug use.

The psychological and emotional aspects of addiction tend to be complicated. Many addicts, including those in this story, struggled with psychological and emotional issues long before they ever found the calming and comforting effects of drugs. The characters in this story are not unique. Many addicts have experienced shame, abuse, neglect, trauma, and a variety of other emotional and psychological wounds. It's no coincidence that they find their way to the most powerful narcotics available—and it isn't because narcotics are fun! Among many things addicts have in common are pain and the need for a powerful substance to soothe it.

As the characters in this story look back on their early days, what seems conspicuous is the dysfunctional makeup of many of their family systems and their acculturation. Given the neighborhood they came from and the qualities of those they looked up to for guidance and direction, it would be hard to blame their addictions solely on their family systems or on the drugs and booze alone. Their neighborhood had more than its share of thieves, thugs, con men, hustlers, and two-bit gangsters.

CHAPTER SEVEN

Standing at the window of his mother's third-floor apartment, Jack, nearly four, watched in amazement as the storm came in. "Mommy, Mommy, look! The sky is getting dark," he said.

"Get away from the window. You're leaving marks and making a mess," replied Phyllis, who was constantly cleaning. The term had not been invented yet, but Jack's mom easily could have carried a diagnosis of obsessive compulsive disorder, a trait clearly passed down from Jack's meticulously clean grandmother, Caroline.

Outside the window, a coal-black funnel a mile wide towered above the entire city of Worcester, writhing and spitting golf-ball-sized hail. The very air seemed illuminated, casting a light on the dilapidated houses across the street that made them seem beautiful somehow. But within minutes, the storm would rip a nasty seam of death and destruction through the heart of the city.

It was June 9, 1953, the fourth day in which a series of tornadoes had torn across the northern United States from Flint, Michigan, to New England. After touching down in Barre, Massachusetts, where it killed two people, the last and deadliest of the tornados churned eastward into Worcester, devouring everything in its path. The paint was scoured off cars. Trees, telephone poles, houses, and everything in them were sucked up into the storm's whirling funnel. Rows of houses simply vanished, and debris was later found more than one hundred miles away.

The storm stayed on the ground for ninety minutes before it blew itself out east of Southborough. By then, ninety-four Worcester residents had died and an estimated ten thousand were homeless. The devastation may have been made worse because there was no warning. According to reports, the National Weather Service, which had recently established a storm warning system, had foreseen a possible tornado but did not share this information because it had not wanted to create panic.

Jack and his family were unscathed by the storm. But another storm, slower-moving but equally capable of destroying lives, was already moving around the child. Like a tornado, it would be visible only when it was too late. Until then, the systems surrounding Jack would project his pleasant, if not altogether perfect, sense of security.

If JD seemed to lack for family, Jack at times felt surrounded by it. The first grandchild on either side of the newly formed Irish Italian clan, Jack by default inherited the attention and celebrity status that goes along with being the first baby in the family. At every family affair, especially on Thanksgiving and Christmas, when the whole family gathered, Jack's mother's younger sisters, some of whom were unmarried and still lived in his grandparent's big triple-decker, teased him adoringly. His auntie Nina seemed to watch over Jack as if he were her favorite doll, and Jack returned her affection as only babies can do, forming a special bond that remains to this day.

The Merrifield Street triple-decker was now home to three generations. Jack's grandparents, Salverio and Caroline, who had immigrated from Italy in 1922, lived on the first floor. Anthony, better known as Uncle Dorsey, occupied the second floor with his wife, Auntie Dottie. Philomena, Phyllis for short, was Jack's mother and the oldest child of Caroline and Salverio. Along with her husband, John, and their young son, she lived on the third floor. The house was full of life and a loving if occasionally boisterous family in which the eldest clung tightly to the Old World, and succeeding generations were thrust further and further into the new. The unifying theme was family, a sense that everyone was in this together. And that feeling extended into the streets of the East Side.

The neighborhood was full of friends and relatives. It seemed like his mother knew everyone. No one ever locked his or her door. The only glimpses that Jack had into a world that was not all peace and love were the shotguns in his grandfather's closet, loaded with rock-salt shells intended for anyone or anything that wandered close to his prized vegetable garden, and the ominous yelling that ensued when his father came home after having too much to drink. These battles were as regular as clockwork: they happened on payday Thursday and late Saturday afternoons. For Jack, they represented the first tear in the fabric of his security, and they spawned transient moments of isolation and loneliness. But in the triple-decker, there was always someone else to spend time with, and no one was more interesting than Grampa.

Short and powerful, Grampa had, in addition to his family, a number of loves in his life. One was the garden, which he tended with a careful hand, growing tomatoes, basil, onions, and garlic for his wife to transform into delicious sauce for pasta. Another was Queenie, his trusty beagle, with whom Grampa stalked the meadows on the fringes of the city for cottontail rabbits to sweeten his pot.

As Jack watched, Grampa skinned and cleaned the rabbits, which had already been field-dressed, and hung them over the basement sink to drain the blood.

"There," Grampa said in his heavily accented, haphazardly constructed English, carefully peeling back the skin of a cottontail and extracting a lead shotgun pellet from its silvery flesh as Jack watched, amazed. "Take-a de-ese out, or you gonna broke you teet."

In the hours Jack spent with his grandfather, he absorbed the nearly unbelievable tales and life lessons of a man who had made the successful journey from Italy to Worcester without leaving the Old World behind. In his basement, Grampa had fashioned a traditional food-production facility that would be the envy of one of today's authenticity-seeking foodies. At the center of the main room, not far from the red-painted closet where Grampa kept his shotguns, was a steel-topped kitchen table that sat on a rather decorative wooden base. When pulled out, the table could accommodate quite a few diners, but ordinarily, owing to the closeness of the quarters, it was kept closed, with a row of chairs squeezed in on one side. Behind the chairs, there stood a huge wood-burning enamel stove on which Jack's grandmother would make anything from pizza to rabbit stew.

Off this main room was the wine room, complete with a large wooden-handled wine press that squeezed out juice for the three hundred gallons of wine that Grampa made—and friends and family consumed—every year. Other than the vegetable patch, nearly every inch of the yard outside was trellised for grapevines, including the driveway. As a boy, Jack loved the seclusion and shade the vines provided, the sweet smell of the ripe grapes that drifted through his bedroom window at night. But even that large crop wasn't enough to produce the amount of wine that was needed, and every year Jack's grandfather had a truckload of grapes delivered to the house in order to guarantee the production of sufficient wine to fill the three large wooden barrels that occupied the entire back wall of the wine-making room.

Today, Jack still wonders whether the quantity of alcohol produced was simply a cultural influence and assurance of having enough wine for every meal or the warning signs of maladaptive use. After all, what self-respecting Italian living in a three-family house would not have a wine-making room in the cellar? Jack still remembers with fondness and not a little bit of pride those moments helping his grandfather make wine.

"Here," Grampa would say. "You a strong boy. Help me push." Jack would place his small, soft hand next to his grandfather's thick, calloused hand on the long wooden handle of the press. As grandfather and grandson walked round and round, a wooden plate would thread its way down the press, compressing and releasing the juice from the grapes packed between the wooden slabs. The smell of the juice was intoxicating, but at age five, Jack found the wine itself less appealing.

One cold winter afternoon, as Jack watched from across the stainless-steel table, Grampa poured a gulp of wine into each of two glass tumblers. Into one of them, he added a shot or so of orange soda and slid it across the table. Jack picked up the cup and put it to his lips.

"Wait," his grandfather said, laying his hand gently on Jack's. "Toast first."

Then in his rugged bass, he began to sing in a mixture of Italian and English:

Signore e signori,
io mi chiamo Pepino Suracilla.
And, what a mulaniana!

The song was "Salute Pepino," an Italian drinking song. Jack laughed aloud as Grampa continued through the song, and then they tipped their glasses to the sky.

Jack had never tasted alcohol before. It felt warm going down his throat, and it began to burn almost immediately in his stomach. He tried to believe he was having fun, as much for Grampa as for himself. But his stomach began to churn, and in a very short time, he found himself outside in the cold winter air, his vomit coloring the snow a bright red. Jack's first experience with alcohol was enough to keep him away from the stuff for a while. He didn't know it then, but that period was to be his first seven years of sobriety; he wouldn't touch a drink until the ripe old age of twelve. In the time between, he had a childhood to live, and he had no idea what lay ahead.

CHAPTER EIGHT

"Hey, Queenie? Come here, girl."
Shaded by the trellised grapevine that covered the side of the Merrifield Street triple-decker porch, Jack approached the recumbent beagle.

She failed to move, and he yelled louder, but nothing. As Jack got closer, he noticed that Queenie wasn't sleeping. Her eyes were wide open, and she had a look of utter helplessness that he had never seen before.

This was Jack's first encounter with death, his first real awareness that terrible things could happen in the world, things beyond his control. Long after his grandfather had buried Queenie in the backyard, Jack would carry the sadness and confusion of this moment. Still, aside from those few dark clouds that always passed quickly, life was good. Living on one of Worcester's Seven Hills provided plenty of opportunity for fun. In the summertime, the streetlights were the signal for the neighborhood kids to return home after hours of playing stickball in the street or rolling homemade "Soap Box Derby" rigs down the steep Gage Street hill. The winter, with its heavy snowfall, brought its own excitement, as the gang tunneled through the snowdrifts and sledded down steep streets, one of which was appropriately called "Steep Gage" and resembled the ski jump from the opening of the once-popular *Wide World of Sports* TV program.

Necessity was the mother of invention, and the East Side kids sledded on whatever they could find, whether it was an old automobile hood, a large cardboard box, or, for the very lucky, a real Flexible Flyer.

Oblivious to any danger, they rocketed down those hills, out of control, often with little ability to change direction or stop. One of the gang, a kid by the name of Tommy, lived up to his nickname of Blockhead when he had the misfortune of sliding headfirst at full speed under one of the parked cars that lined one side of the street. The kid emerged a moment later, his Coke-bottle-bottom eyeglasses mangled and a perfectly round circle cut into his bleeding forehead by the car's muffler. Temporarily stunned, the kids soon collapsed in fits of laughter. True to his moniker, Blockhead had survived, and there was another story to tell.

Of course, not all time was free time for the East Side gang. Like many of his friends, Jack attended Sacred Heart Academy, the neighborhood Catholic school. The closest of those friends was a neighborhood kid named Michael who was known by everyone—except, of course, his mother—as Fudgy, which was a bastardization of his Italian surname. On the East Side, Fudgy was to become a local celebrity, not for his nickname, but for his talent as a performer.

A literal (if not figurative) choirboy, Fudgy had a voice for the ages, hauntingly clear and melodious. On Christmas Eve, a packed house gathered at Saint Anne's Church for hours of singing and praying, and miraculously enough, people never left early, in part because doing so meant they would miss the highlight of Midnight Mass: Fudgy singing solo versions of "Ave Maria" and "Silent Night."

The assembled faithful listened in hushed reverence to that heavenly voice. Many years later, when Saint Anne's Church was closed down and abandoned, an arson fire would hasten its final demolition. Many in the neighborhood would say that Fudgy, in a moment of great despair, had lit the match.

Those days, however, were well in the future, and in his youth, Fudgy shared his talent widely. During his thirteen years at Sacred Heart Academy, his numerous sold-out performances in musicals and operettas single-handedly kept the school in the black. This was no small feat for a school that was free for its parishioners and cost a paltry seventy-five dollars a year for nonmembers of the parish.

Jack wasn't a natural-born performer like Fudgy. In fact, he tended to shy away from the limelight. But the boys shared homes that, while not broken, were often torn and tattered. With lives so similar—their mothers devoted, their fathers distant, their socioeconomic status barely above the poverty line, both second-generation born in America, enough Catholic guilt to last a lifetime—theirs was a friendship waiting to happen.

While Jack constantly dreamed of escape, often unsuccessfully, Fudgy was a master at it. An entertainer at heart, he possessed the talent to make escape a reality. His younger brother, Tony, said in Michael's *Boston Globe* obituary, "He was a pretender ever since I could remember...Acting wasn't something he chose; it was him. He didn't choose it. It had to be." But Tony senior, Fudgy's father, didn't always see his son's penchant for escape from the chores at hand in the same way and would often express his dissatisfaction with the familiar parental admonition of the time, "This is going to hurt me more than it is going to hurt you."

Like many of the fathers on the East Side in those days, Tony showed his affection by simply grunting. Fudgy's mother was another story. Celia doted on her son's every whim. The truth was that Celia was a saint, and she thought her son was one, too. Who was Jack to tell her the truth about their winter expeditions to the old Normal School grounds, snowballs in hand, where they'd wait for the nuns to return to the convent and bombard them with their handmade missiles or about any of her son's less-than-saintly escapades?

Sacred Heart Academy was about a ten-minute walk from Jack's house, so he often met friends along the way. Waking up was always a tug of war between Jack and his mother; he literally had to be dragged out of bed on most mornings. He would barely have time for toast or cereal. His clothes were already picked out and waiting, a fact that Jack thoroughly resented—after all, Jack was a big boy now. Still, he was lucky if he made it to school before the final morning bell rang.

During this time, Jack began a slow, unnoticeable transition from the innocence of childhood to the mischievousness of pre-adolescence. The world around him had not yet begun to change, but his perception of it surely had. His experiences in life were not reconciling with the idyllic relationships and happy endings so often portrayed on *Leave It to Beaver* and *Father Knows Best*. Jack's life was different from those boys' lives on TV. Somehow, somewhere, something was missing.

On the surface, everything appeared fine. Jack was a good student. He scored in the top 10 percent nationally in all his aptitude tests, and he fortified himself with the knowledge that he was smart, smarter than 90 percent of the kids in the country. He had a family that cared for him and loved him and plenty of friends. At school, he was rather popular with his classmates.

Still, on a deeper level, Jack felt dissatisfied. He always measured himself against others, and as one of the smallest kids in the neighborhood and in his class, he often found himself looking up and left wanting. As a kid, Jack was consumed with desiring material possessions. He looked at what everyone else had and he didn't have. This was likely due to the influence of his Depression-era mother, who watched every penny and in his mind's eye forced him to lead a spartan existence. There was a difference between Woolworth's five-and-dime and Filene's. Jack lived a Woolworth's life, and he didn't like it.

Further, Jack began to realize that he was no longer the only favored child of the family. His younger brother, Patrick, was taking up quite a bit of his father's attention. Life no longer revolved around him, and he had a difficult time adjusting to that fact. Before long, his desire for the better things in life—and for escaping from life's sorrows—would lead to trouble.

CHAPTER NINE

S itting in the front row of the classroom, Jack was still lost in his thoughts when Sister Anna Catherine called out from behind her monstrous oaken desk.

"John, it's your turn! Can you come up here, please!"

At the Sacred Heart Academy, where he was now in fifth grade, Jack was always called by his given Christian name, John. Every time Sister Anna Catherine asked for something, her words were more a command than a question. As he rose from his seat, Jack's heart began to flutter then race. The moment he'd been dreading had finally come: it was time for his oral presentation before the class.

To Jack, the ten-minute walk to school every day was drudgery, especially since early mornings were not his favorite time of day and, even more to the point, his final destination was school. Not that he hated school with a passion; he was just like any number of ten-year-olds who would rather be doing other things, especially early in the morning.

Another typical school day, another typical beginning. Jack's mother had just about dragged him out of bed. "Jackie!" she'd hollered from the kitchen at seven thirty. "Jackie! You don't wanna be late again!"

The words had speared through his skull with the sharp pain of an earache. Finally, when resistance proved futile, he'd put a foot on the cold linoleum floor. Jack was lucky if he made it to school before the final morning bell rang at eight. At the second bell at eight ten, attendance was taken for the day, and there certainly would be repercussions and a trip to the headmaster's office if the class was not seated and quiet.

That particular morning in October, Jack's battle against wakefulness was even more difficult than usual, and on his walk, he was too preoccupied to feel the warmth of the morning sun on his face or notice the vibrant colors of the trees. Instead, he was lost in his mental preparation for his presentation. He'd never spoken in front of any group before. And even though he counted many of the kids in the class as neighborhood friends, he was terrified.

"John!" Sister Anna Catherine said, more forcefully this time. "Please be courteous to the rest of the class and get up here!"

Jack walked to the front of the room. For a moment, he stood there in his white shirt and tie and black, twill trousers, staring out across the regimented rows of boys and girls, arranged seemingly by size. He'd known many of them his whole life, yet suddenly he couldn't see a single person he recognized.

"Ummm…" He tried to corner a thought, any thought, but they careened through his head like spilled marbles. "Ummmm."

Somewhere in the crowd, a girl giggled.

"John!" Sister Anna Catherine said, and it was enough to make him focus. At last, he could begin.

Decades later, only a few memory fragments remain of that day. What Jack does recall, and even relive, is the utter sense of despair, shame, and hopelessness that he felt, the disorientation and smallness. The worst came when Jack related a scene from a story they'd read in class. "Then, boat a dem guys came down da street,"

Jack said, his nervousness driving his heavy East Side accent to the fore even more than usual.

A loud guffaw from somewhere in the back of the room broke the spell, and the entire class began to laugh. To make matters worse, Sister Anna Catherine shouted for order, and then unleashed her withering criticism in the resulting silence.

"John," she hissed, "if you could continue your speech in the *English* language, we would *all* greatly appreciate it."

Growing up in a neighborhood populated with Italian immigrants provided little opportunity to perfect the enunciation of the King's English. Jack might as well have been in Brooklyn. In Jack's world, "youse guys," "underwears," and "boat a youse" were common phrases and quite understandable. Jack had no idea that his teacher would be less than impressed with his colloquial Shrewsbury Street dialect.

Beet-faced and ashamed, Jack saw his friends, Michael, Fudgy, and Dermott, as well as the girls, Kathleen, Margaret, and even cute little Mary, covering their mouths and holding back their sniggering. What could he possibly tell them to make them understand? His mind conjured scenarios so quickly that even the new computers being built by IBM would have had trouble keeping up with the flow of self-deprecating thoughts. He could give excuses, but he was too ashamed to verbalize them. His mother never finished the eighth grade; as the oldest of the eight remaining children, she had to go to work to help support the family. His father drank, maybe not as much as some, but his parents argued over it, and when they did, Jack lost sleep.

His head was spinning; his classmates' faces were as distorted as his view of himself and the world. Jack cut his presentation short and again received a disapproving glare from Sister Anna Catherine. He returned to his seat in the front row. The only saving grace was that no one could see the tears welling up in his eyes. Jack was a class clown. Admittedly, he often sought attention and approval. He enjoyed making his classmates laugh but never, never at his own expense. He wished he were anywhere but there.

For the others in the room, the incident meant little—a diversion in an otherwise busy day, a funny story that could be told and eventually forgotten. But for Jack, it was different. In those few moments, a big piece of Jack's self-confidence died. Despite the fact that they were largely self-imposed, the embarrassment and emotional trauma would remain with him forever.

For Jack, that morning would thankfully give way to better ones; he mostly enjoyed his life at Sacred Heart. A small Catholic parish school, it was run by the Sisters of Saint Joseph and supported by the Worcester Diocese and several volunteer mothers whose kids attended the school. Jack's mother was one of those volunteers—which meant that Jack could never get away with anything. But that didn't prevent him from trying.

The school was a four-story brick building with a modicum of ornamentation, typical of early twentieth-century architecture. Its nearly square confines held about four hundred and fifty boys and girls from kindergarten through grade twelve. The headmaster, a diminutive Catholic priest named Father Carelli, obviously suffered from a Napoleonic complex. He ruled the school with heavy-handed discipline and released his frustration with a form of punishment that by today's standards could only be labeled physical abuse and likely would result in his dismissal—a vigorous slap to the back of the head. Jack was able to avoid his wrath for the most part, primarily because his mother worked so hard at the school. Fudgy, on the other hand, was not so fortunate.

"Michael, step into my office," was a familiar refrain. Soon to grow to over six feet tall, Fudgy literally kept Father Carelli on his toes, as the pint-sized priest nearly had to jump to administer his signature punishment. A consummate actor, Michael invariably would emerge from the headmaster's office with a stifled smirk on his face and throw out his best James Cagney imitiation: "Made it, Ma! Top of the world!"

A common feature of the Catholic schools of the day, corporal punishment wasn't solely Father Carelli's domain. The nuns who presided over the classrooms, dressed in full black habit and white headgear, employed it as well, most notably Sister Alice Gertrude, who wielded her "friend," a heavy wooden ruler, with the mercilessness of a Tatar chieftain. It took no more prompting than a bit of idle chatter between two classmates, a disturbance that by today's standard would barely raise an eyebrow.

"You!" Sister Alice Gertrude would bark. "Stop that fooling around back there, and please step up to the front of the class and stick out your hand." Invariably, the sharp crack of wood against flesh followed. Needless to say, this method kept most students in line.

Aside from the intermittent draconian punishment, life was pretty uneventful for the largely homogeneous, white, middle-class student population, as they dressed in their school uniforms and complied with the values and regulations of the strictly run school. As Jack moved obediently through the halls of Sacred Heart, he could never imagine, even in his wildest dreams, the strange twists and turns that life would someday bring.

On a personal level, Jack's life was going pretty well. He was healthy and felt relatively secure about himself, or so he thought. His grades and aptitude tests affirmed his extreme intelligence, and he had a large group of neighborhood kids that he could call friends.

Recovering alcoholics and addicts often say that the thought process that gets many people into trouble is "comparing their insides to someone else's outsides." That's what Jack was doing.

His parents' fighting, which often centered on his father's drinking, also proved troubling. Years later, Jack would write the following as part of his fourth-step inventory:

When my parents fought, I resented them. I was ashamed of their fight-ing; I thought I had the only parents that argued. Looking back, I was scared because I did not know what was going to happen next. It seemed like the argument would never end and the two people that I trusted most would suddenly undergo a metamorphosis before my very eyes. The fight-ing seemed to be out of character for them, my mother with her unwavering religious devotion and my father usually reserved and unassuming. So typically Irish, he seldom spoke more than a few sentences, let alone raise his voice in anger.

If life at Sacred Heart was largely carefree, a few early warning signs had begun to appear in Jack's life outside school. Often, a group of kids from Sacred Heart would gather on the property of the old State Normal School. Originally chartered to educate future teachers, the Normal School offered free tuition for those who intended to teach in the commonwealth; those planning to teach out of state paid fifteen dollars per semester. Its home was the grounds of the former State Lunatic Asylum, which was known locally as the nuthouse and provided fodder for many late-night ghost stories.

The rambling, wooded grounds of the Normal School provid-ed the perfect setting for covert activities, from innocent games of hide-and-seek all the way down to smoking, hanging out while cutting class, stashing stolen treasures, and throwing snowballs at the nuns. While these pursuits may have seemed like childish mischief, an underlying disregard for authority was beginning to percolate underneath Jack's "good boy" exterior.

An ominous sign of this was the stealing. Nearly every day, Jack and his trusted sidekick, Fudgy, would venture out into the world carrying their red school bags, emblazoned in white with "Sacred Heart Academy," to steal anything they felt they needed.

Mostly, the two lifted cartons of cigarettes from Manzi's Market, a small grocery store on Shrewsbury Street. Working in tandem, they had developed a flawless routine. Fudgy, the bigger of the two, provided cover and interference, distracting whoever was minding the cash register. Jack, a diminutive and innocent-looking young cherub, crouched in Fudgy's shadow and stuffed cartons of smokes into his Sacred Heart bag. It was more an act of independence and defiance than necessity. Jack and Fudgy supplied every kid in the neighborhood with smokes and threw away more cigarettes than they actually smoked themselves. But as they racked up successes, their boldness and misguided belief in their own cleverness grew.

Stealing was not just a bad habit; it was becoming a way of life, a means to an unknown end. True, they came from relatively poor families that lacked material wealth, but the reasons they stole were more nebulous, much like a shadow that passes just outside one's peripheral vision, ephemeral and unrecognizable. And they enjoyed a remarkable streak of good fortune—until their luck ran out.

In sixth grade, a combination of arrogance and naïveté led to disaster. At the beginning of each school year, the class elected officers to the Saint Dominic Savio Club. Dominic Savio had been a pupil of Saint John Bosco, founder of the Salesian Society, which helped poor children and educated boys for the priesthood. Savio died at age fifteen in 1857, and Pope Pius XII canonized him as "the classroom saint" in 1954. Only a few years later, Jack was elected treasurer of the fledgling club in Worcester. No one, including Jack, knew at the time of that election that he certainly would not be headed for the priesthood. The voting was primarily a popularity contest; by no means was it a barometer of Jack's saintliness.

In fact, at Sacred Heart, a less-than-saintly approach to life could boost a candidate's fortunes. Jack's antiauthoritarian streak elevated him on the social scale, and his small stature made him a bit of an underdog. Combined, the two traits made him electable.

The beginning of the year passed quite uneventfully, but when Thanksgiving and then Christmas came around, things got interesting. As treasurer, Jack was responsible for collecting fifty cents from each member of the class and purchasing the Thanksgiving and Christmas gifts for their class teacher, Sister Margaret Mary. As a seasoned shoplifter, Jack understood it to be his responsibility to steal those gifts. It also afforded an opportunity to keep the collected funds, a reward for crafting such an ingenious plan. This represented the perfect chance for Jack and Fudgy to expand their repertoire from cigarettes to school supplies, gifts for the nuns, and money.

The local Neiman Marcus offered a wide range of fine school supplies. With a budget of less than twenty dollars, there was very little that Jack could buy. But with his Sacred Heart Academy schoolbag, the sky was the limit. With Fudgy's assistance, Jack swiped the perfect Thanksgiving gift: a marble pen and pencil set.

When gift-giving time came, any discrepancy between the class's budgeted amount and the actual cost of that gift went unnoticed. Buoyed by their success and by the approval of their classmates, Fudgy and Jack were determined to make Christmas even better.

Once again, Neiman Marcus was the store of choice. Being more grandiose than wise, Jack bagged a gold-leaf dictionary, a gold-leaf pen, and an expensive polished-stone paperweight. All three appeared on Sister Margaret Mary's desk at the classroom Christmas celebration. With the exception of Sister Margaret Mary, who had taken a vow of poverty, no one mentioned that the display of generosity seemed excessive. There may have been a few raised eyebrows, quiet murmurs, or smirks, but mostly, the kids in the room kept quiet.

The beginning of the new year heralded new elections of class officers for the Saint Dominic Savio Club. These were not to be ordinary elections, however. Sister Margaret Mary, still proudly displaying her recently acquired gifts on her desk, asked the class to comment on why the current class officers should or should not be reelected. What started to be a promising new year quickly deteriorated when one of Jack's classmates wrote: "Jack should not be reelected as treasurer because he smokes, he steals, he swears, and he drinks."

This traitorous classmate would grow up to be a Worcester police officer whose path would collide with Jack's. Needless to say, Jack was not reelected class treasurer, the gifts disappeared from the nun's desk, and Jack was instructed to bring his parents in for a meeting to discuss his behavior.

At first, Jack was indignant. After all, he had not had a drink since he was five, so at least the drinking was a lie. And the rest? Outrageous untruths, Jack insisted. Under pressure, however, his bravado soon vanished. Being a sixth-grader faced with expulsion and the prospect of being separated from his friends, he delivered a full confession. The other kids implicated had to bring their parents in for a family discussion as well. Jack successfully blamed the classmate who had ratted him out for finking on the other kids, as well. This small victory served as a temporary balm and helped Jack to brush off the incident as a minor bump in the road. He passed through the bright red stop sign and flew right toward the next accident that was waiting to happen.

Today, there is quite a bit of discussion about gateway drugs and behaviors. Risk factors such as little parental monitoring, early onset of risk-taking behavior, early aggressiveness, and a high level of sensation seeking were clearly evident in Jack and his closest friends. Anecdotally, their histories validate the theory about gateways, which states that use of less deleterious drugs precedes and can lead to future use of more dangerous hard drugs or crime. It is often attributed to the earlier use of one of several licit substances, including tobacco or alcohol, as well as cannabis. For Jack and the kids he hung around with, all the gateways were open. They would pass obligingly through each and every one of them.

Too often we hold fast to the clichés of our forebears. We subject all facts to a prefabricated set of interpretations. The comfort of opinion without the discomfort of thought.

—Jack Kennedy

A 1978 experiment called Rat Park, conducted by psychologist Bruce K. Alexander and his colleagues at Simon Fraser University in British Columbia, Canada, suggests another factor in addiction: feelings of isolation.

Previous rat experiments had produced so-called proof of chemical dependency. Rats were stuck alone in small cages called Skinner boxes and taught to self-administer drugs. The rats became addicted and chose the drugs over food and water. Therefore, it was hypothesized that the primary problem with drugs is that they are chemically addictive.

Professor Alexander did not think that this was the correct conclusion. He had another hypothesis and decided to test it. Rats are gregarious creatures by nature, and as with all mammals, social attachment is part of their neural circuitry. Alexander wondered how they'd behave if they were in a more sociable environment. The experiment showed that the rats living communally in Rat Park didn't use heroin, even if the heroin was added to a sweetened solution, while rats isolated in cages did use the heroin and in great quantities.

Then, Alexander and colleagues created a group of heroin-addicted rats and moved them into Rat Park to see if they remained addicted. Their findings were reinforced; the rats stopped using heroin. They apparently preferred to live their lives in a simulated paradise, unencumbered by the haze of opiate addiction! Conclusion: Given the right environment, rats can recover from heroin addiction. Is the same true for humans?

CHAPTER TEN

I n the summer of 1959, Jack and his family moved away from Merrifield Street, the hill, Shrewsbury Street, and his friends. Jack wasn't very happy about moving into a new neighborhood and meeting new people, but his mother wanted her own home, and in Jack's family, neither democracy nor meaningful debate was the order of the day. So off they went to realize the "American dream" of homeownership.

Like many of their friends and relatives, Jack's parents settled on a three-family home very similar to the one they had lived in on Merrifield Street—perhaps because they needed rental income to pay the mortgage. The house, slightly larger and newer than their previous one, featured plenty of open space, a big lawn, and no grapevines. It sat on an incline, on the upper part of Ashwood Street, in a neighborhood that was slightly more affluent than the East Side. Single-family homes and duplexes mingled with the triple-deckers, housing those who didn't live with multiple generations or need the rental income. The neighborhood's inhabitants were just as diverse as the housing was. No longer did every family name end in a vowel, nor did Jack find them easily decipherable. The neighborhood was full of names that he could not pronounce. It was composed mostly of Swedes, Norwegians, and Germans. There were a few Irish families and, notably, only one other Italian family.

Jack's family may have moved off the hill, but their hearts still belonged with their extended family on Merrifield Street. Jack made a few new friends but mostly stayed in touch with his old ones, contact made easy by his continued attendance at Sacred Heart. His only two memories from Ashwood Street are the close relationship he formed with Ricky, a son in the Italian family, and a tragic incident involving a boy named Steven, who lived in the single-family house at the bottom of the hill.

It all started when Steven chucked a rock that hit Jack on the head. And it ended seconds later with a retaliatory toss. In disbelief, Jack watched as the jagged rock he'd thrown traveled a good fifty yards, skipped off the asphalt, and ricocheted into Steven's face, injuring him seriously and permanently blinding him in one eye. The incident was a source of embarrassment and shame for Jack's mother and father, but Jack's ensuing apology was perfunctory and insincere. At twelve years of age, Jack either failed to understand the gravity of the situation or, rubbing the goose egg on his own skull, felt no remorse.

Soon after that incident, the family packed up and moved back to Merrifield Street, back to Jack's old neighborhood and friends. This time, they settled into another Merrifield Street triple-decker almost directly across the street from his grandmother's house. The family had lasted less than two years on Ashwood Street, and Jack was back where he belonged.

In trying to reconstruct the events of his younger life as part of his fourth-step work, Jack wrote, "I am not sure why we moved. Was it my father's continued drinking, my rock-throwing incident, or the fact that my mother simply wanted to be close to her mother again?" Maybe it was a combination of all three, but they never really talked about it as a family. The lack of communication was nothing extraordinary. See nothing, hear nothing, say nothing was an understood code of conduct for everyone, or so it seemed. Like most life questions, this one was for Jack to resolve.

Jack didn't miss a beat socially upon moving back to the East Side. In fact, as a parallel to the widely held belief that addiction is a progressive disease, so too was his deviant behavior. It wasn't long after Jack's return that the frequency of his pilgrimages to the confessional became inversely proportional to the frequency of occasions that required it.

Sex was just one aspect of Jack's life that was worthy of confession. His introduction to sex came rather ingloriously on the back stairwell in the Mount Carmel Recreation Center. The center provided an ideal shelter from the harsh winters of New England. Operated and staffed by the parish priests and a group of parishioners who volunteered their time to help keep their children out of trouble (at least in theory); the center was a logical gathering place for the Sacred Heart Academy kids. Most of the kids used their free time on relatively healthy activities like basketball and bowling in one of the city's premier candlepin alleys, which was located in the basement. Occasionally, they indulged in less wholesome pursuits.

"Is she really going to?" Jack asked, half elated and half terrified. Jack was barely mature enough to know anything about the birds and the bees, let alone the intricacies of love and affection, but for Jack and two of his academy friends, an opportunity had presented itself.

Bucky, one of Jack's classmates and closest friends stationed himself at the bottom of the stairs as a lookout: it would really spell trouble if they were discovered in a stairwell at the back of the Lady of Mount Carmel Recreation Center. At the top of the stairs was Capo with a heavyset girl who wanted to be accepted and was willing to satisfy a young boy's inquisitiveness.

Soon, Capo came down the stairwell, his face flushed and a triumphant but with a somewhat bewildered look in his eyes. "You're next," he said to Jack, giving him a shove toward the stairs.

It was over in seconds. Whether it was the Bible classes he'd attended or just a sinking realization that this was wrong, Jack couldn't say. Neither of his two friends seemed to have the same regret, but somewhere inside Jack knew they were taking advantage of this needy girl. But his need for acceptance and his physical urges overruled his morality. The ensuing shame from this and other early sexual experiences would later define a long period of sexual dysfunction that Jack could only relieve with self-administered medication.

The details of those encounters are less important than Jack's ensuing rationalization, convincing himself that what happened was not really a sin since they didn't have intercourse or that she really wanted to please him and how bad could that be. The absurdity of seeking absolution for these indiscretions was magnified by the fact that this all happened on church grounds.

As a "good Catholic," Jack was well versed in the nuances of confession. He quickly learned that one of the goals was to receive a lenient penance. To that end, one would always search out the priest who, no matter what one did or said, would dole out an "Our Father" or a couple of "Hail Mary's" as a means of reconciling oneself to God. Interestingly enough, confession did not require any reconciliation with the people who had felt the impact of the sin— at least, that was the way Jack understood it.

Sometimes the search for a lenient confessor could take a sinner halfway across the city. Fortunately, for most of their early adolescence, Jack and his coconspirators were blessed with the presence of a priest affectionately known as Father Hail Mary, who handed out one "Hail Mary" for penance regardless of the number or severity of the sins confessed. On Saturdays, it was nearly comical to see the line outside Father Hail Mary's confessional. Resembling the queue at a movie theater in length and composition, the line consisted primarily of young devotees, both male and female. Outside the confessionals of the other priests waited queues of black-clad, elderly women, most of whom had long passed the opportunity for any untoward dalliances.

The sexual misconduct, stealing, and smoking aside, it was still primarily a time of innocence and of local and national pride. In the nation's first televised presidential debate, a young and vigorous Massachusetts senator, John F. Kennedy, lambasted the sweaty, nervous-looking vice president, Richard M. Nixon. On the East Side, many of the residents, and particularly the Irish Catholics, watched their Massachusetts native son with pride. The debate changed many people's minds about Kennedy. He moved into the White House, the first Catholic elected as president, and gave his famous speech: "Ask not what your country can do for you, but what you can do for your country." There was more opportunity for American pride at the Rome Olympic Games, where sprinter Wilma Rudolph won three gold medals.

There were ominous moments, too; many courtesy of the Cold War. In May 1960, newspaper headlines declared an American U2 spy plane had been shot down over the Soviet Union. In April 1961, the Soviet Union launched the first human into space. The United States duplicated the event a month later, when Alan Shepard soared into space aboard the Freedom 7. And in September 1962, President Kennedy promised that the United States would send a man to the moon before the decade was over.

Like the race for the moon, the next few years of Jack's life were full of new challenges and voyages in unbelievable new directions. Jack's teenage years were defined by the code of conduct he encountered on Shrewsbury Street and in East Park, however misguided and antisocial that code was.

CHAPTER ELEVEN

Shrewsbury Street was the center of activity for the neighborhood, and East Park was the site of many of its social events. The park, now officially called Cristoforo Colombo Park, was deeded to the City of Worcester on December 6, 1909, by a vote of the parks commissioners. One portion of the land had been purchased from the former state hospital ten years earlier. Another portion of land had been transferred from the water department by order of the Worcester City Council in 1895. This parcel included a small body of water now known as Bell Pond, which was to play an ignominious role for many in the gang that called East Park their home base.

There was always something going on at East Park, whose entrance was guarded by two huge stone griffins. This ornamental gateway was installed in 1916, using the griffins that formerly supported the arch of the train shed at Worcester's old Union Railroad Station. It is believed the griffins were transported to the park by horse and sled, and today, they still stand as a rather ominous warning to all who enter.

History aside, East Park was the setting for just about every major event in the neighborhood and the centerpiece of the city every Fourth of July. The fireworks display drew residents from the surrounding area, and the park was alive with activity for the entire day. For the neighborhood's Catholics, summer was a time of religious festivals, as well. All summer long, life-sized figures of the various saints, from Santa Maria di Anzano to Saint Anthony de Padua and Santa Rosalia di Palermo, were carried aloft down Shrewsbury Street, their garments adorned with money from the faithful, to arrive in East Park for several days of celebration. The East Park festivities were among Jack's earliest and fondest memories, but by the time he reached adolescence, they had begun to fade away. Gone were the large fireworks displays and the huge crowds on July 4. The saints clung to their positions a bit longer, but they, too, gradually left center stage. The neighborhood was slowly losing its prosperity. Newer generations may have been casting off the ways of the old. These changes did not resonate loudly for Jack, who was undergoing his own silent metamorphosis.

For Jack, Fudgy, and many of their schoolmates, the days of practicing the values of the Catholic saints were replaced by the days of emulating the guys from the Street. The hustle and bustle of Shrewsbury Street soon replaced the relatively quiet confines of the recreation center, and East Park served as a new home away from home. The possibilities for excitement were endless, and there was much to learn from the street-smart kids who seemed to be permanent fixtures there.

Jack's circle of friends was rapidly expanding to include the kids from public school and the guys from Shrewsbury Street who lived right on the main drag: Squeaky, the Greek, Butchie, Big Head, Stan the Man, Jimmy G., Dumbo, Guido, Buddie, Buckie, Jughead, Baba, Toojo, and a litany of other guys whose distinctly uncomplimentary monikers were linked to personal characteristics.

Jack's favorite nickname was Ace, although there were others that were not as complimentary. "Ace" stemmed from Jack's excellence at playing cards, especially poker, a skill made possible by his fantastic memory. Using his ability to recall the order of cards from the previous hand, Jack soon learned that the shuffle, intended to randomize the order in which the cards are dealt, is not a perfect system. Depending on the determination, dexterity, and skill of the dealer, cards often appeared in exactly the same order in which they'd been gathered. It wasn't a perfect system, but paying attention to the order of the cards before the shuffle often gave Jack the advantage he needed to win.

Gambling was exciting, immediately gratifying, and, for a young teenager, extremely lucrative. Jack seldom lost, and his winnings enabled him to show off a wad of one-dollar bills ostentatiously, many of which he spent foolishly. Perhaps more important, Jack's skill with cards enabled his assimilation into the group and gave him status.

With his friends, Jack found it difficult to be himself; his home life had conditioned him to be the adult and just being one of the kids was challenging. When his parents fought, he was the peacemaker, the one who had to make things better. It was a role that no child should have to assume, but all too often, intentionally or not, children do. In the gang, Jack was becoming overly responsible but in a dysfunctional sort of way. He was like the surrogate parent and often played the role of mediator. But he also used cards as a means to gain power. Gambling was not pure enjoyment; in fact, it was very hard work. But it gave him money that he could use to keep some control over the gang. Jack would be the one buying the sodas and the cigarettes—if he wasn't stealing them, that is.

A gambling habit was just one of the changes in Jack's life. For Jack, hanging out and getting into trouble replaced doing homework and being a good student. He used his intelligence to create mischief. One of his earliest brainstorms was to drain Bell Pond and flood Shrewsbury Street. Draining Bell Pond was not an original idea. Jack had overheard one of the older guys telling a story about trying to drain the pond but failing. That story had rekindled one of Jack's most vivid memories from childhood.

In the early 1950s, a hurricane had battered the area. Shrewsbury Street was situated in a valley between two hills and was submerged in two or three feet of water. Jack could recall seeing small rowboats navigating the floodwaters and local residents rowing past the stone griffins at the park entrance. Even after a heavy rain, Shrewsbury Street often flooded, and many residents needed boats to leave their homes. Eventually, a new drainage system put a stop to the flooding by preventing much of the runoff from the surrounding hills.

Longing to recreate those exciting days, Jack took it upon himself to direct the waters of Bell Pond downhill and return recreational boating to Shrewsbury Street. He would succeed where others had failed. It didn't take too much convincing to enlist several of his friends to join him in what would be a historic achievement. If they accomplished their goal, their stock would surely rise with the older guys on the Street.

At the time, Jack believed planning to be one of his strong suits, and foolishly enough, so did most of his friends. The plan, as Jack envisioned it, was to dig a canal into the raised embankment that separated the pond from a swampy runoff area below. From there, the watercourse would lead down a steep hill until it began to level off at East Park before hitting its final destination, Shrewsbury Street. Once the water was set free, gravity would take care of the rest.

Those who had previously attempted this feat had failed to dig deeply enough, but Jack insisted that his team would not make that mistake. He reasoned that by digging inward from both sides of the embankment that held in the water and meeting in the middle, they could create a trench that would be deep enough to drain several feet of water from the pond. Rudimentary engineering suggested that if they created enough runoff, the erosion from the fast-flowing water would deepen the ditch and complete the job. As Jack explained it, his early education in earth science at Sacred Heart assured them of success.

The level of excavation required digging by night, which necessitated lights—something the gang didn't have. To solve that problem, they decided to break into the East Park Community House and steal the emergency lights.

The Community House was a large granite building situated in the middle of the park. In its lower level were restrooms and storage for maintenance equipment. Its upper floor was a large community room. For years, the older men of the neighborhood had used the room as a gathering place, but like the crowds for the fireworks and the feasts, their numbers were dwindling. The park's battery-operated emergency lighting was now stored in the upstairs room. Draining Bell Pond wasn't strictly an emergency, but the lights would serve the purpose. After gaining entry and access to the lights, the gang gathered other tools. Butchie, a member of the construction crew, borrowed some picks and shovels from his dad's cellar. George borrowed a pair of wading boots that his father used for fishing.

The gang waited until dark, and with emergency lights illuminating the work site, began to dig. The excavation of the dirt on the dry side of the pond's bank was slow and difficult. Even more laborious was the dredging in the water. As the foreman and strategist of the group, Jack volunteered to wear the borrowed waders and dig the trench at the water's edge. The boys dug from both sides, taking turns with the shovels and picks. Jack, Fudgy, Butchie, George, Squeaky, and Little Guido all worked for what felt like an eternity but was no more than a couple of hours. At thirteen and fourteen, everyone had an eleven o'clock curfew, so after a while, the gang decided it was time to call it quits and get home before it was too late. They agreed to return the next night to finish the job.

The next evening, the gang waited for darkness to fall and re-sumed working on the ditch. They were close to collapsing the last patch of dirt that separated the excavations and celebrating the completion of the trench when flashlights appeared and a voice called from the darkness, "Nobody move! You're under arrest!"

Standing knee-deep in the pond in fishing waders, shovel in hand, Jack couldn't have fled if he had wanted to. Cops with their guns drawn surrounded them. One can only imagine what the po-lice expected to find, but it wasn't a group of young teens. Drawn guns aside, the gang's apprehension was perhaps the most notice-able aspect of the bust. Jack and his friends didn't have the faintest idea that they were doing anything seriously wrong. This was just a little fun and excitement. They were only digging in the dirt, after all.

In a few moments, the police realized that the only weapons these kids had were construction tools and the only thing that was going to be buried was any hope of draining the pond without get-ting caught. The cops would make sure of that. For the police, there was a sigh of relief and some good-natured chiding as they told the kids they were all going down to the station. George, Butchie, Squeaky, and the rest were dreading the perfunctory phones call to inform their parents that all was not well.

One of the first to leave the police station was George, and his departure left a lasting impression on the rest of the gang. George's father was a big man, and when George left the room and the door started to close behind him, all one could see was a sweeping right hook heading for George's head. Mercifully, the door closed before George hit the floor. In those days, the cops did not need to rely on the courts to dole out justice to unruly kids; that is what fathers were for.

Jack was one of the lucky ones. His father was not prone to physical punishment; that was the upside to his emotional sto-icism. Jack's mother, on the other hand, was constantly boiling with pent-up emotion, and she eagerly assumed the task of discipline. Jack was not too worried about his father coming to the police station. Jack knew there would be a lecture, a shake of his head in disgust, but no beating, and that's pretty much what his punishment amounted to—along with a bit more of a lecture from his mother.

Still, life at home was not without its problems. Jack's parents were still enmeshed in their weekly fights, and their arguments were escalating into physical contact, mostly pushing and shoving, with his mother being the aggressor. The arguments often spilled out of the apartment and into the neighborhood for everyone to hear. Jack felt embarrassed and ashamed, but he could do nothing to change the situation.

His dad's ability to tolerate the booze continued to deteriorate, and his mother's reaction to the drinking continued to escalate, especially around the holidays. This made Jack uncomfortable and even angry. His aversion to his dad and his drinking finally boiled over one bright summer day during a trip to Fenway Park to see the Boston Red Sox. Of course, going to Fenway started out as a lark. It was not often that Jack and his father spent time together alone. Jack's father had been a promising ballplayer and had had a tryout with the Red Sox, and Jack was anticipating a day filled with special moments that only a father and son might share.

The day that started out with so much hope slowly began to turn hopeless, much like a typical Red Sox season. As the innings passed and the drinking escalated, Jack's dad became more and more intoxicated. Eventually, Jack's embarrassment and shame became intolerable. He could no longer remain in his father's presence. He needed to run and hide.

On one of his father's journeys to the beer stand, Jack simply left. He had no idea how he was going to get home; he figured he could always walk, so that is what he began to do. He must have been in some sort of blackout because he can hardly remember the details of how he managed to get home that day. He can, however, recall hitchhiking.

He was picked up by a man who, at first, appeared to be very kind. The ride went well until the driver made a comment about the lump in Jack's shorts. Immediately, Jack asked him to pull over, stop the car, and let him out. The man was good enough to comply, and Jack was lucky to escape any further molestation. When he got home, there was a brief sigh of relief and the obligatory scolding. When his father got home, the argument about the drinking and the neglect of a son went on for way longer than Jack would have liked.

Most people tend to learn from bad experiences; it usually doesn't take more than one encounter with a hot stove to realize that touching it is unadvisable. After the dredging incident, some of Jack's friends stayed away from the park. Others simply never entertained any of Jack's bright ideas again. But for most of the gang, including Jack, that one bad decision led to more, all in the search for immediate gratification and under the guise of fun. Jack was young enough to believe that nothing could destroy him and nothing could control him.

People who study normal human development, if there is such a thing, say that adolescence is when young people acquire the cognitive, social, and emotional skills and abilities required to navigate life. Literature on the subject suggests that adolescence varies for everyone, since gender, socioeconomics, and culture influence development. Young people are shaped by formal institutions, such as church and school, and by relationships with peers, parents, mentors, and bosses. Jack, whose world was shifting from the early positive influences of home and school to the more worldly and fascinating influences of the Street, would likely have agreed with this sentiment.

Strangely enough, however, it appears that many of the early psychologists failed to integrate or fully understand the impact that early substance-abuse disorders could play on development. Twentieth-century psychologist Erik Erikson identified adolescence as a time of identity formation and said that "behavior changes in response to biological maturation and changes in the social environment." But what happens when adolescents view the use of mind-altering substances as a necessary ingredient to social activity?

In East Park, the changes in the social environment came to include more and more drinking. One of the gang's favorite hangout spots—overlooking the park and littered with empty beer cans—was around a large oak fondly referred to as the "Drinking Tree."

In a way, it was appropriate that the primary symbol of identification for the kids of East Park centered around drinking. After all, alcohol and alcohol-related events took center stage in most of the park's activities, despite city ordinances prohibiting alcohol in recreational areas.

For Jack and the gang, every Friday night held the potential that something great was going to happen—and that something great usually involved alcohol. The beer bottle known as GIQ, or giant imperial quart, was the beverage of choice for many of the kids in the park. The GIQ was affordable enough, and it packed a sufficient punch to provide a desired level of intoxication. For Jack and his friends, consumption of a GIQ occasionally led to a condition known as the bed spins, which meant a leap from bed and a mad dash to the bathroom for a session of vomiting or the dreaded dry heaves—a sure way to get caught by your parents and get grounded until the next Friday arrived.

The people of the East Side loved their gossip, and this had repercussions as well. It was embarrassing enough for Jack to have his parents find him in the bathroom hugging the toilet bowl and retching. Infinitely worse to young Jack's fragile male ego was to have his mother go down to the corner hangout and tell his friends, "Jackie threw up all night last night; he really cannot handle drinking"—especially since Jack had told everyone that he was fine and would have no problem holding down his booze. In Jack's neighborhood, holding your liquor without puking was a badge of honor, even at thirteen.

So where did such young kids get alcohol? Despite laws designed to prevent it, obtaining alcohol was not difficult for the kids of East Park. Dumbo and his best pal, Buddie, were the surest connection to alcohol, being the only members of the group who looked old enough to buy at the local liquor store. Fake IDs were easily obtained, and most liquor stores didn't bother to check IDs anyway. As for the local police, one needed only to look at the piles of beer cans littering the park to know that enforcement of alcohol-possession laws were not a priority. In fact, most people considered drinking by the local youth to be normal, and complaints were few.

At first, drinking didn't seem like a problem for Jack, either. As he remembers, alcohol meant a chance for a group of friends to get together and talk about the Red Sox or brag about sexual conquests that were yet to come. Despite the occasional puking session, the times seemed to pass uneventfully, except when events bigger than the neighborhood intruded.

The assassination of John F. Kennedy on November 22, 1963, was one such event. In the halls of Sacred Heart Academy, girls wept openly, but for Jack and his friends, the real implications, notably the loss of American idealism, were pushed aside by discussions of conspiracy theories and, eventually, more local concerns. Life continued to march on, and for most of the inhabitants of East Park and the Street, the things that made front-page news had little impact on their everyday affairs. Instead, life was defined by what happened closer to home.

To underscore just how insulated many of the guys were from the world and its machinations, consider the story of the Mark Five

Band, which was made up primarily of kids from the East Side. Dumbo was the lead singer and rhythm guitarist. His older brother, Freddie, was the bandleader and played the organ and piano. Rounding out the band was a drummer (the group's only African American), a lead guitarist, and a bassist, all of whom were excellent musicians. The Mark Five hit its peak on April 30, 1965, when it opened for the Rolling Stones at Worcester Memorial Auditorium. For Jack and the gang, the big deal was not the Stones, but the Mark Five, and the fact that they were given the privilege of setting up the Worcester combo's equipment on the Aud's magnificent stage.

Even the arrival of the Beatles had little effect on the neighborhood culture. Beatlemania may have overtaken the country, but in East Park, "The Lion Sleeps Tonight," as rendered a cappella by Dumbo, Fudgy, Buddie, and Guido, was still the music of choice. The four also perfected their rendition of "Bird Land" in four-part harmony, their only accompaniment a steady supply of Budweiser or Schlitz, "The beer that made Milwaukee famous."

The guys' attempts at evening entertainment usually resulted in some sort of vandalism to the buildings and grounds of East Park. For Jack, the presence and use of alcohol was becoming more than a ritual. One fall evening, drinking became the catalyst for one of the most significant events of Jack's young life. He cannot recall the date or the details, but he does remember that some sort of epiphany took place.

The night started innocently enough with a large group gathering in East Park for a weekend drinking party. The group included a number of girls, whom Jack wanted to impress. His beverage of choice was a half pint of sloe gin, a sweet and syrupy liqueur that went down easily, without burning the esophagus and stomach as whiskey and scotch did, and often prompted vomiting.

As the chill of the fall air descended upon them, the kids decided on an exciting course of action: breaking into the Community

House, which was a good deal warmer. After they'd pried open one of the rotting wooden doors, they gathered comfortably in the warm, dark confines of the building, and the talk drifted. Buoyed by the euphoria of the sloe gin, Jack began to weave a tale that captured the attention and imagination of all of the hideaways present. The embarrassment of his fifth-grade speech and his fear of public speaking somehow magically disappeared. Jack felt empowered with some mystical ability to communicate with his peers in a way he had never imagined, and he was able to maintain that spell over his friends for what felt like an eternity.

To this day, Jack cannot recall the subject or the moral of his tale. He may have talked about President Johnson ordering bombing raids on North Vietnam, or the beginning of the subsequent war protests. He may have told a story about life in the neighborhood. But what he would never forget was the satisfaction that filled him completely. For that brief moment, Jack was the center of attention, the target of affection for the girls in the audience, the storyteller extraordinaire. He felt confident, invincible. He had shed, however momentarily, the shame that was his constant companion. It was more than the fifteen minutes of fame that Andy Warhol would later promise; it was, for Jack, a rebirth. But it came with a price. Jack was becoming a fledgling alcoholic. Sadly, he was too young—and too smart—to know it.

CHAPTER TWELVE

J ack's first experience with alcohol, at age five, had resulted in physical illness, providing an inoculation against drinking that lasted for seven years. His experiences with his family, and particularly his father, offered further proof of alcohol's damaging effects on human relationships. But that moment in East Park, with his friends gathered around and listening raptly, his self-confidence rising, and his social anxiety melting away, gave Jack another perspective. Alcohol contained a power he could not seem to find elsewhere.

Perhaps more important was the message that the culture he lived in provided daily: drinking was a part of life, a rite of passage, and something that everyone did. If Jack and his friends got a little hammered and took it a little too far on a Friday night, didn't their parents do that as well? And if they found themselves in the company of a crowd that didn't have the highest standards when it came to behavior, what other choices did they have? They were surrounded by people like these. They came from the same neighborhood, the same social stratum. Their families were so close that there were marriages among their extended clans.

The kids in East Park had been together for years; they had yet to splinter into subgroups based on the drugs they used, although some had begun to experiment. Many continued only to drink alcohol. But some liked to bolster the effect of alcohol with marijuana, and others found that they liked different drugs more than alcohol and decreased their drinking significantly or even quit drinking.

Yet at least early on, drinking played a role in many kids' lives, and not just inside the boundaries of East Park. A gang of them would get some alcohol, find a secluded place to drink, and have a party. Often drinking was a prelude to dances, concerts, sporting events, and other social functions. Some kids drank more heavily and frequently than others did, but never did they view themselves as alcoholic or in trouble with booze. It was what they were accustomed to. An imperial quart or a bottle of sloe gin in the hand of a teenager was never really frowned upon by those in the community—unless, of course, that teen couldn't "hold his liquor," in which case the individual, not the drinking itself, was considered a problem.

No matter where, when, or what they were drinking, the alcohol served a critical purpose: it helped to lower their inhibitions. Drinking or getting high allowed the kids to overcome anxiety and become more comfortable in social situations, especially those involving the opposite sex. Miraculously, alcohol and drugs allowed them to be social and chat, be comfortable and funny, suave and witty, or at least less afraid of social rejection. For Jack and his friends, the die was cast. What began as curious experimentation soon became their main method for dealing with the stresses of life. And over the years, it would become a preemptive tool for anticipated stress as well.

Although many of the East Side kids could see how a little alcohol made social situations easier, many could not or did not look deeper to gain an understanding of the more subtle—and therefore dangerous—effects of booze: it also masked their feelings of inadequacy and low self-esteem. Like the dark canal that ran below the city of Worcester, the emotional currents that surged through them—fear and envy, anger and shame—remained hidden from the light of day. They endured personal, painful experiences, often within the confines of their own homes. It was all there—verbal and physical abuse, alcoholism and poverty, infidelity and illegitimacy, depression and anxiety—but they never talked about it. You kept your business in the family and avoided, denied, or lied about it if ever asked. But standing at the Drinking Tree and surrounded by friends, Jack and the gang could numb the pain, escape to a fantasy world they created together. In that world, they were somebody's—operators with a hustle going on, feared or envied by the people around them. They lived together in this place of delusion, thinking they knew how to cope with life and its challenges, that everything would be good as long as they could make the liquor store connection for the party that night. They couldn't have been more wrong.

CHAPTER THIRTEEN

J D arrived on the East Side in the early 1960s. Although new to the neighborhood, he had connections through his father that made the transition a bit easier. Nonetheless, everything seemed new and exciting, especially the smells coming from the Italian bakeries of fresh-baked breads and pastries and the sounds of loud men arguing or playing the street-corner game of morra, which consisted of throwing out fingers while simultaneously trying to guess an opponent's choice.

"Cingo!"

"Quarte!"

"Duo!"

It seemed that the louder one yelled, the more distracted one's opponent became.

JD's dad, Muggsy, was a very well-known figure in the community, not for his civic or philanthropic activity but because he was "connected" to the "right" people and lived his life in a way that seemed very appealing to many of the younger guys. From a tiny restaurant storefront called Muggsy's Lunch, and later from his dry-cleaning store, he worked as a bookie, collecting bets from gamblers who hoped to hit the number and get lucky on any given day. At that time, state-run lotteries hadn't begun to harness the desire for gambling's illicit thrills. Atlantic City would not make gambling legal until 1976, and Native American casinos wouldn't exist for decades. But on the East Side, as in many urban neighborhoods, betting on numbers, horse races, sports, card games, and dice was common, and it generally remained low in the enforcement priorities of the local police.

Those who suffered gambling losses beyond their means relied on a system of illicit borrowing and lending. Bad luck usually was accompanied by a high interest rate (known as the juice or vigorish) to be paid as a fee for the loan. This created lucrative opportunities for anyone willing to risk a little money and self-respect to get ahead, and many of the neighborhood characters were involved at varying levels. Through the activities of his father, JD made a connection to the people who moved in that world.

JD's newspaper route, which he shared with his brother, bordered the east end of Shrewsbury Street. That, too, allowed him to get to know and develop relationships with many East Side residents. In seventh grade, when his family moved even closer to Shrewsbury Street, JD enrolled in the neighborhood's public school, and his East Side affiliation became official. Among his new friends were two boys who would soon become his best friends, Stevie the Sailor and Joe Arts. Both lived on the Street and were well known to all. They introduced JD to the neighborhood and many of their friends, including a kid with a razor-sharp tongue, quick wit, and a gift for calculating numbers, especially percentages and odds, named Hank.

Hank was two years JD's senior, and the Street was his front yard. Hank was constantly trying to find his place among the young people in the neighborhood. Already, his efforts were paying off. Many of the younger kids on the Street viewed him as a leader. Hank attended the Adam Street School, the same school as JD. Part of a close-knit Italian family, Hank lived in a triple-decker owned by his grandmother and his great-uncle, who lived on the third floor. A tenant occupied the first. Hank and his siblings lived on the second floor with his father, a union cement finisher, and his mother, a nurse at the Adams Street School. Hank thought his family was prosperous. They had two cars, when many families had no car at all. And they had a big garden with fruit trees in the back.

"Outside of my old man bein' drunk," Hank says of his young life on the Street, "I was the richest guy in the world."

Beyond the triple-decker's yard was the neighborhood. Hank loved everything about the East Side; most of all, the constant action. The place was alive with kids of every age, all looking for fun. And East Hill Park, especially on weekends, offered baseball, basketball, and even a swimming pool. But there was no action he loved more than gambling.

In retrospect, it's little wonder that Hank today describes gambling as his "first love." While no one in the family had any involvement with illicit betting, it surrounded the family home. From the window of his bedroom, Hank could look across the street to the candy store that fronted an operation that booked numbers and horse-racing bets. Two stores down was the dry-cleaning establishment where JD's father ran a bookmaking operation. The old woman who ran the book there was the best friend and a cousin of Hank's grandmother. Just a couple hundred yards down Shrewsbury Street on the same side as Hank's house was a ceramics shop that fronted as a sports-betting operation.

Too young to lay down sports bets, Hank fed his affinity for gambling in open-air card games on street corners and park benches: seven-card stud, five-card stud, and three-card murder for nickels, dimes, and quarters provided the forum for his "first love" to blossom. At a time when the minimum wage was $1.10 an hour and a schoolteacher took home less than one hundred dollars a week, throwing several quarters into a pot was risky, but with the risk came a huge rush, and that made it all worthwhile, win or lose.

A few quarters weren't the only losses young Hank experienced. Many times, he felt as if he had lost a real father, too. Hank's dad was hardworking and well liked in the neighborhood, but most days, he drank. Early on, Hank learned about the trouble drinking could cause: the arguments, the yelling, the hard-earned money wasted on liquor. Worse than Hank's father not being there for him most of the time was Hank knowing how wonderful it could be to have a sober father. Every year for Lent, his dad gave up drinking for forty days. But as soon as Lent was over, the drinking started again, and Hank made a promise to himself: he would never let alcohol rule his life.

Like Hank, JD and other friends in the neighborhood came from families that were troubled in some fashion, regardless of surface appearances. For many, it was safer to be with each other than it was to be at home, and they accepted one another regardless of the crazy or shameful places they came from.

Yet if they wanted to escape from families damaged by alcohol abuse, irresponsibility, and poverty, they had already begun to look in the wrong direction for role models. JD and his new group of friends didn't aspire to be like the hardworking adults they saw pouring their hearts and souls into their businesses, or those who showed up at their boring, low-paying, or menial jobs every day, year after year, so they could provide for their families. The East Side street kids mocked these folks as "ham-and-eggers" because they were practical, predictable, reliable, and honorable—the kind of people who ate the same old ham and eggs for breakfast every day but would never get a taste of the high life.

Instead, the young East Siders admired the wise guys, the toughs and hustlers too slick to have to work at regular jobs, or those who, like Hank's cousin, Tony, who made big money—in his case by managing a used-car lot—and flaunted their material success.

On the East Side, legit could be hard to find. The area had more than its share of these men: thieves, thugs, con artists, hustlers, and other two-bit gangsters. They carried big rolls of cash, drove fancy cars, and wore dapper clothes and the flashiest jewelry. Soon, JD and his friends began to mimic them in small but telling ways. They talked and acted as if they were smarter and slicker than everyone else, attitudes and behavior that felt as natural as breathing.

Although there were many different clusters of local characters in the community, it was a small geographic area, so the attitudes and behaviors were similar whether you lived or hung out at East Park, Muskeego Street, or near the diners (the Boulevard and the Parkway). Everyone seemed to have some type of connection or relationship that classified him as a "Shrewsbury Street" or an "East Side" kid. JD didn't hang out with Jack, Fudgy, the Greek, or the rest of that crew yet. But he, Hank, and their other friends began to do the same things—drinking, stealing, and gambling—in different places.

Like their heroes on the Street, JD, Hank, and their running mates had an attitude, an arrogance that helped them to justify their actions. If they wanted something, they took it and felt entitled to do so. They stole things they didn't need or use. They made bold raids on trucks being loaded at the neighborhood soft-drink-bottling plant, and then carried their booty to the railroad tracks, where they drank the stolen soda and smoked cigarettes until they were sick and smashed the full bottles left over. The rush of adrenaline was another high, and they developed a need for that, too. Their risk-taking behavior was progressive, and they always pushed the envelope. During another binging episode at the railroad tracks, they thought it would be cool and exciting to see who could stand closest to the tracks facing an oncoming train.

That game of "chicken" was cut short when Al S. got too close. As the other boys watched in amazement, a speeding locomotive sent him flying through the air. He landed in a rumpled heap along the tracks.

Was this a sign that they should change their ways? Maybe for some it would have been, but not for this group. Once the ambulance and the police left the scene, they collapsed in fits of laughter. What a dumb ass! Al ultimately recovered, at least from his physical injuries, but his emotional and psychological damage seemed to worsen over time, and he would be dead a few years later, taken down by addiction. At the time, however, the train accident was just another adventure.

Of course, soda wasn't the only beverage of choice for JD and his new friends. When JD was twelve, he and his buddy, Joe Arts, stole a huge jug of rotgut Parma wine from Joe's nearly comatose grandfather. It went down fast, and hours later, it came back up. Having returned home, JD vomited purple from one end of his house to the other. His mother's fury was nothing compared with how awful he felt. The next day, his hangover was worse, and he found that big pieces of the previous evening were missing from his memory. This first blackout became a topic of conversation in the gang—at least until the next one. JD's passion for escape, which began in early childhood and continued to grow over the years, outweighed the punishment for doing so. Getting drunk and crazy with his friends was what living was all about. He was living the dream.

Although kids on the East Side tended to hang within their core groups, cross-pollination occurred at social events and by casual coincidence. In 1964, JD and his friends ventured into the East Park area, just two blocks away. There, JD met Jack and his friends Fudgy, the Greek, and all the rest. It felt like a natural fit; soon, the two blocks that separated their hangouts evaporated, and they merged into one big, happy family.

Expanding their group also opened up new opportunities for them to practice newly forming talents, such as gambling and handicapping. Those behaviors were part of the culture of the Street, and it seemed that everyone participated. Even guys like JD, who didn't really like gambling, partook because that's what seemed normal; after all, his dad ran a bookmaking operation. In addition, JD felt social pressure: if he didn't gamble, the group might reject him, and that was too painful for him to contemplate after being emotionally rejected by his own father.

Fortunately, Muggsy's occupation provided not only the opportunity to participate in the world of gambling but was a convenient gang hangout as well. By then, Muggsy had moved his operation from the restaurant to Astoria Cleaners, a dry-cleaning business across the street. The "cleaners" had the look and feel of a shady business. Little light filtered in through its dirty windows, which were usually steamed up by the boiler and pants press machine. Smoke from Muggsy's Pall Malls stained the ceiling and mixed with the sharp tang of dry-cleaning chemicals to create an odor that clung to more than one's clothes. Few of the "customers" who visited Astoria carried clothes in or out, but some did; there were times when Muggsy was actually in the shop pressing clothes as JD and his siblings sorted and counted wads of money from the day's gambling action. The shop was usually alive with the sounds of laughter and ball busting by friends and neighborhood characters and tempered by the ever-present fear that the local vice squad would bust through the door and put a halt to all the fun.

Generally, Muggsy operated without interference, yet he still took precautions. At one point, the cops swooped in on Muggsy in front of the store. He frantically tried to eat the betting slips while police choked him to prevent him from destroying evidence. They succeeded, but as usual, the charges failed to stick. Many of Muggsy's regular customers were cops, and his connections higher up—friendly lawyers, judges, and elected officials—made the charges mysteriously disappear. Still, after this temporary setback, Muggsy took care to memorize as much of the action as possible and minimize the paper trail.

Muggsy was on the road most of the day and had Stevie's eighty-year-old grandmother, who was distantly related to Hank, working the phones and holding down the "business" until early afternoon, which was when JD, his sister, and his brother would take over. They ran things while Muggsy did his "route," paying bets from the previous day while booking new action. He would return promptly at 2:05 to use the "safe" phone to call in his action to the main "office," then be gone again until closing time.

If Muggsy got sidetracked and ended up drunk, as he often did, JD and his siblings would have to decide who would work until closing time. They pretty much had free run of the place, and there wasn't much "dry-cleaning" business to distract them from what they liked to do: gamble, bullshit, and plan their next adventures, which is what they did every day after school and all day on Saturday.

The cleaners also provided cover for another type of illicit activity: the use of drugs. Within a couple of years of his cough syrup experiment, JD was a regular drinker, and he and some of his friends begun to test other drugs for inclusion in their repertoire. Working at the cleaners provided them with a clubhouse atmosphere where they could hide their behavior from the public. In the bathroom there, JD had his first (and last) experience sniffing glue, and they would occasionally smoke weed, but his true love was alcohol. Again, emulating his role models, JD acquired a taste for scotch. He drank it to excess for the next twenty years, bolstering it with a multitude of other drugs as time went on and his addiction grew more out of control.

Working for Muggsy also gave JD an opportunity to act out his unresolved feelings toward his father by stealing his money, which, of course, he used to buy drugs and alcohol. This created a cycle:

drinking and getting high to soothe his feelings, then stealing money to buy more drugs and drink. The stealing created guilt, which in turn needed to be tempered by alcohol and drugs. For JD, the situation was unique. But all across the neighborhood, it was being echoed—by the grownups already gripped by addiction and young people who would either enter its clutches or be lucky enough to escape.

The chief cause of unhappiness is trading what you want most for what you want now.

—Zig Ziglar

Throughout the story, there were several opportunities where early interven-
tion may have prevented the eventual descent into hell for both the addict
and the family. One can see risk factors throughout the characters' early
development. In the isolated episodes, these factors were simply associated
with normal growing pains. The cumulative effect surely indicated that
some sort of intervention was warranted, but it went largely unnoticed.
Risk factors such as gender, peer pressure, family attachment or lack thereof,
loneliness or isolation, the age at which substance was first consumed, so-
cial stressors, and the nature of the substance were all, if not obviously ap-
parent, easily uncovered. Of course, shame, stigma, and society's ignorance
at that time trumped any thoughts of asking for help. Other, harder to
identify risk factors, such as the way a person's body metabolizes (processes)
the substance and mental illnesses and conditions, may someday, through
genetic research, lead to early identification of the most susceptible cohort in
the population.

What's interesting and possibly another but less obvious risk factor was
that JD, Jack, Hank, and their friends didn't look up to or aspire to be
like the hard-working adults they saw pouring their hearts and souls into
their businesses, or those who showed up at their jobs every day year after
year regardless of whether they liked their job, those who provided for their
families. Instead their role models were the guys that hung around the street
corner trying to manipulate through life. An aspect that gives a great deal
of credibility to the epigenetic theories and the role of the environment on
eventual outcomes.

CHAPTER FOURTEEN

W*est Side Story* won the Academy Award for best picture in 1964. Beyond the amazing singing, dancing, and acting, there's a reason the musical took the country by storm: what played out on the screen was playing out in ethnic neighborhoods throughout the country. If it wasn't the whites against the Puerto Ricans in New York, it was the blacks against the whites in Boston, and, at one time in the not-too-distant past, the Italians against the Irish in Worcester. The film depicted an abridged version of our nation's history of conflict at its most rudimentary level: an established group fighting to maintain its territory against new immigrants.

No one involved in *West Side Story*'s production could have imagined the impact the movie would have on Jack and his friends. For them, East Park became the set of "East Side Story," which featured them against the rest of the world, especially authority figures as exemplified by the local cops. And the kids didn't need any cues from the director to give them ideas on what to do.

Jack, Fudgy, Squeaky, and their friends acted out *West Side Story* not only figuratively but literally, rehearsing and playing the most dramatic fight scenes over and over. Fudgy could sing every song on key and with panache, and he often did. Jack served as his perfect foil. They exaggerated their disdain for Officer Krupke, directing their songs at the local police, whom they viewed as repressing their First Amendment freedoms by trying to stop their repeated bouts of vandalism.

A typical get-together would start with Fudgy singing, "Dear Officer Guy Guerry, You're going ta understand."

Then Butchie would chime in and try to stay on key, singing, "Just 'cause I'm Italian, doesn't mean you shouldn't shake my hand."

Then the whole crew would sing—occasionally and miraculously in decent harmony—"We're no good, we're no good, we're no fuckin' good. But don't fool with us in our neighborhood."

At this point, Jack would slam Fudgy over the head with a rolled-up newspaper, exactly as depicted in the movie, and guys would continue with the charade, exhausting all possible variations of the song in their own words. After collapsing in laughter, they would move on to other, more mischievous pursuits.

There is an adage, "Necessity is the mother of invention." But if the kids from East Park exemplified an adage, it would have been, "Alcohol is the father of poor judgment." Days in East Park were measured by the absurdity of the delinquency. It was a weekly ritual to devise a scheme, usually including some form of destruction, to enliven the evenings of drinking and harmonizing.

Much to their delight, several of the gang's escapades made the news. This notoriety was seen as a great achievement, and it fueled their imaginations to create even greater mischief. One effort, reported with photos in the evening *Worcester Telegram*, involved removing all of the furniture from the Community House and casting it adrift in the park's wading pool. The wooden chairs and tables were heavy, but the cast-iron stove put the prank over the top. For Fudgy, Dumbo, Jack, and the rest of the boys, it was a publicity triumph.

Another "labor of love" occurred after the parks department decided to resod the softball field immediately in front of the Community House. Before the resodding took place, Jack and the gang used the rolled strips of grass to reupholster the porch and granite steps of the Community House. Once again, they put maximum effort into the job.

The Community House was constructed of huge, rectangular granite blocks and built to last forever, as were many of the structures built in the early 1900s. It resembled a government-style meetinghouse or city hall with large stone steps leading to a large stone porch, surrounded by stone walls with stone pillars buttressing the overhanging slate roof. But, as the boys found out, it wasn't completely indestructible.

Using iron poles discovered by Dumbo during a cursory break-in, the boys dislodged several of the huge granite stairs leading up to the porch. Using rudimentary fulcrums and levers, they arranged the blocks into small fortresses in front of the steps and laboriously carried the rolled strips of grass from the softball field to redecorate the porch and the new construction. To top things off, they once again removed the tables and chairs from the building. This time, they arranged them convention-style on the softball field with a sign attached to the backstop reading "Knobby's Convention," adding insult to injury by mocking the caretaker of the park.

Their antics, as hoped, once again appeared in the next day's newspaper. Jack and his friends shook each other's hands and congratulated themselves as if they had just finished first in a team competition. That article highlighted the cost of vandalism to the community. But Jack and his dim-witted friends missed the point. The story only served to reinforce the delusion that they were local legends.

These acts of defiance may pale in comparison to the antics of today's youth, but the parks department and the city police did not appreciate them. And in those acts, one can see many of the "isms" that are often talked about in Alcoholics Anonymous meetings. Defeatism, fanaticism, narcissism, know-it-all-ism—all the self-centered behaviors and thought processes of the susceptible were quite evident during the East Side gang's developmental phase, and the boys' environmental influences were an accelerant in bringing these selfish traits to maturation. Connecting the dots in a person's life can be a daunting if not impossible task, but if one has the time for introspection, a pattern of behavior often appears that indicates a foreseeable direction. For many of the gang, that course was taking a distinctly negative turn.

As the years passed, the people of Shrewsbury Street, East Park, and the East Side had their share of joy and sadness, happiness and sorrow, elation and tragedy. But for many of the gang in the park, life remained constant and predictable. Young and irresponsible, they were isolated from the waves of emotion that so often accompany the passage of time. In their own little world, they were impervious to the burdens of life, the weight of depression, and the grief that seemed to be constant companions of the adults around them. Emboldened by the notoriety of their destructive acts, they sought even greater notoriety with each passing weekend. It got to the point where Fudgy, Jack, Dumbo, et al. were no longer satisfied with juvenile pranks. They were like drug addicts who build up a tolerance with continued usage and then need more of the drug as the pleasure it returns diminishes. No longer were they satisfied with having their nocturnal activity go unnoticed until the morning; they desired more immediate gratification.

Fire was a great way to get a quick response. One of the first flame-driven pranks involved wrapping the thick ropes used for crowd control during the fireworks displays around the pillars of the Community House, soaking them in gasoline, and setting them ablaze. Of course, the kids called the cops themselves. What fun would it be if no one saw the fire? In these new nighttime games, success was measured by the size of the city's public safety response and the number of flashing lights that illuminated the dark sky.

The reader might ask how was it that a group a kids could manage to stage these destructive events with such regularity and not suffer the consequences. The park offered a number of quick escape routes and secure hiding places, from the top of the rock face that towered over the softball fields to the wooded hill near Bell Pond, and, of course, the nearby neighborhood where many of the kids lived. When the flashing lights arrived, the East Side kids usually hid and watched from a safe distance.

Sure of their invincibility, their daring was only limited by their imagination. They would often booby-trap the three park entrances, using spikes nailed upward through planks laid across the driveways. Often, the kids delayed their escape until they heard the hissing of the tires or the cursing of the officers as their cruisers drove over the nails.

The cat-and-mouse game continued through the summer of '64, as both the gang's bravado and the frustration of the police continued to escalate. For a while, the nightly escapades were looked upon with a mixture of amusement and annoyance, but that balance was beginning to tip. What pushed it over was another brilliant but ill-conceived plan.

Every summer before the Fourth of July, a wide assortment of illegal fireworks magically appeared on the streets of the East Side. That summer's offerings featured the M-80, an explosive device that looked like and was advertised as a miniature stick of dynamite. This newfound toy became a source of entertainment and discovery for many of the young men in the park, from the sadistic blowing up of frogs and cats to the less-than-scientific taping together of multiple M-80 to create a greater bang for the buck. The boom of detonation was heard nightly throughout the neighborhood, distressing both animal and human residents.

Dumbo and Quido, two of the older guys in the park, often came up with the ideas for stunts, but this time one of the younger kids provided the inspiration. The plan was to once again ignite gasoline-soaked ropes wrapped around the Community House pillars and call the cops to the scene. But this time, instead of laying out the usual planks with nails, Jack and Fudgy would be waiting for the cops high atop the rock ledge near the Community House, ready to rain bombs down on them as they arrived.

"We're gonna scare the shit out of them coppas," was the battle cry as Fudgy, Dumbo, Little Mikey, Big Head, Buddie, Squeaky, BaBa, and the rest of the crew scurried around preparing for the evening's entertainment.

To fortify their resolve and solidify their criminal fraternity, the preparations included alcohol, of course. Much like the old Westerns that depicted Native Americans sitting around a campfire, putting on war paint, and whooping and hollering while slugging down a fifth of whiskey, the gang's prebattle planning revolved around who was buying the beer and, just as important, what time it would arrive.

That night, as Jim Morrison sang "Light My Fire" and "The End" on their cassette player, Jack and the others sat beneath the Drinking Tree and psyched themselves up by bragging about their fearlessness and their commitment to each other. The participants' exhilaration and the complete exasperation of their pursuers seemed to be equally important. It was all part of the plan.

When darkness fell, they made their first move. After they wrapped the gasoline-soaked ropes around the stone supports, most of the crew dispersed to a vantage point from which they could observe the festivities, but a few remained to light the fire and taunt the police by running at the last possible moment.

The blaze immediately lit up the darkened park. Quido hustled across Shrewsbury Street to the pay phone to report the fire. Jack and Fudgy, their courage fortified and their thinking distorted by liberal quantities of beer, scaled the ledge to wait for the police and fire trucks to arrive.

As the sirens grew louder, they gained the top, where they had a bird's-eye view of the activity below. Jack was confident of the plan. He had his best friend at his side. They had the advantage of safe distance and higher ground. They were heavily fortified with a half dozen M-80s taped around a piece of wooden fence. It was the Sharks and the Jets, amplified and real.

As the fire was being extinguished, the cops set out on their customary recon of the park in search of the perpetrators. Just as expected, one of the cruisers drove to the foot of the ledge and began searching the area with a spotlight. That was Jack and Fudgy's cue to light the fuse on the M-80s and hurl them into the darkness below. After several seconds, there was a flash of light, followed by two loud explosions. As the echoes died down, a man, his voice shaking with fury, roared into the night, "When we catch you little bastards, we'll break your fucking necks!"

It was mission accomplished; Jack and Fudgy fled deeper into the night.

On it went. To the gang, it all seemed so innocent. No one was getting hurt, though there were plenty of near hits. No one was getting arrested, or at least not for anything serious. Underlying it all, however, was a slow and nearly imperceptible escalation: as the pranks grew in scale, so did the level of alcohol consumption. No longer was drinking solely a Friday night ritual; getting drunk—and frequently—was becoming part of the social fabric at the park. The Drinking Tree began to look more like the town dump. Beer bottles and cans littered the area, piling up until only small patches of earth or grass peeked through. It was another sign of trouble, and the East Park gang blithely ignored it.

CHAPTER FIFTEEN

In the heart of the 1960s, JD straddled, as many young American men did, a cultural chasm: the more traditional blue-collar culture on one side and the growing hippie movement on the other. On the streets of the nation, young people, feeling constrained by the social strictures of 1950s America and simultaneously terrified of and furious about the tragic war in Vietnam, had begun to rebel in any way they could. Although change came slowly to most of the East Side, everything was fair game—from the length of a young man's hair to the length of a young woman's skirt. Beer and highballs gave way to marijuana, LSD, and heroin, and traditional patriotism was rejected in favor of marching on the halls of power and burning the American flag. Police became "pigs." Anyone over thirty was too old to trust, and sex became a free-for-all. To be young meant to make the choice between the old life and the new freedom. Everything you did, from the clothes you wore to the substances you used, became a political statement.

There was fear, distrust, and a lack of confidence in the country's leaders, and anger was erupting. Once these emotions began to bubble over, it was almost impossible to contain them. No longer were people quiet about seeing friends, family, and loved ones returning from war physically or emotionally devastated or in coffins draped with the American flag. People grew tired of hearing the daily news reports of the death toll in Vietnam. The emotional, psychological, and spiritual weight of the war could no longer be tolerated, and something had to give. People needed some relief from the pain and fear, from the anger and heartache.

In a sense, the situation in the 1960s created a perfect storm of social pressures and addictive substances. When humans are in pain of any kind, they look for something to relieve it. Although we have traditionally used prescribed medications for this purpose, we also have used alcohol and other illicit substances. In the sixties, self-medication became a way of life. It wasn't that drugs, especially hallucinogens or "psychedelics," were new to the world; traditional cultures had used some of them for thousands of years. In search of relief from distress and discomfort, young people explored and experimented with LSD, PCP, marijuana, cocaine, heroin, and other illicit drugs at a rate never before seen in American society. From where they stood, JD and the other kids on the East Side couldn't have understood the impact that the countercultural revolution would have on their lives and their community. It would deliver both freedom and devastation, and the community and its children were largely defenseless against it.

No aspect of the sixties affected JD more than the lax attitudes about substance abuse. In fact, his family history and life on the East Side had prepared him for it. JD's family tree included both alcoholism and mental illness, and in the neighborhood, alcohol was a part of everyday life. It was, or so it seemed, typical for kids to pool their resources to purchase and consume alcohol—mostly beer—on the weekends. Everybody drank, some to get drunk, and others simply to feel like part of the group. The consequences seemed minimal, or so JD thought. Every now and again, people might hear of a drunk-driving accident in which teenage drinking took lives, but those stories were rare. For JD and his compatriots, alcohol-related problems were limited to arguments or fights, minor injuries due to falls, or drunken mistakes, such as being caught by police or punished by parents. Still, drinking seemed like innocent, almost adolescent behavior.

While Jack and most of the kids in East Park had thus far avoided any drugs beyond alcohol, JD and the kids from Muskego Street were ahead of the curve. Alcohol, of course, was the first substance to make an impact. Like many of his friends, JD partook early and often. He learned to love alcohol's comforting effect and its social benefits. It made intimate communication and even casual socializing easier and tamped down his feelings of anger and insecurity, even if its side effects—blackouts and head-pounding, cotton-mouthed mornings after—gave him momentary pause. Nothing put those bad effects behind him like another night of partying, and although JD didn't know it then, he had to go back to alcohol. He had no defense against it, and he needed it desperately. He had long practiced other means of escape, weaving elaborate fantasies about his life and lying about the reality of his circumstances. But alcohol provided a new and even more effective means of relief. Life was intolerable without drinking, and even in his teens, he found no real pleasure in anything else.

At first, JD kept his partying to the weekends, but before long, drinking became a daily routine, even on school days. Worse, no one told him that this behavior wasn't normal. One afternoon, during his senior year at North High School, JD dropped by a bar near his school with his trusty fake driver's license. Down the bar, he spied one of his teachers, who was also knocking back a few quick ones before heading back to school.

JD had never heard of detoxification, rehabilitation treatment, or Alcoholics Anonymous, nor does he recall knowing anyone who had to go into treatment because of drinking. It wasn't that he was sheltered from the effects of alcohol, but the antics of those who drank too much were understood and explained in ways that didn't include concepts like addiction, disease, treatment, or self-help support groups. JD admired and aspired to be like the sophisticated individuals he observed enjoying a good glass of scotch whiskey or a fine wine without dramatic or sloppy results—even if his own drinking had no such element of control.

If alcohol was an acceptable part of life on the East Side, drugs were not; many in the neighborhood viewed them as satanic temptations. Still, when marijuana, LSD, and other drugs began to hit the streets of Worcester, the boldest of the partiers discovered what thousands of other kids across America had—that for all practical purposes, an intoxicating substance was an intoxicating substance, sanctioned by society or not.

The illicit allure of drugs played a role in breaking up the group. Friends began to split off from the group to engage in seemingly closed rituals. It almost seemed like a private club or secret society to which only the select kids were allowed access. Insiders enjoyed a mysteriousness and excitement that went along with being part of the group. Outsiders often had mixed feelings: they were scared and confused by this new culture, but also intrigued. They envied those who were bold enough to take the plunge.

Soon, JD succumbed to the allure. He began to indulge in a variety of other substances—marijuana at first, then prescription drugs and LSD, although he managed to sidestep heroin and cocaine. Using drugs provided a different means of escaping from life's issues. In a way, it was often quicker and "cleaner" than alcohol. At the same time, taking drugs also allowed many people to give a big "fuck you" to traditional society and the world. "Tune in, turn on, and drop out" was the mantra for many during that time.

By age fifteen, JD had become a card-carrying member of the "escape from reality" club, using any means by which he could escape from life and himself. In time, it didn't really matter what substance he chose to use; it only mattered whether it could transport him to a better place. He used and abused most of the drugs available, liking some more than others but ultimately using what was there when he needed it, which, by then, was always.

As bigger social changes swept the nation, JD felt caught in the middle. He loved his country but had no desire to go to war. He liked to get high, but he wasn't about to head off to Haight-Ashbury to join the countercultural revolution. There didn't seem to be a place for him, and sadly, he didn't have any solid male role models to guide him in making decisions. He was alone trying to figure it out, which proved to be a major disaster.

He gravitated toward those like himself and followed in the footsteps of the only role models he had, living the make-believe tough-guy role while wandering aimlessly through life.

Like JD, many of his friends started to change the way they looked and acted, the music they listened to, the way they spoke, and the values and beliefs they held. It was beginning to get somewhat crazy, but they were caught up in a movement that was in some ways slow and subtle and in other ways, fast and furious. Looking back on it now, it seems like a tidal wave or tsunami had hit the shore, affecting everyone in its path, innocent or not. Some of the guys held out for as long as they could while others jumped in with complete abandon. Almost overnight, or so it seemed, a small but growing group on the East Side was smoking dope, experimenting with harder drugs, or dealing. Drugs were all around, and people were talking about them, singing about them, or displaying their effects in some pretty strange ways.

Not surprisingly, heavy drug use created problems, and JD was not immune to them. All of the telltale signs were visible: the attitude, school problems, work problems, social problems, and legal problems. He experienced them all, but he never slowed down enough to catch his breath or to pay much attention to what was happening to his life. What had begun as innocent exploration with beer or marijuana to be hip and cool turned into a nightmare.

It was easy enough to laugh when a friend told a story about struggling through a geometry test while tripping on LSD. And when another friend used the same drug (or at least one purported to be LSD), became convinced that he was a dog, and ended up in the mental ward at the state hospital, it was scarier but still worth a chuckle. But when that same person committed suicide by jumping from a highway overpass, or when another friend not even known to be an addict was shot and killed while robbing a pharmacy, it might seem logical for JD and his friends to reconsider their relationship to drugs. Still, they didn't, and these two tragic incidents simply became neighborhood stories about good kids whose lives went bad. As tragic story piled on top of tragic story, the impact was blunted. There simply seemed to be too much trouble to pay attention to any one incident.

Of course, drugs played a role in the reworking of the larger cultural order. Some on the East Side lost interest in trying to do the right thing as far as work and school was concerned. They no longer aspired to follow the lead of their fathers and grandfathers in joining the military after high school or going to work, paying bills, and supporting a family. That life was for ham-and-eggers. Instead of finding a partner and settling down to raise a family, they wanted freedom to experiment with as much sex as they could without emotional strings, responsibilities, or expectations. They wanted to live as unconventionally as possible and, of course, to get high as often as they wanted to, with no restrictions. It was a rebellion against the values handed down by previous generations, the ones their parents lived by. The life of the Old World—large close-knit families, spending Sundays in church, and going to work on Mondays—would soon be gone forever.

CHAPTER SIXTEEN

In 1967, as the summer after high school graduation came to an end, Jack and many of his friends prepared to leave the neighborhood and the security of their friends and families. Those headed to college did not realize how lucky they were for making that choice. Jack left home for the Lowell Technological Institute in Lowell, Massachusetts, to study chemical engineering, a vocation that would one day play a role in his life—but not in the way he imagined it then. Big Head was off to Holy Cross College. Fudgy split for Boston to try his luck as an actor. Leo the Crusher and Johnnie Baba joined the US Marines. Those who didn't head for college or the military joined what could be jokingly called the gangster apprenticeship program. This nonaccredited major consisted of finishing high school, hanging around, playing cards, and for those looking old enough to play the part, going to Foxboro Raceway or Suffolk Downs Race Track, more appropriately called Suffering Downs, to run tickets and place bets for the neighborhood's semiconnected hoodlums, the remnants of the once-influential Patriarca organized crime syndicate.

Jack's arrival at Lowell Tech was not memorable. In retrospect, there were no moments that defined his future, but he did find a home of sorts there. Comfortable with making new friends, he played an instrumental role in the formation of a small community known as Brand X. The kids, most of whom were from New England and as far south as New Jersey, lived on the fourth floor in Bourgeois Hall, a brand-new residential complex situated on the bank of the Merrimack River.

Among the activities that drew the group together was poker. Jack started a regular game that provided him with a venue to show off his skills, which by this time were quite formidable. His uncanny knack for winning, his East Park mischievousness, and his history of bridging the gaps between the Irish and the Italian cultures made him a natural for forging connections. He became a leader on the floor.

Still, Jack's new status had its drawbacks. Engrossed in the social scene, he neglected the primary reason he had come to Lowell in the first place. He attended his chemistry, physics, and calculus courses only sporadically, showing up just often enough to perform miserably on tests. But he never missed an opportunity to play cards, drink, or socialize with his floor mates.

In the fall of 1967, Lowell Tech's homecoming festivities featured a concert by pop-rockers Frankie Valli and the Four Seasons, then at the height of their popularity. Jack's neighborhood sweetheart was anxious to visit the school, see one of her favorite bands on stage, and spend some time alone with Jack without parental supervision. On the surface, this seemed ideal, but Jack soon discovered the drawbacks of spending a weekend without his friends and playing cards. During the day, while his friends were out playing football and horsing around, Jack was in his dorm room with his girl, listening to the Beatles, a group that was popular with everyone but Jack and his Shrewsbury Street friends. The evening proved less problematic, as the allures of a young and willing girl proved a sufficient distraction from thoughts of what he might be missing. Some pre- and postconcert coitus and a remarkable performance by Frankie Valli and the Four Seasons helped lessen Jack's feelings that he was missing out on the real action.

The first semester at Lowell Tech also brought Jack's first exposure to drugs. Taking an occasional hit of weed seemed innocent enough, and it enabled Jack to live the way he liked living—a bit on the edge and outside the norm. At the same time, Jack started learning how to play the guitar, and between that, the card playing, and the dope smoking, his academic performance took a nosedive. In high school, Jack had had the ability to party plenty, then put his nose to the grindstone at the last minute, and do fine academically. In college, he discovered, that wasn't possible.

By the end of the first semester, Jack found himself on academic probation. His grade point average was under 2.0; at eighteen, he had no clear direction except to have fun and avoid responsibility.

The second semester did not start out much differently. Many of Jack's dormitory buddies became close friends as they shared some of the more intimate details of their lives. Their family dysfunction and, on occasion, even their own shortcomings created a foundation for friendship; taking the risk of revealing a less-than-perfect background paid off in a bond of trust. As a group, Jack and the guys of Brand X spent more and more time together—much of it, to Jack's delight, playing cards. His luck and his skill continued to hold out for most of the semester, and he actually had to temper his winning streak to let the games continue.

As the school year progressed, Jack applied himself to everything but school. Albert Einstein is often credited with saying that insanity is doing the same thing over and over and expecting different results. Undoubtedly intelligent, Jack could have been a poster child for that definition. He continued to focus on the social sphere, partying hard and rallying the fourth floor to form a Brand X softball team. Meanwhile, he hoped that his meager academic efforts would be keep him afloat. But when his grades came in at the end of the year, they were once again poor, and he was expelled from Lowell Tech. The notice indicated that Jack could reapply to Lowell if he was able to complete a course of study satisfactorily at another college, but that was hardly a silver lining.

To add to the ignominious distinction of flunking out, Jack also lost a game of poker for the first time all semester. He didn't understand it at the time, but the loss of a couple of bucks and his enrollment status were the least of his worries. Since students had to advance academically to maintain their draft deferments, Jack was now eligible to be drafted into military service in Vietnam. He never bothered to consider the implications of this; he pushed it to the back of his mind. He lived for the present; the future was distant and undefined. His only thoughts were on returning to the East Side and reuniting with his friends.

When Jack returned, the East Side seemed to be frozen in time. Most of its inhabitants still clung to their traditions. Nowhere was this more evident than in the Italian community, especially those who constantly reminisced, romanticizing the good old days. This was especially true for the criminal element that lived on the fringe of society and by the pirates' code of honor: the see-nothing, hear-nothing, and, most importantly, speak-nothing philosophy that was understood to be the true measure of a man's character. The park itself was a bastion of conservatism; foreigners, long hair, marijuana, and all things not Italian were considered disgraceful. Playing cards and drinking were still the order of the day, although this soon would change, seemingly overnight.

For Jack, some things had already changed. For one, the gang was not his only nexus. He found himself splitting his time between his friends and a now steady girlfriend, and the glory days of running from the cops seemed far behind him. This was probably a good thing, as the world outside Shrewsbury Street had begun to unravel. The assassination of civil rights leader Martin Luther

King in April had kicked off race riots in cities across America. Two months later, Robert Kennedy, John F. Kennedy's brother and a Democratic candidate for the presidency, was assassinated, too. The war in Vietnam had intensified, American casualties were at their peak, and America's young people were expressing their opposition to the war in the streets. Of course, the East Side was not immune from these outside forces, and in 1968, the remains of the first neighborhood kid killed in Vietnam were returned to Worcester.

Still determined to get an education, Jack soon returned to school, this time at Central New England College, a hometown school formerly known as Worcester Junior College. At Central New England, Jack was under a little more scrutiny. He lived with his parents, which gave him two options: show some effort at school or drop out and get a job, a fate Jack considered worse than going to war. Without the distractions of dormitory life and under the watchful eyes of his parents, Jack applied himself to his studies, at least to some degree. Gone were the guitar playing, the pot smoking, and the nightly poker games. This was a step in the right direction, but Central New England would not be enough to gain Jack a new draft exemption. The two semesters on probation had sealed his fate.

At Central New England, Jack passed some of his free time playing ping-pong in the student lounge. Most often, his opponent was JD's friend, Hank, another neighborhood kid who attended Central New England. Jack and Hank had met the summer before, while playing cards in East Park. Gambling and drugs brought many of the neighborhood kids together, but the two had more than just the neighborhood in common. Like Jack, Hank had gone to Catholic school, although he attended Saint John's in Shrewsbury. Hank's mother had been the school nurse at Sacred Heart for several years. Like Jack, Hank liked to party. He'd tried alcohol for the first time at thirteen, drinking until he blacked out.

Like Jack, he had already tried other drugs and was using a drink or a drug as a way to fit in with his friends on the Street. Like Jack, Hank felt ambivalent about college and gave little thought to what the future might hold. His parents had always preached the value of education as a way of getting ahead. Hank was smart; his facility with numbers and his storytelling skills were evidence of that, as was his insight into the social conditions that surrounded him. But from early childhood, Hank had struggled with reading comprehension issues. This left him feeling ashamed, and he dodged classroom participation whenever he could. Hank's mother tried to get help for her son, even taking him to a program called The Reading Institute. But he continued to struggle, and eventually this led to trouble. Unable to keep up academically, Hank transformed himself into the class clown, which created problems in the classroom, which then extended into the family home. Hank's mother tried as hard as she could to keep her son on the track academically, with little success.

Perhaps the most important factor Jack and Hank had in common was growing up in a household headed by an alcoholic father. The young men knew the rules of engagement: what to talk about and what to keep private. As the white ball snapped back and forth across the ping-pong table, they wove stories about the characters of the neighborhood and their drug- and alcohol-fueled adventures. Other, more intimate, information remained unspoken.

CHAPTER SEVENTEEN

"Jesus Christ, Jimmy! Did you see the look on that fucker's face?"

JD couldn't answer his friend's question with anything more than a laugh. He was too drunk to think about it, too drunk to care, out of control, and moving through the environment on pure instinct, his right hand in his pocket, gripping the gun. Off to the side, JD noticed an older man staring at him and his three friends as they stumbled toward the exit of the Boston Garden, shouting and cursing, cigarettes in the corners of their mouths, and cups of beer in their hands.

"What the *fuck* are you lookin' at," JD barked, and watched with satisfaction as the man cringed and turned away. This was power. The man was an adult, as old as JD's father, as old as one of his teachers, yet JD had made him afraid. More important, he was the leader of the group, the one with a gun in his hand, the one with the strut. Adrenaline sizzled up his spine as they stumbled out onto Causeway Street.

The trip, which took place in spring 1968, had started out as something that every New England kid dreamed of—a school trip to Boston Garden to see his team play basketball. A sophomore at Worcester Boys Trade High School, JD was trying to do the right thing—learn the plumbing trade so that he would have a skill that mattered, paid well, and would provide a future. But for JD and his friends, the trip to the Garden represented another opportunity to party. They'd left Worcester well supplied with pocket bottles of liquor, and in the Garden, the lax enforcement at the beer counter gave them a source that would last as long as their cash did. JD also carried a fake .25-caliber pistol to intimidate, never realizing that it was more likely to cause trouble than to prevent it.

Within an hour or so, the situation had spiraled out of control. A beer vendor had hesitated to serve them, and JD had pulled the gun. The terrified vendor had backed down, and the group had the good sense to leave the Garden, but the trouble wasn't over. Across the street from the Garden, at the corner of Canal, was a liquor store. The gang tumbled into it like a slow-motion explosion, drunk, loud, and stupid, insulting patrons and stuffing liquor bottles into their pockets. By then, the Boston police were on the move.

Luckily for JD, the police could not find them. They returned to Worcester with their school group, not yet sober enough to care about the consequences of their actions. Soon enough, JD would feel repercussions. None too gently, he was advised that he should find another school. His career as a plumber had ended before it had begun, and he was out on the street, confused, angry, and secretly ashamed. He could muster no response but the most familiar one—drink more alcohol, take more drugs, and push his feelings of guilt and shame away.

His school year over prematurely, JD began another summer on the East Side with little change in attitude. Summer in Worcester offered a seemingly endless series of parties in East Park, on the shores of Lake Quinsigamond, and on the porches of triple-deckers across the neighborhood. There was always somewhere to be, somewhere to go, and somewhere to get wasted and see what crazy shit might happen.

One of the biggest party weekends was the one that ended the summer: Labor Day. For JD, that weekend offered a double dose of potential. His birthday fell on September 2, just a few days away. And his family had already organized a combination Labor Day/birthday party, with JD as the guest of honor. At the last minute, however, another opportunity arose in the form of a trip to Cape Cod with his friend Leo (aka the Crusher). It was a chance to catch the last weekend of the summer in the place where summer really happened, and JD couldn't resist. This spontaneous decision may well have saved his life.

JD was in Dennis Port, Massachusetts, at the summer cabin owned by the parents of his neighborhood buddy, the Crusher, when he got the news. After leaving the party drunk, JD's cousin, John, had crashed his car on a winding country road in the small town of Boylston, Massachusetts. Somehow, John had survived, but three others had died. They were JD's cousin, William (Chucky), John's friend, George, and JD's seventeen-year-old brother, Tom.

JD's relationship with his older brother had been a rocky one, a combination of sibling rivalry and jealousy. Ever since JD could recall, Tom had received all of Muggsy's attention and affection. Tom was being groomed to attend law school while JD was unceremoniously advised to "learn a trade" so he could be assured of gainful employment, code for "you're not college material." JD felt slighted as he watched Muggsy's friends and cronies (lawyers and judges) offer their support and assistance to his brother. But that didn't prevent a devastating tidal wave of emotion from sweeping over JD. In the absence of a real father, Tom had served as a surrogate, someone to look up to, someone to turn to for counsel. Added to the loss JD felt was guilt. Had he not gone to the beach, he might have been in the car. He escaped, but maybe he didn't deserve to. As summer faded and the sun sank lower on the horizon, JD descended deeper and deeper into the morass of drugs and alcohol.

How we communicate with each other does make the difference between life and death. The way we treat each other makes all the difference in the world and is how we find a way to actually develop the ability to use our minds.

—Daniel Siegel, MD

For the kids from the East Side, the die was cast. What began as curious experimentation soon became their main method of soothing themselves and coping with emotional and stressful situations. Then, over the years, drug use became preemptive. The guys and gals from Shrewsbury Street used drugs to prepare for stress they hadn't even faced yet.

Drugs definitely helped them to manage their social anxiety and awkwardness and provided courage to face their fears. What they didn't know was that drugs also masked feelings of inadequacy and low self-esteem for many of them. Getting high allowed them to avoid facing those emotions and the shame many of them felt about their lives. But the beginning of dependence also meant a critical loss of self-control.

What lessons can be drawn from the characters in this book, the latest findings in neuroscience, the definition of addiction as a brain disease, the prevalence of risk factors, and the descent into a life of pain and suffering, not only for the people who misuse substances but also for those who know and love them?

Addiction is a complex disease. Treating it requires knowledge about addiction, an understanding of the neurological processes that have been compromised by drug use, and the expertise to restore them to a state of equilibrium or good mental health.

CHAPTER EIGHTEEN

For Jack and Hank, 1968 and 1969 passed by with few lasting impressions, although some events stood out. On July 20, 1969, Apollo 11 touched down, and Neil Armstrong made "one small step for man, one giant leap for mankind" by walking on the surface of the moon. This moment punctured the cynicism that characterized many young Americans' attitudes about their country but not for long.

For many young Americans, it was not the moonwalk but the August 1969 gathering of nearly half a million people on a six-hundred-acre farm in upstate New York for the Woodstock Festival that would be remembered. Many of the top rock musicians in the world performed at the three-day event. It marked both the high point of the counterculture movement and the beginning of its end. But on the East Side, it didn't have as great an impact. The only guys from the neighborhood who went to Woodstock were Stevie the Sailor and Joey A., less affectionately known as the Mad Ghoul or Joe Ots. They began their journey from Muggsy's dry-cleaning shop, leaving behind JD, who had to work. The Sailor and the Ghoul returned with some great stories, but the tales were soon lost in the turbulence of current events.

That turbulence was magnified shortly after Jack's nineteenth birthday, when he received a letter from the local draft board advising him to report for a physical to determine his eligibility to serve in the armed forces. As the Vietnam War became increasingly unpopular, recruitment of volunteers to the military dried up. It was time for the government to call men to arms, whether they wanted to be called or not.

As Jack understood it, the period between passing a physical and induction into the service was rather short. Many of his more patriotic friends simply joined to avoid the process altogether. But Jack was in no rush to do anything except stay home.

The draft board letter caused Jack to regret suddenly and profoundly his poor choices while at Lowell Tech. Desperate, he reluctantly turned to the one person who might be able to help him.

"Dad," Jack said, looking at his father across the kitchen table. "You know your air force buddy, Joe, is on the draft board. You gotta talk to him. You gotta get me out of this."

If Jack's father had had a few beers in him, he would have delivered a sarcasm-laden diatribe about his son's shortcomings and his failure to live up to his responsibilities in school. But he was sober. In 1969, more than thirty Americans were dying in Vietnam every day. He didn't want his son to be one of them. During World War II, Jack's dad had served with Joe for twenty-three months in England, France, and Belgium as part of the US Air Force's 323rd Bombardment Group. Joe was now the head of the Selective Service Board in Worcester, and Jack's father hoped that friendship would guarantee some loyalty, and it did.

Unfortunately, bureaucracy trumped the loyalty. "There's nothing I can do," Joe said. He simply couldn't rig the game.

There were other options, of course. A few guys from the neighborhood had already headed for Canada to avoid the draft. Hank, who had flunked out of Central New England College after one semester, had joined the Air Force National Guard. At the time, National Guard service nearly guaranteed a domestic duty assignment. By signing up, Hank would avoid both the draft and a likely trip to Vietnam.

Shortly after receiving the letter, Jack made the trip to a military medical facility in nearby Springfield, where he was herded, poked, and prodded through a series of medical tests. Despite his best effort to fail, he was branded 1-A, a prime candidate for military service.

Shortly after passing the physical, Jack received his official 1-A status from the draft board along with a letter telling him to report in twenty-eight days for military service. Canada may have been an option, but he did not have the inclination, resources, or the courage to act. His father empathized, but he also believed that a man should do his patriotic duty. With no better alternatives, Jack prepared himself to do exactly that, but then fate intervened.

On December 1, 1969, the draft was broadcast live on network television from Selective Service National Headquarters in Washington, DC. In a large glass container were 366 blue capsules, one for each possible birth date in any given year, leap year included. The purpose of the capsules was to select men for eligibility in the compulsory military draft.

As families across the nation watched with a mixture of hope and fear, Representative Alexander Pirnie (R-NY), who served on the House Armed Services Committee, drew the first capsule from the container and opened it. The date inside was September 14. This meant that all American men born on September 14 between 1944 and 1950 would have a draft number of one and would be the first to be called to service when the new draft began on January 1, 1970.

Jack's birth date, August 14, was assigned the number 198. The draft cutoff was 195, which meant the letter asking him to report for active duty was no longer valid. This reprieve warranted celebration, and Jack did his duty, celebrating first with his family and later getting drunk with his friends. Jack may have felt that he was free of adult responsibilities, but he wasn't, not by a long shot.

CHAPTER NINETEEN

"I'm pregnant."

With these two words, Jack's life took another dramatic turn, and in December 1969, he found himself hastily married and an expectant father. Maybe escaping military duty in the draft lottery was not that lucky after all.

Just as unexpectedly, Jack found his niche academically, and on June 6, 1970, he graduated from Central New England with an associate's degree in engineering and the academic distinction of membership to the Phi Theta Kappa fraternity for superior scholarship. That ceremony took a backseat to an even bigger milestone in Jack's life, the birth of his beautiful daughter, Gina Marie.

In the early morning hours at Memorial Hospital, Jack unceremoniously witnessed the pains of labor, mostly endured by his new bride, and the slurs, mostly directed at him, of bringing a new life into this world. Thankfully, an ample dose of medication helped to ease the delivery and the diatribe, while across town, the first graduate in Jack's class was walking down the aisle to receive his diploma. Without the slightest realization of the world around them, a tiny Gina Marie and an exhausted Theresa were resting quietly, with Jack looking on in amazement.

Buoyed by fatherhood and his recovered academic prowess, Jack once again embarked on his career path. "I'm gonna be a rocket scientist," he jokingly told his friends on the Street, where higher learning was generally considered suspect. But in fact, he felt excited about his new opportunities, especially after being accepted into the University of Massachusetts at Amherst's School of Engineering.

Neither Jack's marital status nor fatherhood were going to prevent his move to UMass, but his financial limitations dictated some adjustments. His problem: What to do with the family? He could not afford to live on campus with his wife and his newborn daughter. Instead, Jack would migrate to Amherst alone and live in a dormitory, while the rest of the family would stay behind in the safe and secure home of his in-laws, Artemio and Rose.

The summer before school began was such a whirlwind that Jack had little opportunity to get into any trouble—or to adjust adequately to the responsibilities of fatherhood. Still a child emotionally if not chronologically, Jack struggled with the idea of being married, let alone of having a family. He could have decided that these new responsibilities would strengthen his resolve to apply himself in school. But living outside his parents' supervision, Jack soon found himself backsliding.

At UMass, Jack's roommate was a red-haired Jewish kid from Brookline, Massachusetts, named David. Years more hip and mature, David was steeped in the drug culture that had been making news for some time but had not yet developed fully in the isolated enclave of East Park. But at the progressive University of Massachusetts (or Zoo Mass, as it was affectionately referred to) the use of marijuana, LSD, and even heroin was nothing new.

With David as his mentor, Jack soon shifted his educational focus from engineering to drugs. He learned to identify the exotic varieties of hashish—blond Moroccan, brown Lebanese, Nepalese fingers, temple balls—and to enjoy the pleasures of each. Jack's appearance, though not drastically altered, reflected the times, complete with shoulder-length hair and tattered and patched blue jeans.

Jack became an expert in the logistics of marijuana cultivation. There were pot plants in every window at Zoo Mass. At least, that is how Jack perceived it. He spent most of his waking hours under the influence of some kind of mind-altering substance—pot, hash, barbiturates, and speed, individually or in combination. This time, he managed to keep his grades up, despite keeping his prime focus on the party lifestyle.

Oddly enough, Jack excelled in one activity that did not involve getting high: ping-pong. He spent hours playing and developed enough skill to win the undergraduate championship, one of his few positive accomplishments at UMass. That was one bright spot in a tumultuous year.

Jack struggled to adjust to independent living, new surroundings, dorm mates, and friends. His drug use eventually eroded his desire for academic achievement and replaced it with apathy. Then, his wife of less than a year arrived unexpectedly on campus but not to visit him; she was there under the guise of spending the weekend with her brother who not so coincidently shared his dorm room with her ex-boyfriend from the East Side neighborhood. Jack may have skipped quite a few calculus classes, but it did not take a rocket scientist to put two and two together. This was not going to be a match made in heaven. Jack did not need another reason to get high, but his wife's infidelity and the eventual breakup of his marriage accelerated his decent into the abyss of drug use.

This personal crisis was further complicated by the general unrest of the times. UMass became a hotbed of antiwar sentiment, resulting in the suspension of classes in the spring of 1971. The only silver lining for Jack was the elimination of final exams, which did wonders for his grade point average.

Back on the East Side, things were slowly changing. Some of the guys still hung around the Street, but many of Jack's friends were now in the military. Long hair, once strictly forbidden on the Street, was not readily accepted, but it no longer automatically elicited a beating. More devastating changes were soon to come.

CHAPTER TWENTY

I n fall 1971, JD experienced his own brush with the Selective
Service System. His birthdate was assigned the number seventy,
low enough that he could be expected to be drafted and likely
would end up in Vietnam. He had three options: join the military,
enroll in college to defer the draft, or be drafted.

Scared to death of being sent to Vietnam, he made quick arrangements (with the help of a friend) to enlist in the US Air Force
Reserves. Other guys he knew, including his good friend, Hank,
had done the same, reporting for six months of training, followed
by a six-year commitment to monthly weekend service and two
weeks of summer camp each year, with little chance of being called
into combat. JD thought he could live up to that arrangement and
avoid going to war. Had he been a gambler, he might have taken a
chance on a poker game or on the fortunes of the Boston Bruins.
But he had no interest in war, nor would he gamble with his life.

That life was about to change quickly. He'd become a regular
user of alcohol and was experimenting with marijuana, LSD, and
a variety of other drugs, but he had yet to try cocaine or heroin.

He smoked Parliaments at the rate of two packs per day. JD kept the hours of someone who partied hard late at night and into the early morning and paid no attention to his health. His girlfriend and first real love had just dumped him, and his friends were fellow travelers—the long-haired, drug-loving miscreants and wild children of Worcester's East Side. Now he was off to boot camp at Lackland Air Force Base in San Antonio, Texas, for eight weeks of basic training.

Nothing could have prepared JD for the rigors of basic training, the scorching heat of the Texas sun, or the furious barking of the drill sergeants. Rising at dawn, pounding the parade ground, cranking out the push-ups, and learning to respect authority without question. Yet oddly enough, JD not only survived but prospered. He was a smart kid who knew enough to get with the program, and after the first painful week, he learned to enjoy the military lifestyle, including regular sleep, three meals a day, and abstinence from cigarettes, alcohol, and drugs. He gained a suntan, some muscles, and an improved frame of mind. He even made some new friends.

When boot camp ended, so did JD's enforced abstinence. He headed to Chanute Air Force Base in Illinois for thirteen weeks of technical training, and while there, he resumed his love affair with cigarettes and alcohol, although not yet with drugs. The military and drinking traditionally went hand in hand, and JD's training schedule created the perfect scenario for overindulgence—classes went from eight to noon, followed by lunch; the afternoons and evenings were free. JD's intelligence allowed him to handle his classwork easily, and he and his buddies lived the party life with little fallout.

After tech training, JD returned to Massachusetts's Westover Air Force Base, where he was to serve out his weekend and summer obligations as a reservist. Westover wasn't far from Worcester, and he spent most of his free time back in Worcester, hanging with his old friends.

The drug culture was in full swing on the East Side; almost all of JD's friends were using and/or selling drugs. It felt like a new phenomenon had taken over the Street.

With his broken heart nagging him once again, JD felt caught between the wise-guy role, the hippie movement, and trying to find his own path in life. He'd soon fall back into his bad habits, with predictable results.

CHAPTER TWENTY ONE

"Gayle, Joey. Come on, wake up!" Jack wanted to scream, but he knew better than to draw attention to the situation. "You're gonna get thrown out of school."

It was fall 1972, Jack's last year of college—but he was not at UMass. After his last semester there ended early due to war protests, Jack made two adjustments to his academic path. He transferred to Worcester State University and changed his major to teaching. At first glance, those moves seemed sensible; since the end of his marriage, Jack was missing his old neighborhood friends and the student protests that had swept UMass ensured the likelihood that there would be a scarcity of job recruiters on campus. Big chemical companies such as Dow and Monsanto were heavily involved in the creation of a chemical defoliant called Agent Orange, which was one target of student actions. This disenchantment with the industry made a chemical engineering career less appealing to Jack, especially when you couple that with the sparse job prospects for a long-haired, pot-smoking engineer. So instead of working in a Monsanto lab, Jack found himself doing a teaching practicum as a counselor at North High School in Worcester.

It turned out to be a mixed blessing. Heavy drugs were gaining popularity, especially among the younger kids, and finding two kids slumped over and nearly unconscious on the steps to the guidance office was not unusual.

"Hey, Joey. You have to get up. Look at me!"

Jack knew both kids well, and he knew the source of their inebriation: Seconal, a powerful barbiturate, had swept into the East Side, and kids were eating them like candy.

"How many reds did you take?" Jack asked, knowing that too many could be lethal.

"Just…just…two," Gayle stammered.

Two too many, Jack thought. "Joey! Come on, stand up," he said, grabbing his stoned young friend by the arm. "You get busted, it's gonna be big trouble."

Joey gave a lazy moan and staggered to his feet, wearing a mischievous smile.

"OK, Jack," he said. "Thanks for the heads-up, man." He swayed down the stairs and out into the corridor, his wasted neighborhood friend rising and following a few seconds behind.

For Jack, working at the school was about the blind leading the blind. Most of the kids he knew from the neighborhood were constantly high—or low. If a kid had his head down on his desk, he was more likely snoozing because he had swallowed a couple of Seconals or Tuinals and not because the lecture was boring. Jack grew adept at shielding the wasted from trouble. He cajoled a kid on acid to go outdoors, where he could groove on nature until he came down, and he kept kids stripped of their good judgment by what they had ingested from flagrantly betraying their intoxication and getting thrown out of school. How anyone ever managed to graduate was beyond Jack's comprehension, and his own problems with drugs were progressing, although imperceptibly to him.

Back living with his parents, Jack managed to keep the detrimental effects of his addiction in check. Smoking marijuana was his primary activity during the school week. Jack thought he did a pretty good job with his schoolwork and his internships. His professors agreed. Jack never thought about getting high for class or while teaching; he couldn't see the utility of it. He reserved total blackout partying mostly for weekends and special occasions, but his definition of "special" was growing broader by the day. It wasn't long before Jack started to believe the slogan, "A good day to get high is any day that ends in Y."

School wasn't the only place to get wasted. By the summer of 1972, Shrewsbury Street was locked on full-tilt boogie. The uncertainty of the times meant letting go of local traditions; the first to be abandoned was the longstanding prohibition on drugs. While Jack had been away at college learning his ABCs (amphetamines, barbiturates, and cocaine), those on the East Side had embraced drugs with equal enthusiasm. The seemingly benign affectations of marijuana use among the flower children and cocaine use among the more affluent resulted in a laissez-faire attitude toward drug use among the general population on Shrewsbury Street, as residents glimpsed for the first time the Pandora's box of the drug culture. This rapid deterioration was immediately evident in some of the neighborhood kids' preference for shooting heroin and taking dangerous doses of barbiturates. It was time to turn on, tune in, and drop out, but in far too many instances, dropping out turned into dropping dead. The accidental overdose of two of the gangs more spirited members failed to slow the inevitable descent.

The East Park drug contingent was steadily growing, too. Not only were the returning Vietnam veterans swelling the ranks, but also quite a few guys from the hill were spending their Friday nights at the park's Community House. Girls were also beginning to appear with regularity—in numbers and not just from the neighborhood. Whether it was the boys, the lure of abundant alcohol and drugs, or both, no one asked or cared.

Fudgy and Dumbo, singing a cappella, were the nightly headliners, but instead of tuning up with imperial quarts of cheap beer, they were using pot, hashish, reds, or Quaaludes. On the weekends and on many weeknights, twenty-five to thirty kids would gather on the steps of the Community House, hoping to get high.

It is often said that alcohol and drugs hinder emotional development, and nowhere was this more evident than in East Park. The group ranged in age from sixteen to twenty-five, with the older members naturally becoming the leaders. Jack didn't let his aspiration to be an educator influence his interactions with any of the teenagers, who he regularly saw at school. Fun was the only goal of the night; professional decorum was not given a second thought. It was from the older group that most of a night's activities would evolve, and often games like kick the can, jailbreak, and relieve-e-o took the spotlight. But these were not the innocent games of childhood; drinking and drugging influenced the intensity of the games, and the rules of engagement changed.

The guys and girls would all run off to hide, and for a few of them, it was the perfect opportunity to allow "a teenage crush to flourish. For the Vietnam vets, it was back to the jungle. The Crusher, twenty-three, having already survived the tunnels of Vietnam, epitomized the lunacy of it all. Addled by drugs and booze, he tried to swing down from the Community House roof to the porch like some superhero crashing through a skyscraper window into a room full of hostages. His attempt, however, had a less-than-heroic outcome. The Crusher seriously miscalculated the jump, dropping about ten feet, hitting his head on the granite wall of the porch, and tumbling the remaining fifteen feet to the ground. A bump the size of a lying Pinocchio's nose grew on his head, and he lost consciousness for what seemed to be an eternity.

The Crusher recovered, but his was only one of many foolish and outright dangerous escapades in East Park, and the young women took equal part. It was relatively common to find one of the sixteen-year-old girls from the neighborhood passed out in the park from too many barbiturates, but fortunately, predatory sexual behavior was one of the few remaining taboos. It was frowned upon in a neighborhood where everyone was considered extended family.

In a strange way, drugs brought many of the smaller, isolated neighborhood groups together. Like the merchants and customers who drove the development of early trade routes to Africa, India, and China, the East Side youth were united in the search for products that would provide a new peak experience. In many recovery groups, addicts talk about the quest to replicate the exhilaration they experienced when they took that first drink or that first drug. That feeling often proves to be elusive, and it drives the user in a constant search. On Shrewsbury Street and in East Park, scoring and using drugs drove nearly every activity.

Groups of searchers on the Street and in East Park soon broke down into subgroups based on their drug of choice. The Muskeego Street gang had earned an early reputation as the junkies of the neighborhood; they were intravenous heroin users, at the bottom of the food chain—or at the top, depending on your viewpoint. The girls tended to take pills, mostly downers, allowing them to lose their inhibitions along with their virginity in the age of sex, drugs, and rock and roll. The older East Park boys still hung on to their cases of beer, but the college-age kids were smoking pot, popping pills, and sipping Boone's Farm wine.

A change in the East Side's personality and behavior was evident on every street corner. The antiwar movement had been in full swing since National Guard troops killed four demonstrators at Kent State University. Young men wore their hair shoulder length. Miniskirts revealed more leg than some bathing suits did, and string bikinis left hardly anything to the imagination. The names Lilly, Merck, Abbott, and Roche were slowly but surely replacing Schlitz, Budweiser, Narragansett, and Carlings Black Label as the makers of the most popular recreational drugs. In a relatively short period of time, Jimi Hendrix, Janis Joplin, and Jim Morrison had all died drug-related deaths at the tender age of twenty-seven, but public policy makers and the nation at large generally ignored these and many other warning signs. And if the deaths of these megastars had little impact on the national perspective, one could only imagine how insignificant the heroin overdose deaths of the Street's hippest denizens were on the East Side. Already, deaths by overdose of kids from the neighborhood were catching up to the combat deaths in Vietnam, but no one on the street seemed to notice.

The criminal behavior that came along with the use of hard drugs did capture some attention, particularly the robbery of local pharmacies for their precious inventory. Jobs were hard to come by for many on the Street, and the drug trade was beginning to blossom, opening up new avenues of income. As the demand for pharmaceuticals went up, so did the street value of the pills that could be grabbed by smashing a pharmacy window.

The most notorious of the East Side's pharmacy bandits was Joey, the boy Jack found semiconscious on the steps outside the guidance office of North High School. He had graduated to shooting heroin and using other drugs. Now known as "Joey Drugstore," he liked getting high so much that he couldn't wait until he left the scene of a robbery to start ingesting his bounty. In the aftermath of one of his many robberies, the police found him passed out on the floor, a needle still in his arm, and an empty bottle of hydromorphone next to him on the floor.

Always a performer, Fudgy took the robbery show to a higher level. One morning, Jack got an urgent phone call from Dillie, another neighborhood kid who was among the first to hear about Fudgy's latest attempt to hold up a local bank.

"Jack, Fudgy's in trouble." Dillie's frantic voice was trembling.

"What the fuck?" was all a sleepy Jack could mutter after a typical Friday party night.

"We need to go pick up Fudgy. He just robbed a bank in Westborough. Joe Marks was driving the getaway car, but he took off and left Fudgy there."

"Come and get me," Jack said and hung up the phone.

Ten minutes later, Dillie pulled up in front of Jack's Plum Street apartment and off they went. Fudgy had already robbed two banks by this time, both small jobs. In fact, while they were driving to Westborough, Jack and Dillie joked about the first bank Fudgy had hit: Laraia & Ermilio, a small neighborhood concern at the corner of Plum and Shrewsbury Streets.

Fudgy's entrance had startled the teller, which was not a difficult accomplishment at the mostly somnolent facility. Not wanting to advertise his distinctive voice, Fudgy passed a note to the teller stating that this was a robbery and she was to give him all of her money. Loot in hand, Fudgy had fled on foot to the safety of his own familiar and unsuspecting neighborhood. That haul resulted in a whopping $200, which Fudgy used to buy a wedding ring for the first of his several brides.

For the Westborough job, Fudgy had decided that a getaway car was in order, and he put local hood Joe Marks behind the wheel. When Marks bolted, Fudgy once again used the shoe leather express as his transport, beating feet to nearby woods to stash the cash and toss his easily identifiable shirt. The disrobing proved to be a double-edged sword; walking shirtless down busy Route 9 was a sure way to attract attention, and by the time Jack and Dillie arrived in the vicinity, Fudgy was safely under lock and key at the local hoosegow, where he was charged with bank robbery. Somehow, Fudgy managed to keep it together during his interrogation, and eventually, the charges were dropped due to lack of evidence—closed-circuit video at that time was of very poor quality, and Fudgy could not be positively identified. Everyone back in the neighborhood attributed Fudgy's good fortune to his remarkable acting ability. If you listened to Fudgy telling the story, you knew that he believed his own lies.

In childhood, Jack's life seemed to pass by excruciatingly slow as he waited with urgency to become an adult. But in reality, his life moved more like a DVD on fast-forward as he headed toward the addiction bottom, where things get worse faster than you can lower your standards, as people in recovery say. Jack wasn't alone in his descent, and some bottomed out faster than others.

The Crusher still had a few more misadventures to come with the East Park gang. But soon, his heroin habit and a broken heart would cause him to flee the home turf for the Los Angeles area, where he became a car salesman like his father. The Crusher had talent and charisma, and he managed to keep his addiction at bay long enough to haul in some serious cash and set up residence on beautiful Laguna Beach. But eventually, his drug habit overwhelmed his ability to do business, and he lost his plush digs. Exposure to Agent Orange, a toxic defoliant used during the Vietnam War, resulted in his premature demise from liver disease.

Dumbo, once a member of a band that opened for the Rolling Stones, had had his fifteen minutes of fame, but he was playing and singing in a new band, along with a few other guys from the East Side. As the shows wore on, the effects of alcohol and pills would deteriorate his performance. Luckily for him, most of his audience would be just as wasted. In between the bank robberies, Fudgy filled in as a guest vocalist for Dumbo's band or found theater work in Boston. But the need for drugs prevented his star from rising as high as it should have.

Using wasn't the only way in which drugs influenced the lives of kids in the neighborhood. Many answered the siren song of easy cash and entered the drug business as dealers. Some moved to South Florida, a hotspot for young entrepreneurs with a taste for contraband. Miami was the major port of entry for smuggling pot from Colombia, which provided a greater potential for profit than did the lower-grade Mexican bricks or the homegrown plants that were better utilized for rope.

After Jack's graduation from Worcester State in June 1973, his career in secondary education took a backseat to a more lucrative profession. That summer, Jack, now divorced, and Hank moved into the top floor of a triple-decker on Grafton Street, a middle-class neighborhood, and set up shop as reputable dealers of exotic, high-potency marijuana. They actually viewed themselves as doing a public service and developed business practices that would have made the godfather, Don Vito Corleone, proud: no selling to kids, no selling to addicts, no cheating on the weight, and handling only the best product on the market, guaranteed to make you smile and give you the munchies. They gave their grass fancy names, such as Rainbow, Panama Red, Santa Marta Gold, Black Afghan, and Maui Wowie. The more elaborate the title, the higher the effect and the price. Business was good; they never lacked customers, and only occasionally did they experience an interruption in supply as the various interdiction efforts and an unpredictable hurricane season caused smugglers to alter their patterns or delay sailing until more favorable conditions arose.

The success of their operation gave Hank, who was the generous one of the pair, the opportunity to help a friend in need. Stevie the Sailor had not been the same since he started shooting up; he had tried to remain an innocent flower child, but in the world of intravenous heroin use, such innocence wasn't possible. Stevie had been Hank's next-door neighbor growing up, so Hank tried to help Stevie out by paying him for drug-selling duties or making an exception to the "no selling to addicts" rule and selling Stevie the best pot at wholesale prices so Stevie could make some money by reselling it. In Mafia terms, Stevie was a good soldier. For those who stayed on the Street, a definite pecking order had begun to develop. At the top of the order were those who had the best drugs.

Of course, there was never a lack of younger wannabes on the East Side, and they emulated the older guys through drug use, among other things. They required no coaxing or salesmanship, and the drugs they took came without warning labels. It wasn't long before most of the East Side's young adults were experimenting with some form of substance to escape or, in many cases, just to fit in.

The transition from the wonderful, innocent little boys that their mothers still believed them to be to antisocial, personality-disordered hoodlums was different for each of the kids from the Street. Anecdotally, it could be said that their descent was directly proportional to their involvement with drugs, but that would be an oversimplification. For some people, the fall was so rapid that there was no chance of recovery. All hope was erased by drug overdoses. For others, especially those who were able to remain functional, it was a staged disaster, unfolding in plain view but with no remedy in sight.

There is a saying in the recovery movement that goes something like this: "If the addiction doesn't get you, then the lifestyle will." These words perfectly describe what was to come for Jack and many of his friends from the Street. The supposedly enlightened group, those "who knew too much for their own good," as their parents would often say, set the bar for the antics, the drug use, the entrepreneurial spirit, and eventually the pain. Their parents could only watch helplessly as the tragedies unfolded.

Jump into the discomfort. Challenge assumptions that you have about addiction. Bring rationality back to this segment of health-care.

—Denny Morrison

What could easily be characterized as self-evident or, at the very least, a reasonable hypothesis is the correlation between the social dysfunction exhibited by many individuals and the delayed development in many of the primary functions attributed to the prefrontal cortex. Neurobiologists tell us that "attunement," the ability to sense another's feelings; "emotional balance" or "affect regulation," the ability to feel fear, sadness, and anger, and change it to ease and peace; "response flexibility," the capacity to pause before action; "empathy," the conscious awareness and sensitivity to the mind of someone else; and "morality," the ability to think of the larger social good and act accordingly, even when no one is looking are all functions of the prefrontal cortex. We also know that this area of the brain develops during one's midtwenties and that substance abuse can greatly alter it.

What conclusions, if any, can be drawn from this? Anecdotally, at least, the stories in this book support the hypothesis that many of the primary functions of the prefrontal cortex are severely impacted by drug use. There can be no argument that morality, response flexibility, emotional balance, and empathy were casualties of the repeated negative experiences endured by the guys from the neighborhood.

Does knowing this help us in any way to develop strategies to relieve the suffering or contribute to superior outcomes?

CHAPTER TWENTY TWO

For Fudgy, Jack, Dumbo, and the rest of the gang from the Street, the point of no return came with no clear delineation but in a slow, almost unnoticeable erosion of their moral fiber and their innate ability to discern right from wrong, good from evil. Even representatives of the law enforcement community were having a hard time sorting out this new world and its confusing array of new intoxicants and new lifestyles. Particularly in the rural areas, law officers often proved easy to fool—but not always. Which is why, on a lovely day in September, Jack found himself in the backseat of a police cruiser in Bellevue, Nebraska, frantically trying to unload a pocketful of illegal prescription drugs.

It had started a year earlier, in August 1972, when Jack joined three friends from the neighborhood—Craig, Smithy, and Juney— on a cross-country drive to Los Angeles to visit Toojo, a neighborhood kid who had joined the navy and was stationed at Seal Beach, just outside of LA. For kids who had never left the East Coast, LA might as well have been the moon.

Before LA, however, the quartet stopped off at the Strategic Air Command base outside Omaha, Nebraska, where Craig's older brother was stationed. During a tour of the most remote parts of the base, the East Side kids had gazed in jaw-dropping awe as Craig's brother pointed out one of the local sites.

"Yonder in that field over there," he said in what sounded like a Southern drawl, "marijuana grows wild."

Possibly for the first time, the four travelers had not one but two thoughts in unison: "Free!" and then "High!" As Jack was already dealing in marijuana, there was also a profit motive to consider. There was no question in his mind that they'd be stopping in Omaha again on their return from LA, which is exactly what they did.

Unprepared for such a stroke of good luck and afraid of being caught, the friends harvested a few trash bags full of the leafy green plant and stuffed them in the trunk of their car. Later, they would learn that what they'd harvested was industrial hemp, a variety of cannabis with very little THC. When smoked, the main effect it produced was a headache. But it wasn't much worse than some of the legit weed being brought up from Mexico, and the price was certainly right.

When they returned to the East Side, the boys discovered that they'd harvested mostly stems and stalks, which were useless to smoke and worthless to sell. But six pounds of the headache-producing weed turned a profit of a few hundred dollars, which immediately fueled Jack's ambitions for a return trip to the Midwestern field of dreams.

It's critical to understand that the maxim "quit while you're ahead" means little to an addict. Recovering addicts frequently talk about "denial" and use it as an acronym for "Don't Even Notice I Am Lying." This phrase accurately portrays the absence of rational thought and the often-precarious nature of an addict's misguided pursuits.

Jack and his friends didn't see it then, and if they did, they wouldn't have done anything about it, but a bright-red warning sign was flashing. In just a few years, a drug overdose would claim Smithy's life, leaving the rest of them to mourn, and of the four, only Jack would eventually escape the ravages of addiction. But in 1972, it was game on, and Jack soon began to plan a harvesting expedition for the following summer.

The second expedition included a largely different crew: Jack, Leo (the Crusher), Johnny Two Fingers, and Hank. It was planned in advance and, in a few ways, well thought out. Of course, much of the planning centered on the types and quantities of drugs the crew would need to sustain them on their cross-country journey. In this case, pocketsful of barbiturates and amphetamines from a recent pharmacy robbery fit the bill nicely. Nothing was left to chance, or so they thought.

Johnny Two Fingers, a kid who'd become fast friends with Jack after a low-impact fistfight at age thirteen, provided his brand new Oldsmobile Grand Prix, which he'd bought with the money he'd earned as a Marine, crawling through the jungle looking for the Viet Cong, as the means of transportation.

The Crusher cast his lot with his friends because he thought he had no place else to go. Leo grew up in a single-family home on the outskirts of the neighborhood, and though he'd had a few more opportunities than Jack and his friends, ended up in Vietnam anyway. While risking his life crawling through tunnels in the jungle, he got a Dear John letter from his childhood sweetheart, who, to add insult to injury, was dating a kid that received a draft board designation of 4-f, signifying a medical, psychological, or moral exemption from military service. Despite all this, the Crusher still had the innocent face of a sixteen-year-old. His deep-rooted yearning to belong sealed his passage on the trip.

The remaining coconspirator was Hank, Jack's closest friend. Hank started smoking marijuana and taking pills and LSD with some kids on the Street before joining the Air National Guard.

One of Hank's best Guard buddies had cut his time short by pleading insanity and going to the "nut house." Hank, whose parents had both served in the military, had enough pride to stay in the Guard, but he served only in name, not in spirit, and was making up for lost time as far as drugs were concerned. A true flower child, Hank was nonviolent to the core. He belonged to a group of guardsmen who wore short-haired wigs to conceal their shoulder-length hippie hair on active-duty weekends. That politically charged hairstyle, just beginning to blossom on the two recently returned marines and totally evident on Hank and Jack, would play an ironic role in the unfolding events.

The trip west started with the usual excitement and the added euphoria brought about by the celebratory swallowing of several amphetamines commonly known as Black Beauties and T-20s. Soon, communication became problematic, as everyone talked incessantly and all at once. Hank was a chatterer by nature and had a voice that needed no amplification. This contributed to his ability to dominate the conversation, and if the tone of his voice didn't work, he would grab an arm to make sure he got your attention.

Johnny Two Fingers, Jack, and the Crusher, all tried in vain to interrupt Hank's soliloquies by steering the conversation to harvest strategies: maximizing the haul, cleaning the "grass," and assigning the duties of chopping, cutting, cleaning, and bagging. The buzz of the speed wore off after several hours, and the ride, though still filled with promise, settled into drudgery.

After twenty-four hours of nonstop driving, an utterly exhausted crew checked into a motel near the Strategic Air Command base and more importantly, a short distance from the field of weed. It was quite logical, at least to this group, to employ a cocktail of barbiturates, such as Seconal, Tuinal, and Nembutal, commonly known on the street as reds, stripers, and yellow jackets, respectively, to offset the discomfort of crashing off the speed and to induce a good night's rest. As the sleeping pills worked their magic, an eerie quiet descended over the travelers. Even Hank stopped talking long enough for everyone to fall asleep.

When morning came, they were still feeling a bit sluggish from the downers, but the excitement of the upcoming mission and the possibility of a big payday proved to be sufficient motivation. They packed their supplies: hatchets, knives, plastic bags, and, of course, plenty of pills. Jack's engineering studies were finally beginning to pay off; he had carefully measured the volume of the trunk so they knew how many bags of marijuana they needed to fill to maximize profits. They brought a camera along as an alibi. If anyone asked them what they were doing out there in the middle of nowhere, they would simply explain their interest in photography.

They left the motel and headed in the direction of the recreation area. Johnny Two Fingers searched for a spot to park the car, as the plan was to harvest the marijuana and then wait for nightfall to go back to retrieve the bags. It was so perfectly planned, nothing could go wrong. Two Fingers parked the car in an unoccupied lot next to what appeared to be a small and abandoned manufacturing facility.

Making sure there would be no repeat of the mistakes made last time, the guys spent most of the day in the hot sun, cutting and cleaning marijuana leaves from their woody stalks. Greed and the false euphoria of amphetamines trumped engineering calculations, and soon they had filled fifteen contractor-sized trash bags. They had enough pot to yield tens of thousands of dollars in sales, but way too much to fit into the trunk. Worn out and crashing as the speed wore off, they decided to stash their bounty, head out of the field, rest, and await nightfall.

They were leaving the field just as a patrol car arrived on the scene. It seemed that a concerned Nebraska citizen had alerted the police that four hippies, possibly spies, had parked a car with Massachusetts plates in the vicinity of the Strategic Air Command base and quite possibly were up to no good.

The patrol car stopped next to them and a lanky, sunburned cop rolled down the window.

"What are you boys doing out here?"

Inwardly, Jack smiled and thought, *Careful planning, piece of cake.* "Just out here taking some pictures of the area, officer," he explained, holding up the camera.

The cop stared straight ahead for a moment before gesturing toward the group. "You boys better get in the car. I have someone who wants to ask you some questions."

The mind of an addict can be an amazing engine of delusion; Jack's confidence in the plan remained strong. After all, what could possibly happen? There was no law against taking pictures. They were free and clear—except, maybe, for one small problem.

In Jack's pockets were several plastic prescription containers full of Tuinals, Seconals, T-20's, and Black Beauties. Luckily, Jack was riding in the back of the police car, so he was able to stuff the plastic bottles of drugs into folds of the backseat. Hesitant to leave everything behind, Jack, despite struggling with the child resistant cap, managed to dump a bottle of barbiturates into his pocket before depositing the empty container into the backseat crevice.

The four Massachusetts hippies arrived at the police station and were asked to empty their pockets and show identification. The identification was no problem, but the pills in Jack's pocket would raise a few eyebrows; somehow, he needed to discard the pills. Putting on his best Sacred Heart schoolboy smile, Jack turned toward the cop at the desk.

"Officer, would you mind if I used the bathroom?"

"Go ahead. You aren't under arrest."

Inside the public restroom, Jack chose one of the industrial steel-gray stalls and dumped the pills into the toilet, but not before swallowing a few of them. There was no reason to let them all go to waste. Jack was beginning to feel some relief until he flushed the toilet. After the flush, the gel capsules remained, bobbing in the bowl like little red ducklings.

Suddenly, panic began to set in. Flushing repeatedly would surely alert even the least intuitive cop that something was going on. Reaching into the toilet with his hand felt unthinkably disgusting and undignified, but time was passing; at any moment, an officer would be wondering what was taking him so long. Jack eventually decided to cover the entire surface of the water and the pills with toilet paper, hoping the weight of the paper would be enough to sink the remaining pills. Asking God for help and promising never to sin again, Jack flushed once more. Miraculously—or not—the last of the pills vanished, and he finally was able to breathe a sigh of relief.

After Jack returned to the holding room, he and his friends were escorted into an interrogation room, where an air force colonel was waiting. In a matter of minutes, the colonel was able to determine that the young men were no threat to national security, they were not agents for or from another country, they obviously were not too bright, and they were lying through their teeth. The first two conclusions likely came from the two marines' service record; the latter two came from the absence of film in the boys' camera.

Satisfied that the country was safe, the colonel ordered their identification returned, and they were driven back to Johnny Two Fingers' car. Once back in the car, it was decision time. They'd had a close call, but all that marijuana was still out there in the field just waiting for them.

The four were divided on what to do. Hank and the Crusher thought they should consider themselves lucky and just drive back home. Two Fingers and Jack wanted to leave, too, but with a trunk full of marijuana.

Hank objected most vociferously. "You guys are out of your minds. Going back into the field can't work out any way but bad."

But for Jack, the decision was easy. The barbiturates were beginning to alter his thinking. He had no fear, and he had effectively lost touch with reality. He wasn't slurring his words yet, but he was making superhero-level promises. "You guys stay here. I'll run up the road and carry the pot back on my back."

It all made sense to him. Obviously, he was not thinking about the half-mile run into the field and the hundred-plus pounds of weight that he would be carrying. Evidently, the others were convinced by Jack's willingness to volunteer. They all decided to go back.

Two Fingers steered the Grand Prix down the dirt road leading to the field, and once they got there, Jack jumped out of the car, intending to run up that dusty dirt path and return victorious. Head down, arms and legs churning, Jack suddenly looked up to see a police car heading straight in his direction.

Jack pivoted and ran for the car at full speed, screeching at the top of his lungs, "Johnny, for Christ's sake! Start the fucking car! Let's get the fuck out of here!"

They tried to make a getaway but were soon surrounded by the Bellevue police force and taken into custody. This time they were arrested, locked into a small row of cells in the Bellevue police station, and charged with harvesting and possession of marijuana. Bail was set at five hundred dollars.

Given the customary opportunity to make a single phone call, they each called home. One by one, they talked to their parents—their mothers, if at all possible. The kids were not newcomers to trouble; there would be no fainting on the other end of the phone. Still, they knew what pain and embarrassment their new trouble would cause their parents. As each took his turn at the phone, he told as little of the story as he could and pleaded for understanding and, most of all, bail money.

The Crusher was the only one who had trouble reaching his family. They were vacationing on Cape Cod. He was both embarrassed and afraid to ruin their vacation. Quite often, bad situations only get worse, and so it was for the Crusher. After agonizing about whether to call his parents, he did. Their day in the sun was interrupted by the beach's public address system informing them loudly and all too publicly that their son was calling them from jail.

Hank was the first one to make bail and secure at least temporary freedom. But he was still fifteen hundred miles from home, and his friends were still locked up. Having no one to talk to, no means to travel anywhere, and no place to stay made going back to jail look attractive. Hank considered his options and convinced the cops to let him stay the night in jail with his friends. The officers agreed and even let him out for the evening to grab some dinner and maybe shoot a little pool before returning to his cell. Hank brought back McDonald's hamburgers for everyone, even the cops.

The next day, the four harvesters all had received their bail money and were able to leave their cozy little home away from home. With a court date in eleven days, they holed up at the Bellevue YMCA, which was cheap, functional, and in close proximity to the courthouse. Their attorney was a local defense counselor whose main attribute was that he was affordable.

The eleven days at the Y went by uneventfully, but the four heard the local maxim, "Hard on harvesters," whenever they sought advice or opinions about their upcoming court date. Harvesting marijuana carried a maximum penalty of five years in prison and to make matters worse, they were told that if they appeared in front of one particular magistrate, who was described as "older than fire," he would lock them up and throw away the key. According to Hank, who lost ten pounds from worry in the days before the trial, everyone was terrified. None of them had ever been arrested. They were fifteen hundred miles from home without their families or neighborhood friends. And they were facing a possible five-year sentence.

When their day in court arrived, they walked into the court-room and confronted their worst nightmare. On the bench and wielding the gavel was the older-than-fire judge. Any hope that their attorney provided evaporated, and before long, they were asked to adjourn to the judge's chamber for a pretrial interview. This was their first encounter with the legal system, and they had no idea what was in store. Things started roughly, but the tone of the interview began to change when the Crusher and Baba, the two Vietnam veterans, detailed some of their experiences during combat. As much talking as they had done in the car on the way to Nebraska, these stories were new and harrowing and impressed the judge. These new revelations from their good friends propelled Hank and Jack, a National Guardsman and an aspiring teacher, respectively, to paint themselves as typical all-American kids in an effort to distance themselves from the drug-harvesting prototype.

The dark mood soon lifted, and the jocular old judge bantered on about his recent visit to the home state of the accused and the wonderful clam chowder he had tasted there. A collective sigh of relief traveled around the room, probably unnoticed by anyone who was not from Massachusetts. "Hard on harvesters" was not how it would play out on this day. The East Side boys were slapped with a two-hundred-dollar fine, and Johnny Two Fingers' car was not impounded. The chowder-eating judge ordered the boys es-corted to the city limits and did not invite them to return. Best of all, news of the arrest never made the Worcester papers.

What lesson did the four East Siders learn from all this? Instead of being grateful and realizing their good fortune, the conversa-tion on the way home focused on lost opportunity, lost money, get-ting high as soon as possible, and vowing that the next time, they would not get caught.

CHAPTER TWENTY THREE

J D had tried to work in the plumbing trade once he returned from his military training, but his drinking and drug use made it difficult. He drank daily, including on the job, and he also began smoking more marijuana and using any other drug he could find. He was a Muskeego Street boy, tried and true, which meant partying harder and with less restraint than anyone else on the East Side did. For many of the kids from Muskeego Street, that meant heroin.

JD had begun to hang out with an old high school buddy named Kirbstone, who lived in a nearby neighborhood and worked for a distributor of cigarettes and tobacco products. Kirbstone was a heroin user.

One afternoon, as they sat in the back of Kirbstone's van, JD curiously watched his friend prepare to shoot up, and he was struck by an overwhelming desire. He had seen those he knew inject heroin and sink into the warm, euphoric embrace of the drug immediately, and he wanted to experience that for himself. He didn't plan on becoming addicted or even using it on a regular basis. He merely wanted to see what the big deal was.

In a voice subdued by fear and excitement, he said to Kirbstone, "I want to do some." Following the customary warning about the evils of the drug and the guilt-laden rationalizations for not doing it, Kirbstone, in his drug-induced haze, prepared and injected JD with a small dose. Within seconds, the drug collided with JD's conscience and sense of right and wrong, and the drug won. JD immediately knew what the big deal with heroin was.

Heroin opened up a strange and exciting new world for JD; he couldn't have imagined the eighteen years of pain and struggle that would follow. Once again, any thoughts of the future were subsumed by his present needs, which now included daily doses of heroin and the cash to obtain it. Soon, waiting for a measly paycheck at the end of a week wasn't getting the job done for either JD or Kirbstone, so they turned to a more nefarious way of producing cash: stealing cases of cigarettes from Kirbstone's employer and selling them to a local fence. For a while, they made lots of money, enough to support their habit, buy new cars, and take trips to Florida. What they didn't know was that progression is a key aspect of addiction, prompting the addict to need more and more of the drug to achieve the necessary result. In order to keep up with the addiction, they had to steal more cigarettes, which meant more risk. Fortunately, JD's father had connection in the halls of power, and that would save him from a fall.

"Jimmy, I got word from a buddy of mine who is on the vice squad," Muggsy said, sitting across the table in the family kitchen, his voice elevated with concern. "He's a good guy, and he is looking out for you, which is why he called me. They've been watching you guys, and they're about to bust your fence and take you guys down with him."

JD's parents already knew their son was in trouble. They'd spoken to him about it directly, but he'd insisted that everything was fine. When Muggsy confronted him about the thefts, JD once again issued a denial.

"I don't know what you are talking about," JD said. "Me and Kirbstone aren't up to any bullshit."

"Look, Jimmy," Muggsy said, pointing a thick, stubby finger at him. "The cops know Johnny S is fencing those cigarettes you've been lifting from Kirbstone's boss. Now you can sit there and lie about it; that's your choice. But they got pictures. Of you, Jimmy, unloading the truck at Johnny's. They're gonna bust you all."

JD was pretty messed up on drugs, but he could put a couple of things together: the end of the cigarette scam was near, and prison probably did not offer a heroin concession. So he did what any addict does when the heat is on. He ran.

Ironically, JD's escape would be made possible by Tony, the stepfather he hated. Tony's brother, Peaches, was an original East Side hood who now made his home in Florida. On the East Side, Peaches was a legend, a character most everyone knew. He made his nut with two-bit hustles and outright theft, and he often passed himself off as some sort of talent agent as a way to get women.

Peaches had visited the East Side in 1972, and he dropped by the house to see his brother, Tony. JD happened to be home when Peaches visited, and while sitting at the kitchen table, Peaches had confronted him bluntly. "So Jimmy, what the fuck are you gonna do with your life?"

After fumbling with a bogus answer, it became obvious that JD had no clue.

"Get the fuck out of Worcester," Peaches told JD. "This place is dead. Come down to Florida. That's where it's all happening. I'll put you up, and I got some local connections. We'll get you a job, and you'll be all set."

Back then, JD had been reluctant. But the situation had changed. Florida seemed much more appealing than jail. It took a little scrambling, but JD managed (or more accurately, his mother managed) to scrape up enough money to buy a plane ticket to Florida. But there was a big fly in the ointment: JD's remaining obligation to the Air Force Reserve.

For the previous six months or so, he'd been trying to live up to his commitment, but the progression of his drug use had made it nearly impossible. He had spoken to the folks in charge, telling them that he was having problems. He even produced a letter from the well-known Dr. Mario, a family physician and childhood friend of Muggsy's.

Dr. Mario was another local legend from the Street. He had made something respectable of himself, and nearly everyone in the neighborhood was his patient. He was reminiscent of the old-time docs who made house calls, visited his patients if they were in the hospital, and respectfully attended their funerals and those of their family members. So when JD's drug use escalated to the point where he couldn't control it any longer, he went to Dr. Mario for help. After a good tongue-lashing about being so stupid as to get "fucked up with dope," Dr. Mario gave JD a script for Dilaudid to wean him off heroin, and wrote a letter to his commanding officer at Westover Air Force Base stating that JD was addicted, under his care, and unfit for military duty.

JD could have waited to see what effect this communique might have, but he decided not to stick around while the military bureaucracy ground slowly forward. So off to sunny Florida he went. He hid out for the winter, working at the job Uncle Peaches had found for him, parking cars at a resort hotel with ties to Boston wise guys. Thankfully, Peaches had an anxiety condition for which his doctor prescribed Valium, which helped JD wean himself off heroin. Still, he was drinking as much as ever, taking Valium regularly, and using whatever else he could get his hands on. Life seemed good, and JD gravitated to a group of friends and associates who were just like him.

It was the early 1970s, and in South Florida, cocaine was king. JD fit right in with those who were stealing, dealing, and hustling, including Uncle Peaches, who, as always, was working scams of his own. Peaches had studied the trade of locksmithing; he knew how to read codes from manuals and manufacture keys for just about any kind of lock, and he used that knowledge to steal. His favorite targets were vending machines. Every hotel, motel, beach, and high-traffic spot had them, and cracking them open was a piece of cake. It was a quick and easy night's work to make a few stops, empty out the machines, and head home with five hundred to a thousand dollars. At Peaches' invitation, JD joined in the scam. Combined with his parking job, the vending machine hustle created a great cash flow. JD's drinking and drug use cost him some money, but nothing like his heroin habit had. He was living large.

For the next two or three years, JD moved surreptitiously between Florida and Massachusetts, trying to fly beneath the radar of the military authorities. During that time, he took another old friend, Chazbo, to Florida. JD had moved up in status on the beach, having made more connections and proved to be trustworthy when it came to stealing and dealing. As a result, he and Chazbo easily got jobs at another resort.

Chazbo wasn't the only East Sider making his rounds in the Sunshine State. Johnny Two Fingers and a few others were spending time in Florida, but for a different reason. They were transporting drugs between growers and processors in Latin America and the markets up north. Since they all nursed addictions at one time or another, JD and Chazbo soon reunited with their old friends.

In summer 1974, JD and Chazbo moved into Johnny Two Fingers's house in North Miami Beach to hold down the fort while he traveled to Colombia and Boston to set up deals. It felt like old home week when guys and girls from the East Side would fly in to do some business, catch some sun, and party. The visitors even included the Crusher, who flew all the way from California to hang with the guys from the neighborhood.

For JD, the good times continued to roll, and he managed to stay away from heroin. He used pot, booze, and prescription drugs to feed his addiction. Of course, there was usually plenty of cocaine around, but oddly enough, he didn't enjoy its stimulating effects, and although he occasionally partook, he usually stayed away from it.

The good times came to a screeching halt in summer 1975 when JD and Uncle Peaches were busted in Myrtle Beach, South Carolina, for emptying vending machines they didn't own. Uncle Peaches made bail, but JD couldn't. The courts ran a records check and found out that he was wanted by the military. So JD was remanded to the county jail.

As mothers have always done for their troubled sons, JD's mom tried to come to his rescue. She flew in for one of his hearings, and almost got him more time when she accused the judge of being a "redneck cracker" who was still pissed about the Civil War. The truth was, short of bringing JD clothes and cigarettes, there wasn't much anyone could do. He had to face the music, and being a white boy from the North in a Southern jail was no picnic.

After a month in the county jail, JD used the last of his cash to pay his fines, and he was released to military authorities at Myrtle Beach Air Force Base, who promptly locked him in their own facility, which, while a country club compared to the county lockup, was still jail. Eventually, he was released with orders to return to his home base in Massachusetts for a military court-martial. Luckily, JD did not have to be present for the proceedings. A military advocate-general defended him and managed to convince the court that JD was too impaired to comply with military life. He was given a general discharge and released.

Free but still shaken, JD was afraid that returning to Florida might mean facing up to some of his other illegal activities and doing more time. He stayed on the East Side, which turned out to be a good decision. Within six months, Chazbo, who had gotten into drug smuggling and dealing, was caught red-handed by the DEA and the FBI on a boat filled with drugs. Like his compatriots on the Nebraska reefer run, JD had dodged a bullet. And like them, that wouldn't be enough to make him stop.

CHAPTER TWENTY FOUR

B y 1974, Hank and Jack's Grafton Street pot-dealing business had grown from selling in half-ounce increments all the way to kilos. The move to the metric system was a sure sign of their upward mobility, which was also reflected in their ever-fattening wallets. Of course, success did not come without risk, and that risk was driven mostly by the ever-increasing dependence upon something to make life more exciting. Without the thrill of danger and the money it brought, they might have had to think about what their criminal lifestyle and addiction meant in real terms, and who wanted to do that?

At that point, Hank had already suffered through and escaped from a yearlong battle with heroin. He had gotten out of the National Guard by faking an injury in 1970, and about six months after that, he shot up for the first time. Soon, he was hopelessly addicted. After shooting drugs for a year, he contracted hepatitis and was hospitalized for thirty days. The doctor warned Hank that if he wanted to live, he needed to give up both his heavy drug use and the needle. Hank ignored the former order, but he had never really liked shooting dope anyway, so he complied with the latter. Plenty of drugs did not require needles, after all.

The expansion of Jack and Hank's dealing business relied on their ability to purchase marijuana cheaply from Frankie, a former intravenous heroin user who was trying a geographical cure. He moved away from the East Side and the temptation of his junkie friends, and in 1974 was living in Casa Grande, Arizona, where marijuana was cheap and plentiful. Jack and Hank would travel to Casa Grande, load up with weed, transport it back to Massachusetts, and sell it at a handsome profit.

The first leg of the return trip involved driving the weed to Las Vegas. Conveniently, gambling junkets from their old Worcester neighborhood to Las Vegas and back provided an economical and nearly foolproof means of transporting marijuana quickly and safely across the country.

For starters, the junkets, which were organized by the casinos and their backers, offered free airfare and lodging, contingent only on depositing thirty five hundred dollars into "the cage" at the host casino. Once that money was deposited, it could be withdrawn at any time, and most people withdrew it to gamble.

Even more critical, in the days before heightened airport security, luggage that traveled on junket trips was never searched. Jack and Hank's bags, stuffed full of marijuana, would be picked up at their hotel at the start of their trip back to Massachusetts and delivered to them curbside at their home airport, which made the contraband nearly impossible to detect.

Life could not be any better—or so they thought at the time. Jack and Hank had money, drugs, and the glamor of Vegas. But given the nature of their addictive personalities, they had occasional scares. One such moment began with an innocent tennis game.

Many people with addictive personalities have a constant need for excitement, for something to entertain them—anything to distract them from being with their own thoughts. Jack and Hank did not know the term "cross addiction," but the concept was certainly applicable to them. They gambled away a great deal of their excess cash and would wager on almost anything that had an unpredictable outcome. Sports, horse racing, card games, and Barbooth, a dice game of Middle Eastern origin, all offered the excitement that was becoming more and more necessary to fill an unidentifiable void. Las Vegas and The Dunes, the hotel casino where they stayed, offered just such an opportunity for Hank and Jack, but they both knew of gambling's potential peril. They figured a friendly game of tennis might keep them away from the gaming tables—at least for a while.

Next door to The Dunes was Caesars Palace and its legendary tennis courts, which had hosted some of the biggest matches and greatest stars of the game. In the early 1970s, Rod Laver, Jimmy Connors, Arthur Ashe, Billie Jean King, Chris Evert, and a host of other tennis greats put Caesars Palace courts on the map.

In Las Vegas, all men are not created equal. Money is king. The more money one is willing to risk on a game of chance, the more status and amenities one accrues. The high rollers" had carte blanche privileges. Hank and Jack were not really high rollers, but they imagined themselves that way. What better fantasy was there than to play on center court? The stakes were low—just two hundred dollars between the two old friends who had thirty-six thousand dollars locked safely in the casino cage and plenty more to come when their latest shipment sold. The midday temperature in Las Vegas tops one hundred degrees, and the sun was beating down unmercifully, but Jack and Hank went at it like McEnroe and Connors, playing as if their lives depended upon it, concerned only with whatever instant gratification they might extract from winning.

Obsession is the trademark of the addictive personality. Hank loved to gamble, but like most people who throw their lives away in pursuit of an addiction, it didn't matter much to him if he won or lost—being in the action was enough. However, no one likes to lose, so he wasn't beyond contesting a call.

"That was out!" Jack said, after Hank smacked a stiff overhand.

Hank's response was reflexive and immediate. "Are you fucking blind?" he replied. "That was in by a foot."

This was not the first difference of opinion between the two Grafton Street roommates, and it would not be the last. The ensuing argument grew heated, but it was nothing compared with the desert sun beating down on them. Their clothes were drenched with sweat, and dehydration was just around the corner, but their focus was on the line call—and more importantly, the winner's prize.

"Hank, I'm not going to cheat you," pleaded Jack, secretly knowing his interpretation was not exactly fair. Eventually, Hank muttered something under his breath, and the play continued. The final point of the match was more the result of exhaustion than poor execution; Hank's return of a second serve failed to make it over the net, and the second set ended six to four in Jack's favor.

This was the end of the match, as Jack had won the first set by an identical score, taking the best out of three sets.

"Good game," said Jack, the gracious victor, offering a handshake.

"Yeah. Good game. You fucking cheated," muttered Hank, ignoring the goodwill gesture.

The two comrades slowly walked off the Caesars Palace court and headed back to The Dunes for a well-deserved shower and a few minutes of rest. After that, it was time to drop by the cage to grab Jack's prize—a two-hundred-dollar gambling voucher. As they walked up to the cage to withdraw the money from their deposited funds, Jack offered Hank the opportunity to join him at one of the many blackjack tables in the casino. Hank declined, said he'd be back, and disappeared, presumably heading back to his room to sulk.

Jack wagered cautiously. After considerable time at the tables, however, he was getting down to the end of his two-hundred-dollar grubstake, and he started to wonder what had happened to Hank. Jack loved Hank like a brother and trusted him with his life, but something nagged him in the back of his mind. Hank was the kind of gambler who bet money he didn't have and always thought he had a comeback in him, which could be a recipe for serious trouble.

More than a little bit worried, Jack grabbed the chips he had left on the table and started out in search of his good friend. It wasn't long before he found him. Hank was sitting at a blackjack table and playing two hands at five hundred dollars each. It took Jack a couple of minutes to realize what had happened. Hank had gone back to the cage and withdrawn the thirty-six thousand dollars that represented their business capital and life savings. It took only seconds more to realize that Hank was losing badly, and that over half of that thirty-six grand was gone.

A strange feeling of familiarity passed between them, and it wasn't love at first sight. Jack didn't just want to end their friendship; he wanted to kill Hank. Fortunately, that's when Hank's luck miraculously began to change. The deck heated up, and in rapid succession, Hank won hand after hand. In the blink of an eye, their lost money was recouped, and they were actually a thousand dollars or so ahead. Before the pendulum could swing back the other way, Jack scooped up the chips and tipped the dealer. They cashed in the chips, secured the money in the cage, and left the casino without saying a word. It was another day in the life of two addicts, and they had barely managed to escape disaster.

CHAPTER TWENTY FIVE

By 1975, JD didn't have many great options left. Life was going nowhere fast for him, and he had started to use heroin again. The handwriting was on the wall: if things didn't change, he was headed for disaster. JD's mother had a younger brother who had just moved to Las Vegas to join the police department there, and during a visit to Worcester, he told JD, "Vegas is a happening place for a young, single guy." He offered to help JD get a new start there.

With few prospects to return to in Florida, JD made the trek west to Nevada to check it out, blowing into Vegas with thirty-five dollars in his pocket. He stayed with his uncle and tried to live a "normal" life, but for a twenty-one-year-old addict, a normal life was not in the cards. In about a month, things started to get shaky.

JD's buddy, Marooch, who had a long history of drug abuse, had moved to Vegas about two weeks after JD arrived. Marooch lived with his sister, Patty, a nurse at one of the local hospitals, and her roommate. Marooch was trying to escape his own madness using the geographical cure. He and JD immediately partnered up, which, of course, was a recipe for disaster.

Between blackouts and nearly burning the house down when he put a frozen pizza in the oven and passed out, JD had worn out his welcome at his uncle's home. He found himself deposited unceremoniously in front of Marooch's new apartment—new because Marooch had been evicted from his sister's place. He had made inappropriate sexual advances toward his sister's roommate after a long night of drugs and booze. Birds of a feather flock together. So began a long run of dope, booze, and trouble for both of them.

Marooch had chosen a likely spot for debauchery. The apartment complex where he and JD set up house was a breeding ground for those who loved to get crazy with booze and drugs. JD and Marooch made connections and found work, and JD even laid off the heroin for a long time. But he drank daily and used plenty of other drugs, and his addiction, like Marooch's, was always in command.

"JD! Yo, JD!"

Hank's voice rose from the street outside the apartment complex, through the window, and into the ear of a sleeping JD, who, half-roused, tried to determine whether he was awake or dreaming of his childhood on the East Side, when he could stick his head out of the window and hear Hank at their hangout spot, a half-mile away.

This was no dream. It was Hank, larger than life, his head and upper body sticking up through the sunroof of a baby-blue Lincoln Continental. Hank was in town after picking up a load of drugs in Arizona and wanted JD to come out and play. Stevie the Sailor had joined Hank on the trip, and he was waiting across the street at his sister's apartment. Jack had stayed behind, trusting Hank and Stevie to conduct their business.

On the surface, that seemed like a good plan. But when you throw booze, dope, and gambling into the mix, plans often fall apart quickly. An innocent breakfast among old friends quickly deteriorated into a gambling spree. Hank always thought he had a comeback in him, and after his tennis match with Jack the year before, he'd had just that. But this time, a good turn of luck was nowhere to be found.

Hank lost the money he'd set aside for their plane fare home. Hank had no choice but to call Jack, who slammed the receiver in Hank's ear after shouting a few choice words, including, "Find your own way to get home!"

Eventually, however, Jack did wire the money, and Stevie and Hank flew home with the two suitcases full of pot.

Jack was furious. The night Jack picked them up at the airport, he locked Stevie out of the apartment, making him sleep on the porch. But Jack realized that he was lucky that Stevie, Hank, and the marijuana had made it back safely, and under the calming influence of drugs, he let the dark clouds pass quickly. Jack forgot his anger, and the trio rolled into a day or two of drinking, drugs, and storytelling.

By this time, JD and Marooch were both using heroin again. They were associating with dope dealers and a variety of other unsavory criminals and putting themselves in extremely risky situations. Perhaps the riskiest arose months later, when JD got a call from Ron, a local dealer and pimp who had been busted. He called JD from jail to ask him to go to his apartment, collect $350 from his stash of cash, and use it to bail him out.

JD dutifully collected the cash, but he got distracted by his heroin habit. Instead of bailing Ron out, JD used the money to score drugs and get high. After being bailed out by another friend, Ron was on the street again, and extremely unhappy with JD. The dealer and another associate made a string of furious phone calls demanding that JD pay up or else. The more insistent JD became in denying that he'd taken the money, the more Ron upped the ante of his threats.

One evening, JD and Marooch were fed up with the game. The ninety-five-degree heat of the desert night had made them more agitated and impatient, and after a brief amount of nonsensical deliberation, they borrowed a shotgun from Oafey, a biker friend, and headed over to Ron's apartment to straighten things out.

On the way to the apartment, they stopped to drink and get high, and by the time they arrived, they were amped up and ready for business. They kicked down the apartment door like the cops on TV. Marooch leveled the shotgun at the dealer's head and screamed like a madman. "You dumb mother fucker, I told you to stop fucking calling and busting our balls about some fucking stupid shit! I got a good mind to blow your fucking head off right here!"

The dealer's sidekick, who had come out of the bedroom to see what the commotion was, got so scared that he jumped out the window and ran for his life. And after a good minute or so of Marooch's screaming and threats of murder, Ron decided to take the loss. JD and Marooch left Ron shaking and sweating, but thankful to be alive. As they headed for the door, Marooch turned to JD with an utterly insane look in his eyes.

"Should I blast this fucking shit-hole place to show them we mean business?"

JD quickly assured him that wouldn't be necessary and would probably bring the cops. Of course, the police were called anyway, more than likely by a neighbor due to the screaming going on, and with a description of JD's Caddy, they stopped them nearby.

Having an uncle on the police force, plus the fact that the shotgun was in the trunk, earned JD and Marooch a get-out-of-jail-free card. It probably helped that Ron and his associate were known to the police, who didn't appreciate their business practices and might have looked the other way even if JD and Marooch had eliminated them.

The shotgun episode was just another crazy event that nearly ended in disaster—like when JD, rendered paranoid by the drugs and carrying a derringer for protection, nearly blew his finger off in the bathroom of a casino bar trying to load the gun while he was wasted. Although JD survived, the wound required medical attention, and he nearly drove his doctor to suicide by constantly hounding him for more Percodan to kill the pain. Finally, the doctor threatened to call the police if JD didn't stop harassing him for drugs. This was crazy, yes, but for JD, it was just another day in the life of an addict. He and Marooch eventually parted ways over a woman and didn't speak for many years. During that time, JD stopped using heroin. But circumstances and mutual friends would once again reunite JD with Marooch and heroin. In the end, heroin killed Marooch. Fortunately for JD, that was not to be his fate.

Although JD's uncle had evicted him from his home, he still helped JD out of a lot of the scrapes he got into, and they kept in touch. JD was devastated when he learned that his uncle was gunned down by a desperate career criminal he had stopped for a driving infraction. Once again, JD relied on drugs and alcohol to comfort him and avoid dealing with the pain while he continued the madness he called his life.

Not that JD had a particular fondness for cops. In fact, he was no stranger to Vegas wise guys and gangsters. During the 1970s, an organized crime presence saturated the town, and JD made a connection, courtesy of the Crusher, who loved to gamble and made frequent trips to Vegas from his place in LA. The Crusher knew people at the Aladdin, a new casino owned and operated by mobsters from Detroit and Chicago, and JD felt right at home working as a bartender there. The club drew top-name entertainment into its theater and lounges, and JD spent many nights among well-known singers, comedians, and musicians, most of whom liked to drink and get high just like he did. Of course, not everyone who came to the bar was rich and famous. JD worked the overnight shift, which meant that after 2:00 or 3:00 a.m., crazies, hookers, and degenerate gamblers occupied most of the barstools.

In Vegas, underworld connections meant everything. Being connected was called having some "juice," and the more juice you had, the better off you were. Of all the people JD met in Vegas, none helped him more than "Uncle Bernie" did. He was a "money guy" for the mob who ran four or five casinos in town, including the Aladdin. For whatever reason, Uncle Bernie liked JD and took him under his wing. Over the years, Bernie made sure that JD always had a good job and could make a living. It probably didn't hurt that Uncle Bernie's daughter, Kathy, really liked JD, and they hung out a lot.

Being connected had benefits that extended beyond employment. Working for Bernie, JD enjoyed complimentary meals and show tickets, even for big-name acts like Jimmy Buffet. Vegas seemed great for JD for quite a while, but things started to change in the late 1970s and early 1980s. The FBI, the DEA, and the IRS began investigating Uncle Bernie and his organization for phony Teamster loans, tax evasion, skimming from the casinos, and a variety of other crimes, forcing many of the mobster's associates to go to jail or underground. This shut down much of the organization, and life became tense for everyone. Luckily for JD, Uncle Bernie and some partners had bought a small, off-strip bar and casino, where JD worked for the next few years.

There had always been a strong dislike for drugs among the "old regime" within organized crime, and if there weren't enormous amounts of money to be made, most mobsters would shun that business. They looked upon drug addicts with disdain. JD's drug addiction didn't sit well with Uncle Bernie's business associates and friends. It was difficult for them to trust JD, whose first priority always seemed to be getting high. So he remained on the periphery, content to make a decent week's pay while living what he thought was a good—even normal—life.

Actually, JD's life at the time resembled a scene from a mob movie. One night, he was hired to tend bar at a holiday party at a private residence at the Las Vegas Country Club. JD recruited his friend, Debby, to work as a server.

As with any other gig, JD had to get good and buzzed beforehand, so he and Deb each took some LSD. Upon entering the house, they both instinctively knew that Gerry, the lady of the house, was higher than they were (at least before the LSD kicked in), and she showed the telltale signs of someone who snorted mounds of cocaine. Gerry, a cute blonde, greeted them and showed them around at lightning speed between visits to the bathroom for a hit, which made JD and Deb feel right at home.

What they came to learn, ironically, just as the LSD was taking hold of them, was that the host of the party, Gerry's husband, was Frank "Lefty" Rosenthal, a well-known Vegas sports handicapper and mobster who would later be the subject of the fictionalized Martin Scorsese movie *Casino*.

As the evening progressed, the house filled with mobsters dressed to the nines. Since the feds and the IRS had broken the connections between the Teamsters, the mobs, and the casinos, Vegas was wide open. New wise guys like Anthony "the Ant" Spilotro, a Chicago enforcer, were trying to take over, using violence and disrespect for the other mob guys who were trying to run their "businesses" quietly.

JD and Deb found it hard to be serious and do their work while laughing like hell at this strange cast of characters, posturing for each other at the party. The extremely violent and dangerous men would not have appreciated being mocked, but it was an interesting experience watching Lefty, who sat in a secluded room like the godfather, receive visitors who paid their respects and delivered holiday gifts and good wishes.

The only conversation JD's brain could muster during his moment alone with Lefty was to ask, "Where did you get the name Lefty?"

Although Lefty told him the story, JD has no memory of it. He does recall that Lefty was pretty engaging, and JD followed him in the news during his remaining days in Vegas, which ended when "they" bombed his Caddy (with him in it) outside Tony Roma's rib joint.

Thanks to a steel plate below the passenger-side floor, which the Cadillac's manufacturer had placed there to correct a balance problem, Lefty survived the blast. But he couldn't ignore the message and shortly thereafter relocated to Florida. Before leaving, however, he settled an ongoing dispute with his then ex-wife Gerry, who had stolen his money to support her cocaine addiction. She was found in a rundown LA hotel, dead from an overdose that some said was a "hotshot," a lethal overdose injected by force. Live by the sword and die by the sword was the order of the day.

For JD, Vegas had been an opportunity to escape insanity, but it was an opportunity lost. Vegas was no more peaceful or sane than any other place he had lived, and like his addiction itself, JD's life got progressively worse. He blew the jobs, the relationships, and the living arrangements and put a huge strain on everyone he knew by stealing or borrowing from them as often as he could. Slowly but steadily, he began to sink.

Through some contacts, JD lucked into a job dealing blackjack at the Hacienda Casino, so he still had an income, but he was on shaky ground there within a very short time. His lifestyle and addiction dictated when he showed up for work, what condition he was in when he did show up, and how long he could stay before he needed to score more drugs to keep withdrawal at bay.

Ironically, the Hacienda was the first casino on the famous Vegas strip, and in a strange, metaphorical way for JD, it was the very last casino as people left Vegas, usually broke. The Hacienda was JD's swan song and his last stab at trying to stay afloat. Nearly everything was gone at that point, his dignity, self-worth, and self-esteem, not to mention his ability to continue the charade. He was bottoming out, living with his former girlfriend, who was as much of a train wreck as he was, at his friend Bo's apartment, and doing increasingly dangerous and stupid things.

One of the dumbest things he did was to bite the hand of the man who had been feeding him, Uncle Bernie. Mob guys are in the business of loaning and making money, and JD made the mistake of borrowing money from Uncle Bernie and promising to repay it ASAP, all the while knowing that he couldn't. By then, every dime JD made was already owed to drug dealers who had fronted him drugs on a promise, or to friends he had borrowed from. JD used every trick he knew to keep Uncle Bernie pacified, but eventually, time ran out. In a desperate last-ditch effort to outflank Uncle Bernie, JD fabricated a tall tale about having to return home to help his sister with a new business venture. He said he would be back in a few weeks. In truth, like any other time in his life when things got too hot, JD ran like a thief in the night. He sold his car and what little else he owned to his buddy, Gouge, who had watched JD's decline over the years and was always there to help him out. With a one-way plane ticket bought by his family, JD flew back to Massachusetts and settled in on the East Side again. Vegas was over, and so was his ability to keep running.

The secret of health for both mind and body is not to mourn for the past, worry about the future, or anticipate troubles, but to live in the present moment wisely and earnestly.

—Jack Kornfield

A funny thing about addiction is that your life can be going down in flames, but you keep thinking that you're doing all right and that everyone but you has a problem. While you're thinking that, your addiction is destroying your world one piece at a time. Coming to terms with this insanity is not easy.

Neuroscientists tell us that "neural plasticity," the ability for neural connections to change, lasts throughout one's life. We also know that neural plasticity is enhanced by aerobic activity, novel experiences, focused attention, and emotional arousal.

It should come as no surprise that these same conditions play a predominant role in the development of the neural connections that deepen dysfunction. Clearly, novelty and emotional arousal were intimately involved in many of the East Siders' experiences. "Focused attention" could easily be understood as obsession, which shaped their motivations and behaviors.

To reverse this journey into decreasing health, one would be well advised to focus on one's ability to overcome or manage one's disease(s) or symptoms; to make informed, healthy choices that support physical and emotional well-being; to find a stable and safe home; to move away from the loss of purpose by participating in meaningful daily activities, such as a job, school, volunteerism, family caretaking, or creative endeavors that provide independence, income, and the resources to participate in society; and to embrace community by developing relationships and social networks that provide support, friendship, love, and hope.

CHAPTER TWENTY SIX

"Barbooth!" screamed Tush, and another $3,000 wager was swept away by the denizens of the club. Jack and Hank could not believe their eyes as their bankroll steadily disappeared. Tush was a seventy-something Greek who had been playing the game of barbooth since before Jack and Hank were born. Tush had remarkable command of the dice, likely perfected with years of practice against the uninitiated—something that through their constant drug-induced haze, Jack and Hank hadn't picked up on and probably never would.

Twenty-five thousand dollars later, in the grimy light of dawn, Jack and Hank walked out of the Plum Street gambling den hearing the rich and gravelly voice of Johnny Ringo as he counted what had been Jack and Hank's hard-earned dope money. Still, it was only a monetary loss, and money could be replaced.

For Jack and Hank, those early days of drug use and drug dealing seemed, by Shrewsbury Street standards anyway, to be innocent enough. No one was getting hurt or killed, at least intentionally. The prevailing sentiment on the East Side was that marijuana was the least of many possible evils. And the dire prognostication of devastation from repeated drug use had not yet manifested itself, despite the fact that small cracks were beginning to show everywhere on the Street. Soon, those cracks would grow bigger, revealing a bottomless cavern into which many would fall.

In rapid succession, LSD, mushrooms, mescaline, downers, Quaaludes, PCP, prescription narcotics, and heroin became the drugs du jour, and with each new drug, a new business opportunity was born.

Jack and Hank's dubious celebrity as marijuana dealers gave them entrée into the world of pill dealing. A couple of ounces of marijuana might bring hundreds of Percodans in return—an offer they couldn't refuse. Neither Jack nor Hank knew they were selling their souls with their step up to opiates or that they would soon find themselves hopelessly addicted to those tiny pills. But money and addiction have a way of adjusting the lens of reality.

This drug naïveté of the sixties and seventies could be seen as an isolated episode in history, but our present-day cycle of addiction occurs in a similar fashion. No one dreams of becoming a drug addict or an alcoholic. No one wakes up in the morning and says, "Jeez, I can't wait to overdose or get arrested today." For such a preventable disease, there is a lack of public will to confront what is too often viewed as a moral failure and to promote the early education required to save millions of kids from a lifetime of heartache and pain. In the sixties and seventies, prevention resources were even less available. The sad fact was that society was overwhelmed with the drug problem and had little idea how to respond.

For the individual addict, the problem—and the response—are always the same. Depression and pain, anxiety and the horrible physical symptoms of withdrawal—sweating, nausea, muscle aches, diarrhea, and vomiting—are familiar companions, but those companions are quickly forgotten, or at least subconsciously repressed, by the euphoria of the next high.

That next high for the Shrewsbury Street gang was getting more expensive by the day, and financing those "good times" was both exciting and infinitely more dangerous. The interstate transportation of marijuana had shifted from Las Vegas to Worcester to Florida to Worcester due to changing market conditions and a not-so-subtle warning. Hank had spun his love of gambling into a side business as a bookmaker, and one of the mobsters he did business with warned him to stop using the junket system to smuggle weed. Getting caught, the mobster warned, would mean more than just Jack and Hank's arrest. It could do damage to the junket system itself, which brought big money to the Vegas mob. Screwing that up could mean a death sentence that would come quicker than any trial for marijuana trafficking. Colombian marijuana was in demand, and it was streaming into Florida by the boatload. Choosing between that and a bullet to the back of the head was a no-brainer. Jack and Hank packed their beachwear and headed to the land of Jimmy Buffet, which would be their new staging area.

A phone call from old pal Johnny Two Fingers helped nudge the move along.

"Jack," Johnny said, speaking from his condo in North Miami Beach, "look at the centerfold of the latest edition of *High Times*. That's my pot you see there, and it's what I got down here waiting for you."

"Don't do anything without me," Jack replied without hesitation, and the die was cast.

Johnny had moved to Florida shortly after the Nebraska weed-harvesting debacle with his girlfriend, Terri, to fulfill his lifelong dream of becoming a wise guy, which he pursued with a frighteningly addictive fervor. Today's clinical vernacular includes a number of types of addiction. The chemical dependency addictions are universally accepted as medical conditions that require treatment. The process addictions, such as sex, gambling, work, and, in John's case, an obsession to emulate Don Vito Corleone, the celebrated head of the Mafia family in the movie *The Godfather*, are somewhat more nebulous in the public's perception. They are subject to treatment regimens of various depths. Yet regardless of the type of addiction, a common thread is the slow deterioration of one's capacity to understand fully the ramifications of one's actions. To the friends and family members who go through hell due to this irrational behavior, the analogy of banging your head against a wall and then wondering why you got a headache can come to mind. For the addict, it's like asking for a heart attack and ignoring the fact that heart attacks tend to be problematic.

As Jack and Hank's dependencies grew, so did their involvement in the commercial aspects of the drug culture, which is a nice way of saying drug dealing. Of course, drug dealing at that level wasn't simple; there was a great deal of risk involved, both personal and financial.

The Florida runs started with trips for marijuana. A pound of weed could be purchased for $250 in South Florida and would bring $350 to $400 in Massachusetts. At one hundred or two hundred pounds per carload, that represented a hefty profit. Not too shabby for a time when the median household income was just a tad over $10,000 annually. It was a nice little return on investment—and tax-free, to boot. Jack and Hank minimized their own risk by employing others to take it for them.

It wasn't hard to find willing volunteers. Addiction disregards socioeconomic status and demands its pound of flesh from everyone. The less affluent, who lack easy access to cash, must become more resourceful, which usually involves some sort of illegal activity.

As Jack and Hank's interstate marijuana transportation business grew, so did their influence on the Street. They became an important source of income for the unemployed—or more accurately, the guys who wanted to make an easy dollar. Prescription drugs, such as Percodan and Percocet, were eating up more and more of the local addicts' disposable income, so easy dollars were in high demand. Stevie the Sailor, Paige, Ship, Riley, and Joey S. were among the recruits, and the list went on. The growth of the business wasn't due to an effective marketing campaign, but rather to the insatiable demand for anything that made a guy look cool and anesthetized his feelings, especially the uncomfortable ones. On Shrewsbury Street and in East Park, cool was king and making money gave people the inside track to the drugs that delivered it instantly.

With the advent of drug-sniffing dogs in the Florida airports, air transport was just too dicey, so cars became the transportation method of choice. It wasn't as fast as air transport, but the risk of discovery was infinitesimally small as long as the driver stayed under the speed limit, and for those who did the job, the anesthetizing effects of the drugs and the powerful attraction to easy money tamped down the fear. For a drug addict, the end justifies the means, and if skirting the law provided the necessary funds to get high, then so be it.

While guys from the Street could often skirt the law, they couldn't skirt the fact that their lives were falling apart, which was punishing their families brutally. It wasn't long before the drug culture began to cast its shadow over nearly every family. Like the creepy, green mist that claimed firstborn sons in Cecil B. DeMille's *Ten Commandments*, drugs often claimed the young and the innocent, whose naïveté made them easy prey.

Kids from surrounding neighborhoods, once considered personae non gratae on the East Side, began to migrate to the Street to make drug purchases. As the provincial barriers came down, new friendships developed, and the greasy tentacles of drug-distribution networks grew. Initiation into the "family" had little or no relation to the ceremony or the seriousness often depicted in the stereotypical Mafia movies. The code of honor for the Street, its roots a modified code of *omerta*, typified the response of many newly migrated groups into a foreign land: see nothing, hear nothing, and say nothing.

In the "How It Works" chapter of the Narcotics Anonymous *Basic Text*, a twelve-step program created for addicts by addicts, there is a sentence that reads, "We didn't become addicted in one day." That sums up the influence of drugs and the natural progression of associated ills. Some of the kids on the Street still participated in traditional activities, such as sports and dancing. A couple of kids even campaigned for neighborhood politicians. Members of the Shrewsbury Street Merchants touch football team, like their professional counterparts before the era of drug testing, ingested more than their share of the analgesic Percodan before, during, and after the games. The longer a guy was on the team, the more "Percs" he required to mitigate the physical and emotional stressors of the game. Many of the young addicts from the Street played for the Merchants. Teddy, Kid Paz, Tommie, Paige, Jimmy C., Jack, and several others would all develop opiate dependencies before their playing days were over.

Jack, now in his midtwenties, was the starting left cornerback for the Merchants, but even football had to take a backseat to drug dealing. With the Colombian marijuana supply forecast to dry up during hurricane season in September, Jack and Hank decided it was a good idea to make one more trip to Casa Grande, visit their old friend Frankie, and return with a trunk load of Mexican marijuana.

One of the first signs of Jack's serious deterioration was the breakup of his partnership with Hank. Their decision to go to Casa Grande led to a hiatus in their business relationship and started to undermine their enduring friendship.

The seeds of the breakup were their differences in attitude. Hank was easily satisfied with his life in the neighborhood. To make his world complete, all he needed was cash for his daily two-hundred-milligram dose of methadone and some sports betting, preferably on a football game. Jack had an underlying desire to do something important, something more.

Hank's life was the Street, and he had few other ambitions, but he often went over the top in his quest to get high, and that was becoming a problem for Jack. For years, Jack had been telling Hank to wait until after six in the evening to get high, to control his drug use, but Jack's admonitions fell on deaf ears. On several occasions, Hank's mother, Toni, found him unconscious when she arrived home after work. Once, he still had a needle in his arm and was barely breathing. Despite her training as a nurse, she was paralyzed and could do nothing but wait helplessly until Hank regained consciousness. The shame and stigma of the situation overwhelmed her. How could her wonderful son be an addict? Frantic and terrified, she made Jack promise to take care of her son. Little did she suspect that Jack was part of the problem.

The trip to Casa Grande, a two-day visit at Frankie's house, and the purchase of one hundred kilos, commonly called Mexican bricks, went smoothly. Jack and Hank filled the trunk of their car with the bricks and headed back to Massachusetts, with Frankie's farewell admonition, "Don't drive through Tucumcari at night," resonating in their ears.

As fate would have it, they found themselves doing just that. There were few vehicles on the highway when a New Mexico state trooper traveling in the opposite direction noticed their car and immediately made a U-turn. Jack's heart sank as he imagined handcuffs, the closing of the jail cell doors, the courtroom, and life behind bars. Suddenly, a sign appeared advertising one of the many motels on the long stretch of highway. The state trooper was still far back in the rearview, so it seemed like a good idea to get off the road.

"Let's stay here for the night," Jack said to Hank. For once, there was no disagreement. They pulled into the Motel 6 only moments before the state trooper slowed but continued past them. Realizing that discretion was the better part of valor, they got a room for the night and grabbed some much-needed rest.

The next morning, Hank shook Jack awake and, uncharacteristically, tried to whisper, "Jack! Wake up! The car is surrounded."

Never an early riser, Jack groggily struggled to comprehend Hank's words.

"Look out the fucking window," Hank said, and Jack did.

Peeking between the drawn drapes, Jack blinked his eyes several times, trying to make the nightmarish scene vanish. His heart began to race; he was no longer sleeping. The sheriff's department, the New Mexico state police, you name it—it seemed as though every law-enforcement division in the state had converged upon them. It took Jack a few more seconds to realize that if they were the targets of this much force, they might as well just surrender now.

"We're fucked," Hank whispered over Jack's shoulder, as if he needed to be told.

But it wasn't over, not just yet, and it was better to be safe than sorry. Rather than leave the room with their hands held high, waving a white flag, Jack lowered himself to his hands and knees and crawled out of their room, onto the second-story walkway for a closer look. What he soon discovered was that this particular Motel 6 had the best coffee around and was the traditional meeting place for every cop in the area. A smile and a country hello quickly dispelled any residual thoughts that they were busted, and Jack returned to their room to assure Hank and his blood pressure that things were copacetic.

They waited for the police to leave before once again embarking on their long journey home. With the passing of each state line, they celebrated what they envisioned as a very profitable journey, well worth some tense moments. After what seemed like an eternity, they arrived home only to find that, in the weeks they were away, Colombian marijuana had become plentiful again, rendering their Mexican bricks all but worthless, at least for the time being. The drug trade, like addiction, places little value on loyalty. It's all about present need and the ability to fulfill that need. With a trunkful of worthless weed, Jack and Hank's celebration quickly turned into a funeral for their business partnership, as they each blamed the other for their miscalculation. And as if that were not enough, Jack's absence during the Merchants' opening games cost Jack his starting cornerback position.

Despite the impact of drugs on the team, the Merchants enjoyed huge success in one of Worcester's most popular sports. The drug culture may have lowered the ethnic and regional barriers between the various neighborhoods, but those differences intensified the competition and fueled most of the rivalries in the Worcester Parks Department Touch Football League. With all that came additional opportunities for dealing drugs—even the legal kind.

The inner city rivalries, while intense on the field, produced even more intense postgame celebrations. Fortunately for Jack, he had acquired a Shrewsbury Street bar in 1976 using some of the proceeds from the marijuana business, and since his demotion from starting cornerback, Jack used this resentment to sponsor his own team.

Even though their pot-selling partnership had ended, and despite the occasional finger pointing, Jack and Hank remained good friends. Jack knew he could trust Hank and asked him to manage the bar. The Grass Roots Pub, as it was aptly named, provided the perfect opportunity to keep the party going after a football game ended.

"Three Heinekens over here," a voice shouted from the crowd. Football players and teammates were standing three deep around the bar.

"Coming right up!" was the reply from the bartender.

Hank was at the cash register, often giving away more than he took in. Easy come, easy go, was his attitude. His real source of income was bookmaking and drug dealing. The bar was just a way to attract new friends and potential customers, a good marketing strategy, tried and true. Let the good times roll.

Kid Paz, Squeaky, Ship, Joey S., Jimmy, Teddy, Gayle, Gina, and the rest of the neighborhood peopled postgame parties that lasted all day and into the night. News of a good party spread fast, and before long, revelers from the surrounding suburbs joined in on the opportunity to get a good buzz on. Needless to say, these Sunday afternoon partygoers all fit the high-risk profile for addiction, none better than Dawn, the affluent, green-eyed daughter of a prominent barrister.

Her life ended in an overdose before she could grow up to enjoy it. There were hushed conversations, a quiet and private funeral, and a parent's unresolved grief. But there was no mention of the disease of addiction ending yet another promising young life. The significance of this tragedy may not have been lost on everyone, but booze and drugs anesthetized the sad feelings among her friends. Nothing could stop the party.

The drinks, the drugs, and the fun were flowing—and so was the money, despite Hank's occasional lack of attention to the till. Adversaries became drinking buddies; rivalries and ethnic differences faded to memories. By late evening, guess who was still left at the bar? The most devout users, the gang from Shrewsbury Street. As the evening progressed, they graduated from the bar to backroom tables, from alcohol to prescription medication and lines of cocaine. Everyone was having a great time, or at least that's what they thought.

CHAPTER TWENTY SEVEN

There is the illusion for many burgeoning addicts that life is just grand, and everything is going exactly as planned. On infrequent occasions, the stars do align and the illusion edges close to reality. Those brief moments of confluence reinforce an addict's misguided decision to continue his downward progression. They keep him in denial. The New Mexico escape, a few football parties, sex, drugs, and easy money convinced Jack and his partners in crime that everything was right with the world.

One thing was certain: they didn't give a thought to the hypervigilance and constant worry that occupied the minds and hearts of their parents, let alone to their responsibilities. Jack's relationship with his daughter, Gina Marie, now six years old, was relegated to weekend visits, with most of that responsibility transferred to his mother, who loved her granddaughter but constantly reminded Jack that he was her father and he needed to be around.

In 1976, Gerald Ford was president, and the United States was celebrating its two-hundredth birthday in a massive wave of cultural hoopla. But to many in the East Park gang, the true cultural high point of that year was Jack Nicholson's portrayal of Randal Patrick McMurphy in *One Flew Over the Cuckoo's Nest*, which perfectly captured their sense of alienation, anger, and hopelessness.

In *Cuckoo's Nest*, forced medication was the order of the day, but the denizens of the East Side willingly self-medicated. The Grass Roots Pub, Jack's only legitimate enterprise, served as an unofficial clubhouse for most of the fledgling addicts on the Street. During the day, many of the guys and a few of the girls routinely gathered at the pub to begin the daily process of getting their fixes. Often, they did not fit the stereotype: the unkempt junkie scoring a bag of heroin, heading out to the alley, and plunging a needle into his arm. Instead, they might be the well-groomed young men sitting down in a bar booth to forge a prescription for Percodan or meeting a connection to purchase a bottle of Dolophine, the brand name of methadone, the long-acting painkiller commonly used as a heroin substitute. For many novice drug abusers, the low cost of twenty-five cents per pill and the resulting relief was of primary importance. But methadone wasn't the only pill available on the East Side; Percodan and Percocet, both morphine derivatives, were everywhere.

The Percodan invasion was made possible by the most tried and true marketing techniques. In the late sixties and early seventies, drug dealers used the marketing model now popular in giant box stores, such as Sam's Club. They offered a free sample or two with the hope that an experimenter would become a loyal customer. Of course, the pleasantly anesthetic and addictive qualities of morphine helped move the transaction along. The drug wasn't named after Morpheus, the god of dreams, for nothing.

Initially, Percodan and Percocet were viewed as the less desirable by-product of drugstore robberies intended to score more powerful and injectable drugs, such as morphine, Pantapon, and Dilaudid. The most common drug store robbery technique was the smash and grab, a rather risky maneuver. With the alarm bell ringing and the nearest police officer responding to the call, there was little time for reading labels. Shelves were emptied into garbage bags with the sweep of the hand. Grabbed in haste, the five hundred- and thousand-dose bottles of Percodan and Percocet were shunned by rush-seeking desperadoes. Initially, they had little value for the injection-drug user; they were either discarded or traded away for little or nothing. Fairly quickly, however, they proved their value as introductory-level drugs for those with a fear of the needle. And fortunately for those who sold them, Percodan was just as addictive as any other opiate.

While many of the denizens of Shrewsbury Street were involved in drug trafficking or benefited from it in one way or another, some ran scams of their own. One popular scam, which today is called doctor shopping, consisted of faking a vague, difficult-to-diagnose, yet painful ailment and using all one's savoir faire to convince a greedy, clueless, or overly benevolent doctor that he could alleviate the pain by prescribing a narcotic, preferably with several refills.

The real art of the game was to cultivate several such doctors simultaneously. One such artiste was Kid Paz, an athletic, neatly dressed East Sider with a penchant for contrived sincerity. As a criminal, Kid Paz was atypical. He was a rather sophisticated and serious-minded young professional—a rarity for a Shrewsbury Street expat. His only flaws were an insatiable appetite for Percodan and denial, which enabled him to believe that he didn't have an addiction problem.

Despite his size and strength, Kid Paz earned his keep not in the dangerous role of enforcer or collector but by acting. The awards for his performance in medical offices everywhere were bottles of coveted opiates.

Kid Paz wasn't the only one on the East Side playing a role. Neither was Fudgy, who by now had sunk deeply into opiate and cocaine addiction. The lines of morality had become so blurred that the gang from the Street could see no lines at all. They became masters at lying to themselves as well as deceiving others.

Most drug addicts lead dual lives, and some display multiple personalities. While their most notorious behaviors make the news, the tragic and human side of the story is largely disregarded. The Shrewsbury Street crew exemplified this dichotomy. Fudgy, Hank, Joey, Dumbo, Jack, and most of the other young men were dutiful and respectful sons to their mothers and did little, at home, anyway, to dispel their mothers' myopic fidelity. But beyond their mothers' fields of vision, they engaged in a constant cycle of hustle and score. Among those who rode the cycle hardest was Hank, who simply couldn't numb himself enough. Long past his prime and a self-proclaimed junkie, he struggled against a gigantic gambling addiction, often gambling away every penny he owned and some pennies he didn't. Beaten out of shape by drugs and alcohol, he still considered himself a superior athlete, and he laid money down on that assertion at every opportunity. He gambled heavily on par-three golf, and when the action got slim, he ran staked foot races against Webster Willie, a young street hustler who took advantage of Hank and other heavily sedated opiate addicts to make his own nut.

Not all of the guys from the East Side played football, gambled, ran races, or became addicted. A few were spared—mostly by the good fortune of leaving the neighborhood. Big Head was one of the few college graduates from the East Side, and one of the few to leave the neighborhood permanently. He had joined the ROTC in college to receive some badly needed financial aid, and he had to fulfill his obligation to the navy upon graduation. Luckily for him, he was stationed in Hawaii and decided to remain there, thereby avoiding many of the undesirable consequences of a life on the Street. Gules went away to school and became an IRS agent; Guido and his younger brother moved away. Stan the Man became a cop after returning from military service. Toojo stayed in California and in the navy for several more years, smart enough to know that he was not missing too much. Jimmy, Charlie, and even Dumbo tried the geographical cure, seeking a more temperate climate as a means of escaping an increasingly problematic life of addiction. Others just stayed behind, content with life on the East Side.

Fudgy was one who vacillated. Shortly after high school, he had packed a few belongings and headed to Boston for a life in the theater. Most of his friends thought he was crazy—not for pursuing a nontraditional profession but for leaving the neighborhood. But he had made the move, and when he wasn't robbing banks, he was often on stage. However, since neither acting nor bank robbery had proved to be very profitable, Fudgy seldom had the kind of cash needed to purchase the costly prescription drugs and cocaine that he loved. Like a moth to the flame, he often returned to the Street and the safety of his mother's house, mockingly clicking his heels like Dorothy in *The Wizard of Oz* and proclaiming, "There's no place like home."

Still, Fudgy didn't return for sentimental reasons. When he met a friend on the Street, his opening gambit often was, "You got anything?" As much as Fudgy loved the theater, it appeared he was developing a love for the high life even more.

During one of Fudgy's many journeys back to the hood, he ended his night at the Grass Roots Pub, catching up with Jack and some other regulars. It was a summer night and getting close to 2:00 a.m., closing time for liquor establishments in Worcester; but the bar's denizens were not ready to call it quits. Still holding down the fort were two alcoholics, Julio and Mary, who, at the age of fifty-five, seemed very out of place among the twenty something group and were looked upon as dinosaurs by Dominic, a slick-haired Italian gangster type; Fudgy; his girlfriend, Laurie, and Jack.

Everyone was trying to figure out what the next move should be. Dim the lights? Lock the door, huddle below the windows, and simply continue to drink? Julio and Mary certainly liked that idea.

Both barely over five feet tall, huddling did not present much of a problem to them. Fudgy, always theatrical, thought of a different idea. He enthusiastically unfolded his plan and carefully laid out the roles each of the characters would play.

When he was finished, Dominic picked up his glass. "See you guys tomorrow," he said, as he walked out the door. Jack wondered why he took the glass, but that question would be answered at a later time. It was now time to put the plan into action.

Fudgy had just finished appearing in a stage production of *Mr. Puntilla and His Man Matti*, a play in which his character had to shoot someone on stage. He still carried the blank gun used in that performance, and he intended to put it to good use—not in a bank robbery, as was his custom, but in a spontaneous, way-off-Broadway production that would be staged not at the Grass Roots Pub but at the Boulevard Diner, a popular late-night eating spot, a short distance away from the pub. Built in 1936 by the Worcester Lunch Car Company, the Boulevard was designed in the typical railroad-car style of all true diners. It was long and narrow, with a counter and cooking area on one side and booths on the other.

Fudgy, like a seasoned director, orchestrated each of the player's roles and staged their positions, entrances, and exits. Jack was to sit with Laurie in one of the booths, and Julio and Mary were to take seats on stools adjacent to the table. Fudgy would then walk into the diner, loudly and angrily proclaim that he finally caught Jack red-handed cheating with his wife, pull out the blank gun, and start shooting. To help with the performance, he suggested that a small plastic bag full of red grenadine be smashed open against Jack's chest at the sound of the gunshots.

The Boulevard Diner was just a few minutes' drive down Shrewsbury Street. Julio, Mary, Laurie, and Jack all entered the diner. As if prearranged, the last booth and the adjacent stools were unoccupied. It was midweek, and the eatery was relatively quiet. Simply put, the staging couldn't have been any better. Jack sat facing the entrance. Laurie sat across the table from Jack, with her back to the door. Julio and Mary seated themselves on the empty stools directly across from the booth.

Jack and Laurie ordered some food, and after several minutes, Fudgy came into the diner. He walked about halfway through place, took one look at Laurie sitting with his best friend, and exploded into rage.

"You fuck, Jack! I finally caught you with my wife!" He pulled out his stage pistol, screaming, "I am going to kill you, you fuckin' bastard!" and fired off several rounds of blanks. Then he ran out of the diner.

In unison with the gunshots, Jack compressed the bag of red grenadine to his chest, causing a bright red stain to appear on his shirt and an explosion of sticky red droplets to spatter all over the wooden booth and the windows. Laurie, sitting on the other side of the table, started screaming and put her hands to her face in disbelief. Jack recoiled as if being slammed by real bullets and slumped under the table. Julio and Mary, seated on their stools, had the closest vantage point, and they confirmed what everyone else thought they were seeing. "Call the cops! Jack has been shot!" they screamed.

The servers all knew Jack well; he was a frequent visitor.

"Jackie's been shot! Jackie's been shot!"

Years of practicing the fight scene in *West Side Story* was finally paying dividends. Jack, slumped under the table, tried to stifle his laughter as he watched the customers scurry from the crime scene, leaving their unfinished meals and unpaid bills.

The only customers who did not vacate the premises were a couple occupying the booth directly in front of him. From his slumped position under the table, Jack saw the woman trying to see what had happened and the guy lightly tap his date on her head, and said in true Humphrey Bogart fashion, "Turn around, shut up, and eat your spaghetti."

The actors involved in the charade could barely hold in their laughter. Mary and Julio had to cover their mouths to stay in character. In a few minutes, Jack got out from under the table and started laughing and joking with the few remaining diners. The staff, though still rattled, were more than a little annoyed but at the same time extremely relieved. Marie, a sister of the proprietor, Johnny Ringo, a regular at the Plum Street dice game, put her hand on Jack's arm.

"Jackie, I'm gonna kill you," she said, but her voice lacked conviction, and the look on her face was relief.

For Jack, Fudgy, and the rest, it was an innocent prank. They never considered the possible ramifications, which is par for the course for fledgling addicts. What would have happened if a cop had been there that night—a likely possibility, since cops dined there regularly? What about the potential trauma to the diners, and/or the loss of revenue and reputation for the Boulevard Diner? These thoughts if they even materialized would never appear on the actors' radar.

The following day, an article headlined, "Actors Empty City Diner," appeared in the *Worcester Telegram*. Jack, Fudgy, Laurie, Mary, and Julio preened and gloated as if they had just won Oscars.

Jack ran into Domenic the next day and asked him why he had not tagged along and why had he taken his glass with him when he left the pub. Domenic, who recently had been released from prison, said, "If I was gonna go, my fingerprints were gonna go me." He was wise enough not to take any chances with that particular group of fools.

CHAPTER TWENTY EIGHT

For Jack, Hank, JD, Fudgy, Dumbo, and the rest of the crew, addiction was their secret life. They all tried to act normal, or at least what they thought was normal, but their obsession with getting high utterly controlled their lives and influenced their thought processes 24/7.

Addicts who are graced with the opportunity to recover often refer to the insidious nature of addiction—that inexplicable preoccupation and desire to use despite the crushing weight of negative consequences. As Jack and Hank's drug use escalated, they spent night after night with small groups of friends, almost reverently passing a mirror bearing carefully groomed lines of cocaine around the living room of their Grafton Street apartment. The stimulating intoxicant fueled conversation that often centered on solving the world's problems and creating world peace. In reality, their addiction, not their altruistic fantasies, drove the bus. But the exhilaration of the camaraderie, hope, and ecstasy engendered by those nights would soon become their all-consuming quest.

The all-night cocaine parties in the company of good friends soon went the way of the dinosaur. It was not that cocaine use disappeared, but fewer people gained access to the party. The benevolence of those who trafficked in coke and could afford to give it away was the first casualty of addiction. Generosity was replaced by drug-driven egoism, in which every personal interaction was intended to guarantee either the funds to get high and/or the drugs themselves.

In fact, as time went by, the notion of actual friendship began to disappear. For those who know addiction intimately, this is no surprise. A chronic cloud of stress and tension constantly hangs over the addict's world. It casts a shadow over everything, joyous or sad, pleasurable or challenging, tainting it and causing it to feel different than it is. There is no relaxing or trusting that things are OK or safe

For these reasons and more, there is a tendency among addicts to associate with people who use, just as they do. For the guys from the East Side, this tendency helped fuel the denial and perpetrated the illusion of normalcy. But increasingly, normalcy was harder to find.

As their involvement with drugs intensified and the cost of that involvement increased, so did the personal risk. For Kid Paz, doctor shopping turned into prescription forgery. This was a big leap for a kid whose family was well known in the neighborhood. Kid Paz's father was once a popular boxer whose pugilistic skills would resurface when any of the boys went astray. In the course of his lifetime, Kid Paz's father hit him "with so many rights that he would be begging for a left," as the saying goes. His mother, like the mothers of most of the gang, was a saint, or at least that was how the story was told. Despite this somewhat unstable combination, many members of Kid Paz's family prospered. His upwardly mobile older brother had made a name for himself in local politics; his bright, caring sister lived a straight life. A couple of cousins even made it to medical school. Needless to say, Kid Paz's family held good social standing, and Kid Paz had a lot to hide and a lot to lose.

Quite frankly, all of these people had a lot to lose. Most of them came from blue-collar families and had parents who prided themselves on being law-abiding Americans and working hard to keep a roof over their heads. The new drug craze had caught them completely unaware and clueless. The innocence of the sixties had long been replaced by the distrust of the seventies. In 1976, Tom Wolfe coined the term "the me decade" to describe the narcissistic focus of American life, and on Shrewsbury Street, young people exhibited it to the nth degree. And when drug supplies got tight, nearly anything would do.

Once pharmacies wised up and improved their security, prescription medication became more difficult to obtain. Because the using population had grown exponentially in a very short time, demand increased. The price for methadone skyrocketed from the IPO debut of twenty-five cents per pill to over five dollars per pill—an expensive addiction in 1975. For some addicts, heroin became the drug of choice, despite the stigma and the danger that came with its use. Heroin was plentiful and relatively affordable, and the lure of that surreal experience, that acquiescing to the obsession to get high, made it all worth the risk. Of those who tried the needle, few escaped the downward spiral unscathed.

Although not addicted to heroin, Jack and Hank were both heavily into opiates by then. To fuel their addictions, they needed more cash, so the marijuana business slowly expanded into more profitable and even less reputable undertakings.

In the 1970s, the federal government's "harm reduction" policies resulted in one important, if unintended, consequence: the proliferation of methadone clinics, at which the growing population of heroin addicts could obtain methadone to wean themselves off the needle. This not only reduced the spread of needle-borne diseases such as hepatitis, but it reduced the criminal behavior associated with heroin to some degree. More clinics meant an increased availability of methadone, a highly addictive, marketable, and sought-after drug. The East Side gang quickly capitalized on this untapped potential.

New York, where there were a number of methadone clinics, soon became the East Siders' drug market of choice. Customarily, Hank, accompanied by Stevie or Ship, drove down to New York with a couple of thousand dollars and stood on the corner of Twenty-Third Street and Third Avenue on the city's East Side. Cash in hand, the boys purchased methadone from those patients who needed money more than the drug. By the end of the morning, their money would be gone, replaced by vials of liquid methadone.

Market price for methadone on the corner of Twenty-Third Street was about twenty-five cents per milligram. Back home on Shrewsbury Street, less than a five-hour drive away, a milligram sold for four times that. Like a hawker scalping tickets outside Fenway Park, Hank would, upon his return to Worcester, stand on Shrewsbury Street and call out "Methadone, here!"

In no time, potential buyers appeared as if from thin air. The hint of impropriety, coupled with the laissez-faire attitude of the New York police, provided just the right circumstances to make the trip exciting, not to mention profitable.

The methadone trade represented a great opportunity for the boys to feed their rapidly progressing dependence. And they justified their dealing by thinking that they were providing a public service. They were saving fellow addicts from the health hazards of injection-drug use and the inherent dangers of haphazardly adulterated heroin. This thought pattern typified the extent to which the horror of the problem pushed people away from trying to solve it. Most people couldn't even bear to talk about drug abuse, let alone deal with it, despite the fact—and because of the fact—that people were dying.

One such victim was Tony B., or Anthony, as his mother always called him, a personable young man who had the reputation of being able to "talk the toothpaste back into the tube." Young Tony, who had been blinded in one eye by a BB pellet during an over-zealous war game as a child, was found dead with a needle in his arm before he reached the age of twenty-three. Although all of his friends from the Street attended the funeral, no one mentioned the drug addiction that had cut his promising young life so senselessly short. Not at the funeral home. Not at the church. Not at his final resting place in the cemetery. Shame and pain silenced the truth, leaving Anthony's family confused, distraught, and agonized. For his friends from the Street, unspoken complicity and continued denial ruled the day.

In hindsight, this behavior seems reasonable. When humans experience chaos, they try mightily to control the situation. But in dealing with an addict, it's like trying to hold water in your hand: no matter how hard you squeeze, it's simply impossible to contain it. Powerlessness over someone else's addiction sometimes makes people try to ignore the symptoms. Yet symptoms are the part of the illness that lets others know that something is out of whack, diseased, or disordered. When we ignore symptoms or pretend they don't exist, the condition usually worsens. This is especially true in the case of a progressive, life-threatening condition like addiction. Still, it is perfectly clear why we don't want to face this reality: it sucks.

To Love An Addict Is To Run Out Of Tears

-Sandy Swenson

How do you begin to describe the impact addiction has on those whose lives are connected to an addict? For starters, no one ever asks that his or her life be turned inside out or upside down by another's behavior; it just happens. Parents, spouses, siblings, loved ones, friends, and coworkers usually bear the brunt of an addict's insane behavior. Strangers wouldn't put up with it, and addicts know this. Addicts often rely on the loving, caring people who are closest to them to validate their nonsense: close friends and, above all, family. Often, these people cosign not only out of love and caring but also out of hope. They hope that the addict will outgrow the addiction, or that it is just a crazy reaction to life's stressors. In the face of all evidence to the contrary, loved ones continue to believe the bullshit lies and look the other way rather than face the truth: that someone they love and care about is going down in flames and taking them down, too.

Addiction changes everything, making it very difficult for the addict's family and friends to trust or let their guard down and experience life as it is. Addiction forces those around it to live in a chronic state of distrust, suspicion, and hyperalertness, always aware that at any moment, something can, and usually does, disturb any semblance of tranquility. Life with an addict is chaotic and generally unpredictable. What is predictable is that someone will get robbed, lied to, or conned in order for the addict to get what he or she needs: the next fix. It's critical, however, to understand that when an addict uses someone to get something he or she needs, it's not a personal affront. The addict would do it to anyone willing to go along with the script. They are merely trying to get what they believe they need.

CHAPTER TWENTY NINE

In clinical terms, tolerance is defined as the diminution of response to a stimulus after prolonged exposure and/or the ability to endure unusually large doses of a poison or toxin. In the broader sense, one of the word's other definitions is the ability to endure hardship and to put up with harsh or difficult conditions. Tolerance is also one of the key indicators of dependence. Although none of the guys from the Street realized it at the time, tolerance was the driving force behind their drug habits and their continuing descent into a world that was dangerous and uncharted. At times, that descent was exhilarating, yet it demanded complete abandonment of their morals. Against this backdrop, their lives uncontrollably steamrolled into situations that they never intended to get into.

By this time, Kid Paz, once an impeccably dressed and sophisticated young man, had turned into someone he never would have imagined. Gone were his refined look and much of the muscle mass he'd acquired from hours of bodybuilding in the gym in preparation for football season.

Kid Paz was not alone in compromising his principles; many of the guys on the Street who got in over their heads with drugs quickly became involved in all sorts of degrading and illegal activity. Stevie the Sailor was to become a Shrewsbury Street version of Wimpy, the hamburger moocher from the popular *Popeye* cartoon series. Wimpy was soft-spoken, very intelligent, and well educated but also cowardly, lazy, parsimonious, and utterly gluttonous. He was also something of a scam artist and could be notoriously underhanded. The nickname Wimpy might not have been the most complimentary or completely accurate description of Stevie, but it was close enough that the gang often called him exactly that. Like Wimpy, Stevie often begged for what he needed—in his case, a couple of pills—and promised future payment.

When begging stopped working, Stevie took more nefarious action. In times of desperation, which always was the case when he was getting dope sick, the Sailor wouldn't think twice about helping himself to others' TVs or jewelry to get the dope he needed. Of course, the people closest to the Sailor were the prime targets. Not only did Stevie use his knowledge of his victims' routines and whereabouts, but he also relied on the bond of the relationship to mitigate some of the adverse legal consequences if he were caught. It was self-preservation at its finest, the true hallmark of an addict. No one was exempt, including Stevie's brother and sister, who were now obliged to guard their possessions closely, even in the confines of their own home.

The Grass Roots Pub on Shrewsbury Street, Jack's only connection to legitimacy, was becoming a burden. Hank was too preoccupied with getting high and the methadone business to manage the bar, and the place was beginning to draw unwanted attention from the police. Jack and Hank received a number of warnings from friends and local officials that their activities were becoming more than a nuisance. More important, Hank's insatiable desire to get high was becoming a huge drain on Jack's ability to maintain a sufficient supply of narcotics. Nothing was more important than that. Given those facts, the pub would have to go.

Still, a big question remained: Who wanted to buy a business that was losing money? Jack did not have to look far for the answer; it was "all in the family." Hank's uncle, the hotshot car salesmen whom Hank had so admired as a boy, was a fledgling cocaine addict by then. And he was ready, willing, and able to step into ownership. Who better to sell the bar to than an up-and-coming dope fiend? That sale pretty much cut the umbilical cord in Jack's partnership with Hank, as well as Jack's allegiance to the Street.

For better or worse, Jack's world was expanding. Simply put, he wanted more. As much as he loved to gamble and get high, Jack had an insatiable need to succeed, to be somebody, anybody but Jack. He was caught in the trap of always judging his insides against somebody else's outsides, and from Jack's vantage point, he constantly came up short. Jack wanted his family, his friends, the neighborhood, and the world to know he was successful, at least on the surface. Deep inside, though, Jack had the sinking feeling that he wasn't.

While Hank and his crew were hustling methadone on a street corner in New York, Jack had been hanging out in Coconut Grove, the Florida Keys, and greater Miami. Johnny Two Fingers had moved several times and now lived in North Miami Beach with his hometown sweetheart, Terri. The house doubled as a staging area for their marijuana transportation business, and Jack was a frequent guest at their home. For Jack, South Florida seemed like paradise: a fantasyland of opulent mansions, gigantic yachts, luxury cars, jewelry, and designer clothes. Jack wanted it all, and he figured that with a few successful smuggling trips, it would be within reach. He would raise his level of affluence, provide lavishly for his daughter, who was eight years old, and lift his entire family into a new age of prosperity. He would also achieve world peace:

an opiate-induced dream, a cocaine-induced psychosis, whatever it was, Jack began to believe it because he desperately needed to.

Once a person sets basic morals aside, few criminal acts seem beyond the pale. Jack had already broken many moral (and legal) barriers with his marijuana business. So it made perfect dollars and sense, to him anyway, that if transporting pot from Florida to Massachusetts was profitable, importing it from its country of origin would be more so. Consequences are things an addict usually thinks about after they happen, so it should come as no surprise that the idea of smuggling marijuana from Colombia into the Port of Miami sounded like a surefire way to an early retirement, a life of leisure, and a never-ending supply of drugs, not necessarily in that order.

Jack was not alone in his delusion. Fudgy, Ronnie, Ship, and all of the other guys from the Street were mesmerized by the tanned, bikini-clad bodies, the warm, azure-blue waters, the sunny skies, and the easy access to drugs that made South Florida notorious. Jack jumped in headfirst, deciding to become an international pot smuggler without the slightest inkling that he was raising the stakes to a much higher level of personal danger. Jack entered that business the way he began using drugs, without premeditation or foresight, and his world slowly collapsed.

In 1977, as he moved into the Florida scene, Jack brought with him a new retail buyer and soon-to-be business partner named Arnie Katz, the son of a past Worcester mayor. Hank had met Arnie through his Worcester bookmaking operations. In many ways, Arnie was unlike the other guys from the Street. In Hank's words, he was from the other side of the tracks—the good side. Arnie had been raised in a prosperous, politically connected family. At twenty-eight, he was a successful businessman who owned a restaurant in Worcester. But like the guys from the Street, Arnie struggled with addiction—first and foremost with gambling, or maybe it was simply money, and then later and to a lesser degree, with drugs. He was already selling pot. For a time, Hank and Jack joined forces with Arnie. Later, as Hank deteriorated, they cut him out. So much for loyalty; it was just another casualty of addiction.

Desperate for a big score, Jack convinced Arnie to invest in one of Johnny Two Fingers's smuggling trips, and their first foray was an immediate success, turning a $30,000 investment into $300,000 and putting Jack into an income bracket he had never imagined. Needless to say, his standard of living greatly improved. Soon, he ventured toward a more permanent residency in Florida, renting a waterfront condominium in North Miami Beach complete with a dock for Johnny's twenty-four-foot Sea Ray.

In Florida, life soon became one endless party. One of the few memories Jack has of those days was a very early morning excursion to purchase a pack of cigarettes. Jack, Ronnie, Suzie, Mary, and several other friends had been up all night snorting coke and chattering about saving the world when one of them noticed they were running out of cigarettes.

Instead of taking the car to the store, taking the Sea Ray across the bay seemed like a cool South Floridian thing to do. The early morning sun was glowing brightly on the eastern horizon, and it looked like the perfect day to be alive.

Jack, Squeaky, Johnny, and Ronnie embarked on what they viewed as a leisurely cruise down the Intracoastal Waterway to Haulover Inlet. They'd motor north along a small stretch of coastline, and then back inshore through Port Everglades Inlet at Fort Lauderdale, where they would arrive at a waterfront convenience store that catered to seagoing adventurers like themselves. The voyage started out unceremoniously enough as they all hopped aboard, started the engine, cast off the lines from the bow and the stern, and made headway en route to Haulover.

A strong breeze created a slight chop on the inland waters, but it barely caused the vessel to rise and fall. When they reached Haulover, the water became quite a bit rougher, but they surmised

that this was a natural occurrence, as they were leaving the pro-
tected confines of the Intracoastal and entering the vast expanse
of the Atlantic.

Despite increasingly turbulent waters and their growing un-
ease, they decided to push onward, hoping conditions would improve. But conditions rapidly got worse, and the high seas began
to toss the boat back and forth.

"Holy fuck!" Jack shouted. "Hold on!"

Everyone grabbed any hold he could find. The waves were sev-
en to eight feet, but to the four cocaine-influenced sea-goers, it felt
like they were being tossed about like the *Andrea Gail* in the perfect
storm. Had they not been too busy snorting lines to pay attention
to the TV or radio, they would have known that small-craft advi-
sories had been in effect since midnight, but as Mark Twain once
said, common sense isn't very common. He might've added that it
was doubly uncommon for drug addicts.

Not that Jack and his crew didn't know at least some of the rules.
Experienced boaters understand that it is critical to recognize the
limitations of the boat and of the skipper. And as an old sea captain had once told Jack, "It's not uncommon to see someone coming out of an inlet in a nineteen-foot boat and facing three- and
four-foot seas. A boat that size doesn't belong in that kind of water,
and the skipper ought to stay home." All of this was lost to the
exuberance of the cocaine-addled brain, but it wasn't much longer
before even they began to realize that they were in serious trouble.

"Holy shit! Oh my God!" Squeaky alternated exclamations with
pleas for divine intervention as more waves broke across the deck.

"Don't worry! Stay calm!" Jack hollered back, but his heart
was pounding—and not just from the coke. The boat, which now
seemed pathetically tiny, had begun to buck like a rodeo bull.

Many books have been written on how to navigate rough water.
A few of the panicked crew had even read some of those books,
but none had ever experienced, let alone mastered, the necessary

techniques. Still, they needed to do something—and fast. The idea that made the most sense was to turn back, and finally one of them said it. But turning, never mind turning back, was not as simple as it sounded, especially in high seas. One hasty turn of the helm would place the boat broadside against one of those huge waves and surely capsize it.

It seemed like an eternity, but they eventually got the boat turned around and headed back to Haulover. Once safely inside the Intracoastal, they all breathed a sigh of relief. In mock celebration, they hugged and slapped each other on the back like soldiers returning victorious from battle. Back at the dock, they climbed off the boat and in a sincere gesture of relief, kissed the ground with gratitude. It should have taught them a lesson. But addiction and learning seldom go hand in hand.

When not in South Florida, Jack rented a house on Lake Street in Shrewsbury with longtime East Side friends Fudgy and Squeaky. The house was far enough away from Shrewsbury Street and the Grass Roots Pub that they could avoid daily scrutiny by the local law enforcement officials, or at least that is what the trio thought. Its attached garage and spacious surroundings provided the privacy required to shuttle a thousand or so pounds of marijuana in and out without drawing attention.

Fudgy had returned from Boston and put his acting career on the shelf in favor of pursuing his drug habit. He was tired of the infrequency of theater jobs and the scrounging for money. He knew there was always "work" he could do in the drug business. For Fudgy, dealing seemed like a relatively safe occupation after bank robbery. Squeaky, the only one of the gang to hold a legitimate day job and for whom addiction wasn't an issue, just wanted to be with his friends.

At the time, Squeaky and Jack dated women who were best friends. Neither woman was from the neighborhood, and they might as well have been from another planet as far as their lives and moral outlooks were concerned. Squeaky dated Carol, a pretty, blond only child who somehow found her way down to the Street. Carol's friend Sandi, a leggy, twenty-year-old Italian American with a million-dollar smile, dated Jack. Sandi, like Jack, had attended Catholic school, but unlike Jack, she practiced. She would become a beacon of hope for Jack, who secretly knew deep inside that his life was not going in a good direction.

Fudgy was now on his second marriage: he had tied the knot with Laurie, the young, vivacious actress from the Boulevard Diner escapade. The three friends and their female partners occupied the house on Lake Street, giving it a somewhat normal appearance. What was eerily inexplicable was how these young and innocent women had ended up with Jack and his friends.

Meanwhile, for many of the guys on the Street, things had started to deteriorate. For a drug addict, the feeling of prosperity is ephemeral. It usually comes early in the addictive cycle, either in the form of euphoria, material success—likely from dealing—or, in rare instances, from both. The effort to re-create the initial ecstasy of their first high extorts a high price from many of them. From AIDS to hepatitis C to a premature grave, the costs associated with the disease of addiction are exorbitant—and these were only the health costs. Unemployment, crime, violence, and a plethora of social dysfunctions were beginning to destroy their lives. Joey S. and Stevie had already been to jail, the result of several petty burglaries. Kid Paz had been busted by the state police for forging prescriptions. Hank had contracted hepatitis and spent a month in the hospital. Jack had been stabbed and busted for driving under the influence on more than one occasion. The list of disasters went on.

Despite the flashing warning signs, most of the crew was still driven by the obsession to get high—and not in a small way. For a drug addict, a little is good, and more is better. There is a limit, an LD (lethal dose) to the number of Percodans, bags of heroin, or milligrams of methadone that one can consume before respiratory arrest and, ultimately, death occurs. For many of the guys on Shrewsbury Street, the goal was to reach LD, but without the graveside service. Some of the more desperate addicts were ambivalent about the possibility of death—it offered a welcome relief from the painful battle of addiction. Perhaps the most tragic aspect of the rampant drug abuse on the East Side was the inability to see life beyond the next fix. People were crying for help but had no clue how to ask for it. Losses, in one form or another, occurred with such regularity that the survivors grew desensitized to the unfolding catastrophe.

CHAPTER THIRTY

In every addict's life comes a tipping point: the point after which the descent toward the bottom becomes too fast to control. For Jack, that tipping point may have been his relationship with Arnold Katz. Arnie had oldest son syndrome, which compelled him to compete with his father, who was not only the ex-mayor of Worcester but a multimillionaire besides. That left Arnie with a lot of ground to make up. Hard work was one way to do it, but the fast and easy route seemed more appealing. And that's where Jack and Arnie's interests matched.

Arnie, propelled by his need to reach a financial status no one from Shrewsbury Street had ever dreamed of, acted as an accelerant, pushing Jack, now close to thirty years old, toward his own dreams of material wealth, power, and respect. And it wasn't long before they settled on a means for achieving their dreams: their own Colombian smuggling adventure, separate from that of Johnny Two Fingers, who was now spending his time in a Florida prison.

Though large-scale international drug transport was then a burgeoning industry, the proportional risk/reward formula is the same as it is today: the higher the risk, the higher the reward. On the risk side, bringing pot from Colombia was no simple task. Aside from the legal implications, it required access to financial and human resources. The reward side, however, was limitless, or at least that was how the potential multimillion-dollar profits seemed at the time.

Jack's greed, coupled with the addict's innate sense of hopelessness, blinded him to the possible dangers that lay ahead. Life was becoming a B movie with plenty of action but literally no meaning, responsibility, or redeeming social value, but Jack was eager to play his role. That twenty-four-foot Sea Ray outside the condominium was soon replaced by a leased forty-four-foot ketch capable of transporting several thousand pounds of Colombian gold across the Caribbean. Fort Lauderdale was the new staging area for Jack and Arnie's operation, and Miami Beach was Jack's new home away from home. Percocet and cocaine were Jack's constant companions. The stage was set for disaster.

It would be easy to either glorify or make light of their first couple of attempts at big-time smuggling. To be fair, certain aspects of drug smuggling were exciting. It was easy to be caught up in the glitz and the glamour of the yachts, the bikini-clad women, and the million-dollar mansions. In South Florida, some or a lot of that ostentatious lifestyle was funded by involvement in the illegal drug trade. The lifestyle was exhilarating, at least on the surface. But on a deeper emotional level, it was a meaningless, extremely treacherous, and even deadly journey. Often, it played out in the style of the Keystone Cops—blunder reinforced by blunder with a net result of failure.

Like all his forays into the drug trade, Jack's first attempt at smuggling started with lip service to altruism. Jack would make a lot of money, take care of his family, and live happily ever after. Of course, most of that happiness would come from having enough money to maintain a constant stupor fueled by opiates and cocaine.

Still, given the nature of the task, some realism was necessary. The leased ketch represented a serious upgrade in seaworthiness and cargo capacity from Johnny's Sea Ray. Jack and Arnie moored the boat in Miami Harbor, pretending that they were among the rich and famous who also harbored there. They concocted a simple plan: hire a captain and crew to sail the vessel to Colombia, load eight thousand pounds of marijuana on board, and then sail back to an early retirement.

It all sounded so easy and so innocent, but the reality was quite different due to a number of factors, most critically, Jack's heavy drug use. Jack didn't think twice about collecting a crew that partied as much as he did. His newly hired captain listed, ahead of food and water, ten cases of Heineken and three quarts of rum on the prevoyage supply list. An experienced seaman would have summarily disqualified this man and his crew, but for Jack, the booze barely raised an eyebrow. Seeing the writing on the wall is a talent often lost on the addict, and this particular endeavor was no different.

One could say that Jack's fate was sealed the moment he fulfilled the captain's supply request, but that would be an oversimplification. It was safe to say, however, that it did not help. Still, thanks in part to cocaine, enthusiasm ruled the day. Jack and Arnie gathered for a little ceremony at the pier and gave final instructions to the captain, including the rendezvous point where the crew would meet the Colombian coconspirators. After solemnly bidding the captain and crew bon voyage, Jack and Arnie returned home to wait for word from Colombia that the connection had been made.

Several days passed, all of them filled with white lines, yellow pills, and high hopes. That optimism turned to pessimism as no word of a rendezvous was received. They had agreed to radio silence, a precaution against an intercepted transmission alerting the Coast Guard to their activity. More importantly, they did not want to have any connection to the vessel should the operation go astray. Instead, it was agreed that phone contact from Colombia would confirm the deal had gone down. As time passed, the silence grew deafening; something had obviously gone wrong.

Several more days elapsed before word finally arrived from a mutual acquaintance of one the crew. The ketch had run aground on a shallow reef near the island of Bonaire and begun to take on water. After being rescued, the crew had vanished. The only cargo remaining on board were the ten empty cases of Heineken and three empty bottles of rum. The boat was ruined, and $200,000 of preparation money was gone. The bright side was that Jack didn't get busted. More importantly, he still had the means to get high. Was a lesson learned? Hardly. There was still a drug habit to support.

As it turned out, Colombia by sea turned out to be a bad option for reasons other than maritime inexperience. As Jack and Arnie were working to get established, a competitor already had a firm grip on the Colombian weed trade: notorious Boston mobster Salvatore Michael Caruana. Sonny, as he was affectionately known, had the resources to do it right. His vessels sailed from Colombia all the way to Cape Cod before offloading their precious cargo. It was a longer but much safer journey, since the sleepy Cape Cod community was oblivious to the trade. Further, Caruana did not partake of the drugs in which he traded. He was clear-eyed and had a good business sense. He could undersell any competitor and employed extreme violence without hesitation.

Jack and Arnie met Sonny Caruana through a Worcester-area car dealer they knew. Soon, they were working as his subcontractors, delivering tractor-trailer loads of marijuana to Vermont from Cape Cod. They made good money, but not the pot of gold that Jack imagined he could get from one big Colombian adventure of his own.

Jack soon headed back to Florida, where once again he teamed up with Johnny Two Fingers, who recently had been released from jail. Johnny's luck had not been good of late, but he and Jack hoped it would turn for the better. Johnny had just discovered a smuggling opportunity that seemed too good to be true.

"Nick just told me about nine thousand pounds of Colombian pot sitting on a deserted island in the Bahamas, just waiting to be picked up and brought to the mainland," Johnny told Jack. "All we need to do to own that nine thousand pounds of pot is to find someone crazy enough go out there and pick it up."

It was a piece of cake, if only they could find a boat.

With his daughter, Gina Marie's, birthday coming up, Jack decided to head back to Worcester. That meant that Jack needed someone to take his place on the boat. He made Johnny promise that "someone" wouldn't be their friend, Frank. "Make sure Frankie boy does not get into trouble," Jack said to John. "He has a family."

Jack's "friendship" with Frank was, of course, based largely on drugs. Frank had access to Percodan due to some phantom back pain and a cooperative doctor. Frank's prescription never seemed to run out. Further, Frank had the perfect profile for driving marijuana to Massachusetts from Florida. He was an older guy, a family man with five kids, who didn't attract the attention of police.

Jack knew the Colombian weed venture would be risky. A huge load of pot just sitting on an island, waiting for someone to show up, could result in any number of bad situations. Now back in Massachusetts, Jack received a call from Frank with the cryptic message, "I've gone fishing."

The remark could only mean one thing. Johnny had found a boat and taken Frank along.

There was no sense in crying over spilled milk. Jack could only hope that everything would turn out all right. But for an addict, hope dies quickly, and before Jack could arrange to get back to Florida, Johnny, Frank, and Charlie were all in custody, the victims of a sting operation. The crew of the boat Johnny had hired were all undercover agents. They went along with the charade until they'd busted every last person involved.

Jack decided that Florida was a little too hot to handle and that it would be a good idea to put any future smuggling plans on the shelf—that is until Arnie suggested an alternate smuggling plan.

In the years that had passed since the Nebraska debacle, the marijuana industry had evolved from the harvesting of a naturally occurring weed that primarily produced mild euphoria, a low-grade headache, and a voracious appetite to the cultivation of highly potent strains of mind-blowingly psychoactive pot. Along with this increase in potency came an associated increase in value. This consumer demand for higher potency and higher-priced marijuana created the ideal circumstances to make Arnie's plan feasible and profitable.

Some of the best of the new weed was coming out of Mexico. Fudgy, Arnie, and Jack packed up their belongings and with a gang of pothead misfits moved to San Antonio, Texas, to set up a base camp from which they would coordinate the smuggling of high-end pot across the United States–Mexico border. This new plan involved not boats but planes, and although the gang had even less experience with this form of transport, they judged the task to be another piece of cake.

The gang, headlined by Jack and Fudgy, started out with the usual due diligence and capital expenditures that were required for most new business ventures. They purchased two small recreational vehicles, a small airplane, and several high-powered two-way radios designed to operate on private frequencies. Finally, they leased two furnished houses for their living quarters. Now it was time for phase two: flight planning.

First, they familiarized themselves with the area and searched for secluded landing sites where they could quickly and covertly off-load their illicit cargo before taking off again and landing at the final destination listed on the official flight plan. After finding a suitable landing site as well as secondary and tertiary backups just in case the first one failed, they camped out in the countryside for several days, observing traffic patterns, testing communications equipment, and rehearsing the plan to unload the plane. Expediency was critical; spending too much time on the ground would cause a deviation from the time parameters listed in the flight plan, and might arouse suspicion.

Although the plan should have worked like a well-oiled machine, in reality it was more like a train wreck. Jack and Fudgy had moved to San Antonio, but they hadn't left their addictions behind. Physically dependent on opiates, they needed them daily, and the fear of withdrawal influenced their every thought.

To provide a steady stream of pills, the ever-loyal Fudgy flew home to Worcester regularly. When he returned, he brought Percocet and news from the Street, none of which was promising. It was like a Who's Who for the pathetically addicted. Who sat in jail? Who got caught breaking into houses? Who just overdosed? Who was dope sick? And who was going to detoxification, a new word that was becoming more popular in the vernacular of the Street. Kid Paz, who had run out of friends to hustle and had no game left, was the first to seek help for his addiction. But not many followed—at least not early on.

Hank, who had reunited with his childhood sweetheart, Eileen, was using more than ever and was starting to have trouble keeping pace with the demands of his habit. He was using more and more methadone, which was making it hard to fund his forays to Manhattan, and he was often so high that he couldn't get off the couch to make the trip even when he did have the cash. He told Jack that he had contracted the widespread disease "Funzalo." Funds were low—but this feeble attempt at humor was not so funny to Eileen. Like the friends and family of many addicts, she watched helplessly as Hank seemed to drift farther out to sea, only to be swallowed up in an ocean of incorrigibility.

Eileen had had enough. "Love Hurts" wasn't just a song on the radio any longer; it was her life, and she couldn't stand the pain of seeing Hank waste his life away. Their five-year relationship, once so full of promise, had lost its childhood innocence and was swallowed up by the deceit and hopelessness of addiction. On a Monday morning, just like any other, Hank's grandmother walked into Hank's living room—actually, his mother's living room, as Hank, closing in on thirty, was back living at home—and said, "Hankie, your bags are on the porch. Eileen said, 'No more.' She's done." And for the first time, Hank's grandmother uttered the words that would repeatedly echo in his mind. "Hankie, you crazy! You need to go to the ocean and wash your brains in salt water."

On the Street, times had turned desperate. Friendships now hinged on who had enough "ammunition," a term endearingly and sometimes accurately applied to one's drug supply: after all, getting high every day seemed like a matter of life and death. In this environment, loyalties shifted from day to day. Friends became enemies, and enemies became friends, depending upon who could supply that next fix. Any solution was acceptable, as long as there was a chance to stay high.

Joey S. was in jail again—another drugstore robbery gone badly. Jimmy O. and Ship were fighting their way out of one jam after another; Dumbo was shooting heroin, something becoming more acceptable due to its affordability and availability, compared with prescription narcotics. Money was always an issue when it came to getting and staying high. If you didn't have it, then you had better do something about it.

Back in Texas, this news made for black comedy, but Jack considered himself different from the rest. After all, he had money and a purpose: pulling the trigger on a monumental score.

Unlike the Colombian sea venture, the preparations in Texas had been extremely thorough, and the gang thought they'd left nothing to chance. What no one could have foreseen, however, was the accident that spoiled everything. The Mexican grower had harvested the weed, but he broke his leg in an accident before it could be packaged. Left to sit in the sun, the green, resin-covered weed withered into a dry, less potent, and exceedingly unattractive brown. Desperate to make at least some profit, the gang succeeded in flying the weed across the border into Texas, but the product was effectively worthless. Once again, fate had intervened, leaving them high and dry. They left the Lone Star State with empty pockets and dashed hopes.

CHAPTER THIRTY ONE

Addiction can make an individual ambivalent about life. In an unspoken and perverse sort of way, the Texas calamity was a welcome relief. The collapse of their smuggling scheme meant that Jack and Fudgy could return home to the East Side, their fellow drug addicts on the Street, and a ready supply of critical narcotics. It also allowed them to continue their downward spiral into hopelessness, although they might not have viewed it that way.

Resiliency is not a trait associated with drug addicts, but addiction was creating a new breed of miscreants who just kept coming back for more. In twelve-step programs all over the world, this seemingly irrational behavior is described by the observation, "Insanity is doing the same things over and over and expecting different results."

For many of the guys on the Street, this inability to see the futility of their choices meant continued pain and suffering. It is misleading to portray their lives as just one sad story after the next, though. There were some ephemeral triumphs—even if they simply kept a user above bottom and allowed his addiction to continue. Despite all of their failures in the get-rich-quick marijuana business, their determination to find new revenue sources did not diminish; after all, they had drug habits to support.

In the distorted logic of a brain captured by addiction, the best way to meet the needs of an addiction was to deal in that drug. There was no better assurance of a ready supply. So, for Jack and his friends, a change in drug preference meant a change in drugs dealt. None of the gang smoked pot any longer because there were more potent highs to be had. On the Street, the drugs of choice were opiates and cocaine.

Opiates were still something you didn't talk much about. Standing on the corner, waiting for other dope fiends to come by and sell you their methadone, while profitable, was nothing close to glamorous. Dealing heroin had a bad reputation, as well. But cocaine? Well, dealing coke was trendy. Before the cartels, the drug lords, and the drug wars, cocaine was considered socially acceptable in many circles. It was a sign of affluence, erudition, independence, and, in the drug culture, a sign of coming of age. Of course, underneath all this superficiality was something simpler: the insatiable and undeniable urge for more and more drugs.

Jack's addiction drove his next scheme: to smuggle cocaine from Peru. And with the help of two Shrewsbury Street transplants, he realized this less-than-lofty goal.

The first of these new associates was Eddie, who was a year younger than Jack and had received a first-class moral education at a rival Catholic school while Jack was at Sacred Heart Academy. Eddie grew up in the Worcester suburbs. He was Irish, with boyish good looks and a touch of eloquence that distinguished him from most of the gang on the Street, who, by this time, showed the hardened realities of addiction on their faces. In love with cocaine and always ready to party, Eddie was fascinated with the pirate's code of conduct as exemplified on Shrewsbury Street. He was attracted to the illusion of easy money. For him, dealing in coke seemed a logical step. Until his premature demise from liver cancer in his early forties, Eddie was a good friend, business partner, and coconspirator to Jack.

The second Shrewsbury Street transplant was Ronnie D., a Hamilton Street kid. Ronnie was a singer in a rock-and-roll band, a long-haired alcoholic who loved chasing women and snorting lines.

Together, Jack and his two new friends developed a smuggling plan that had a number of positive attributes, including simplicity and low start-up costs. First, the plan only required two mules—people willing to assume the risk of carrying drugs across an international border for relatively little reward. To a person who was not addicted and not accustomed to a life of such a precarious nature, the risk would be evident. To Ronnie, who signed on as one of the mules, any risk was offset by the opportunity to snort the best coke on the planet: he would be paid in coke after the goods were successfully transported to the United States. In fact, the operation required very little upfront expense, which, after the Colombia and Texas fiascoes, was a real positive.

Two other elements of the plan made it even more appealing. The first was a route that would bring the drugs in through the customs-free port of Saint Martin, a short boat ride to the US territory of Puerto Rico and then a simple domestic flight to the United States, thereby avoiding a customs inspection for the whole run. The second was an ingenious method of packaging that they thought would foil detection if authorities did become involved.

At the time, instant Polaroid cameras and the film that came with them were popular choices for international travelers. The film was packaged in a slender cardboard box. Inside the box, a sealed plastic sleeve covered the metal cartridge that contained the film. Jack and his associates created a system to conceal cocaine in a nearly perfect replica of a Polaroid film pack. First, they designed a compression system using a small wooden box with a tight-fitting lid and a C-clamp to create small slabs of pressed cocaine. The slabs were vacuum-sealed in a food wrapper, placed inside an actual Polaroid film cartridge, sealed in a replica of Polaroid's plastic packaging sleeve, put in an actual cardboard Polaroid film box, and pasted shut.

The Polaroid packs were a brilliant example of Yankee ingenuity—and believe it or not, they actually worked. The gang managed to smuggle in five kilos of high-quality cocaine without a hitch. It wasn't the million-dollar bonanza Jack had dreamed of in his pot-smuggling ventures, but with a street value of $55,000 a kilo, it was a quarter-million-dollar haul for an investment of less than $25,000—a pretty good return.

With the coke safely shipped, it was time to party. Jack, Eddie, and Ronnie popped bottles of Cristal champagne and snorted lines as they forecast the beginning of a new empire. But in addition to the partying, they had some work to do, namely, selling the five kilos. This wasn't as big a deal as the smuggling was. Street sales provided a good opportunity for some of the guys lower on the food chain to earn a few extra dollars and feed their own habits. The big money would flow back up to Jack and Eddie at the top.

Life was good. In fact, for Eddie, there was even a brief brush with celebrity. During a visit to New York, Eddie had some brief encounters with the early cast of *Saturday Night Live* at a club called PJ's on Third Street in Manhattan. The cast loved the Peruvian flake cocaine, which only served to accelerate Eddie and Jack's delusions of grandeur. Of course, in the drug culture, most relationships were fleeting and based upon need. So when the cocaine stopped flowing, the *SNL* cast bid Eddie adieu.

The good times never seemed to last very long, and the bad times passed by like background scenery. Addiction numbs the soul. The life of an addict is, by necessity, very self-centered and so filled with losses that the death of a close friend or family member can have as little emotional impact as a minor event reported in the morning newspaper. Yet isolation and apathy hide the inner turmoil that is the constant companion of a drug addict.

The death of Terri B., Johnny Two Fingers's one-time girlfriend and one of Jack's closest friends, clearly illustrates this dichotomy. Terri had been Johnny's girlfriend since he returned from Vietnam in 1972. Eventually, they moved to Florida and rented a house in North Miami Beach, where Jack was often a guest. Over long nights of snorting coke and plotting to save the world, the friendship among Jack, Johnny, and Terri deepened. When Johnny and Terri eventually broke up, she went home to Shrewsbury Street, where Jack was living again after the Texas fiasco. In the aftermath of the breakup, she relied on Jack's friendship and cocaine to get her through her emotional distress. Eventually, she began dating Leo F., also known as Frenchy, another one of Jack's friends from the Street. They fell in love and got married. Life changed, but Jack and Terri remained close.

One typical Friday night, Jack found himself alone in his Worcester apartment. By this time, he lived on the first floor of his mother's three-decker, the house he grew up in. His mother bought the house from her father with money that Jack gave to her—at least one part of his dream of wealth and influence had come true. Jack had renovated the first-floor apartment and had quite a bachelor pad—for Merrifield Street, anyway. Jack loved to listen to the melancholic sounds of Air Supply, and with "I'm All Out of Love" playing at full volume, the telephone rang.

"Hello?"

Terri's soft, gentle voice was on the other end of the line. "Jackie, can you please come over? I need to talk to you."

215

Jack loved Terri as much as he could love anyone in his constantly altered state. Being there for her when she needed him was automatic.

"Sure. No problem, Terri," he said without hesitation. "I'll be over shortly." With that, he hung up the phone.

Minutes later, the phone rang again. This time it was Terri's husband, Leo.

"Hey, Leo," Jack said. "Terri just called and said she wanted to talk to me. I was on my way over. Do you know what she wants?"

"She probably just wants you to cash her check." As Jack always had plenty of ready cash, it was a favor he could do. But as the conversation continued, Jack got the feeling that things were not going well between Terri and Leo that evening, and Jack decided not to step into the middle.

The conversation shifted quickly, as it always did, to the familiar topic of cocaine. After a brief, cryptic discussion regarding the next scheduled delivery, Jack hung up the phone. He popped a couple of Percodan, snorted a few more lines, and returned to the romantic melodies of Air Supply. Dismissing Terri's phone call as the fleeting interest of a woman on the outs with her husband, he lost himself in the rapture of the drugs.

Several hours later, however, Jack decided to fulfill his promise to Terri and headed down to Harper's Bazaar, a local bar on Shrewsbury Street. He was walking toward Leo and Terri's house when the flashing lights of an ambulance and several police cars interrupted his euphoria. Jack knew it wasn't good, but he couldn't imagine how bad it really was. Even today, he can't recall exactly what happened next. Did he continue walking toward those flashing lights or simply turn and walk away? He doesn't remember who told him that Terri had hanged herself.

What Jack does remember is that Leo found her in a closet with a rope around her neck, utterly alone. Candles burned throughout the house, and she'd left a note proclaiming her despair. Terri was not the only one taken out by the ambulance that night; Leo overcome by grief, guilt, and suffering from shock went, too. Years later, the scars still remain.

Jack's own grief and guilt is just a shadow of Leo's pain, but to this day, he often replays that last conversation with Terri in his head. Was there something in her voice that he missed? At the time, Jack had no inkling she desperately needed help.

What did Terri's suicide do to Jack? In fact, it made things worse. Once again, he had failed to live up to that higher calling, a remnant of his Catholic school upbringing. It was just the excuse Jack needed to numb himself even more.

How far you go in life depends on your being tender with the young, compassionate with the aged, sympathetic with the striving, and tolerant of the weak and the strong because someday in life you will have been all of these.

—George Washington Carver

Researchers who study personal change say that it happens in stages along a continuum, and that the first stage is the precontemplative phase, in which a person has yet to make the connection between the behavior and the negative consequences of that behavior. People in this stage are ignorant or in denial, and they are unaware that their problems in life might somehow be a result of their drinking or drug use. Some go through life never moving beyond this initial stage; they simply can't or won't accept that their behavior is causing most of their problems. They continue to blame people, places, and things for their misfortune, never accepting any responsibility.

The "wrongs of passage" committed by the guys from East Park underscore the correlation between continued substance use and the loss of morality, response flexibility, and emotional balance. According to ASAM's new definition of addiction, "this [dysfunction] is reflected in an individual pathologically pursuing reward and/or relief by substance use and other behaviors. Characterized by inability to consistently abstain, impairment in behavioral control, craving, diminished recognition of significant problems with one's behaviors and interpersonal relationships, and a dysfunctional emotional response."

As these executive functions deteriorated in the East Siders, so did their lifelong relationships and the associated interpersonal characteristics, such as empathy, insight, and attunement. Once the East Siders traded these important familial and societal ties for the next immediate fix, they quickly became isolated from life and life's meaning.

CHAPTER THIRTY TWO

J ust when Jack thought things couldn't get any worse, they did. The chemical allure and the economic benefit of cocaine dealing were irresistible, and that meant routine business trips to South Florida. In April 1979, Jack and Fudgy headed south to the Miami area to pick up another illicit cargo.

In the cocaine business, one customarily avoided dealing with strangers whenever possible; vetting someone beforehand was a way to sniff out potential police activity and avoid potential rip-offs. This time, Jack and Fudgy were dealing with a new supplier, a man who dated Jack's friend (and distant relative) Diane. The tenuous family connection provided some assurance, but not enough to make Jack foolhardy. He put his faith in the one man he could trust for sure, his lifelong friend Fudgy and left the money in his hands for safekeeping. While Fudgy sat on the loot at a local hotel, Jack drove over to Diane's house to check out the quality of the merchandise.

When Jack arrived, Diane introduced him to her boyfriend, the boyfriend's brother, and a third man, who Jack assumed was the guy with the coke. They made small talk for a few minutes. Then the men pulled out a trio of very large handguns.

"Sit down, motherfucker!"

One of them pushed Jack into a chair, as all three leveled their weapons at his skull.

"The money!" Diane's boyfriend barked. "Now!" As if to emphasize this point, he jammed the muzzle of his pistol against Jack's temple.

Fuck me, Jack thought. *After everything, this is how it goes down.* His mind began to race, channeling every horror imaginable and frantically trying to craft an escape. His head began to pound, more from the feeling of impending doom than from the pressure of the gun against his head. Once again, a scheme had backfired, and he had the biggest problem of his life to solve.

There are instances—not many, but some—when being under the influence of narcotics is a good thing; alleviating serious pain and preventing shock are among them. In this case, the second use came into play, if in an unintended way. In general, Jack dosed up with opiates every morning as a way of warding off the inevitable and uncomfortable feeling of living life on life's terms. On this particular day, being high probably prevented him from literally shitting his pants, which, in turn, allowed him to evaluate this predicament with at least some level of clarity.

These guys might have guns, but Jack still had a card or two to play. First, they wanted the money, and luckily, Jack didn't have it with him. That would have been too easy, the end of the ordeal, and likely the end of Jack. They key was to act sufficiently scared, which wasn't difficult. This wouldn't be as well planned or acted as Fudgy's late-night show at the Boulevard Diner, but in this Florida home, Jack had a whole lot more incentive to put on a good show.

"Look, guys," Jack pleaded. "Let's make some sort of deal here. Honest. I don't have the money on me. You know that; you already searched everything. But with one phone call, I can get it for you. Swear to fucking God."

The performance, which would have made Fudgy proud, convinced the captors that they had the upper hand—so much so that they reversed their initial course and decided against tying Jack up. Then the haggling began. After some heated back-and-forth discussion, Jack managed to bargain for his freedom in return for $10,000. He wasn't trying to be coy with his life, but he believed that if they got their hands on the whole $250,000, they would simply kill him. After all, leaving no witnesses was the safest way to get away with the crime. He was also hoping that calling Fudgy with a request for such a small sliver of the cash would tip him off that something was wrong.

The deal negotiated, Jack's captors handed him a phone, and he dialed the hotel.

"Fudgy, get ten thousand from the hotel safe."

Jack spoke these words for two reasons. First, he wanted his captors to think the money was not in the hotel room under guard. Second, he was betting that Fudgy would realize that something was wrong, since the money was not in a safe but under the bed that Fudgy was likely sitting on while answering the phone. Unfortunately, the nuance of Jack's subterfuge never registered in Fudgy's mind. When Diane came to pick up the money, he handed it over, still failing to smell, as Jack had, the rat named Diane.

Diane soon returned with the ten grand.

"OK," Jack said, "we had a deal. Let me go."

The response was not what he had hoped for. As the thugs counted the money and popped a few more barbiturates, it became apparent that the feeding frenzy fueled by drugs and greed would not end until all the money was in their hands. As if on cue, the words, "We want the rest," echoed in Jack's ears.

During the entire time he was held captive, Jack had been looking for an opportunity to escape to keep alive a glimmer of hope and prevent himself from melting down. He wasn't tied up. And he was in a small Florida ranch house, not Alcatraz. But what if he tried to escape and failed? He envisioned diving through a window, being impaled on a glass shard and dragged back inside, bleeding and still captive. Then there were the guns. He was fairly certain they wouldn't want to attract attention by firing them at a fleeing target, but heavy drug use and large piles of money tended to make people think and act without much thought of consequences. Doing nothing, however, was the worst option and would likely end up with him out $250,000 and/or dead.

Stalling for time, Jack surveyed the room, constantly looking for an escape route. Faced with the increasing odds of a bad outcome, he narrowed down his choices until he reached only one—the kitchen door. It was only fifteen feet away, it didn't involve the risk of impalement, and whatever was beyond it had to be better than this. The door opened outward. The only question was whether his momentum would create enough force to smash the wooden frame and allow him to escape.

His heart pounding, Jack edged toward the door, counting slowly downward. When he reached zero, he exploded, legs and arms churning, leaving one shoe behind on the floor. Like the cornerback he once was, Jack hit the door with everything he had, and it shattered with a tremendous crash.

"What the fuck? Hey, motherfucker! Get back here!" the thugs screamed, but by then Jack was gone, tearing through dank Florida heat, not stopping for blocks until he was sure they hadn't pursued him.

Catching his breath, Jack spied a pay phone. Hands shaking, he deposited some coins and dialed. "Fudgy! Get the hell out of the hotel, now! And don't forget to take the money!"

Fudgy obeyed instantly. But in his haste to get Fudgy out of potential danger, Jack had failed to set a rendezvous point. Cell phones were still a dream in those days, but fortunately, pay phones populated the area. It took a while to make the connection, in part because Fudgy spent time calling friends across South Florida, trying to level the playing field by finding a gun. Meanwhile, Jack was busy trying to regain his senses, find a safe place to lie low, and find his friend. Eventually, they connected by calling Laurie, Fudgy's wife, who was living at the Lake Street House back in Shrewsbury. Concerned that Jack still might be followed, they agreed to meet in a public place. The reunification resembled a scene of two long-lost brothers returning home from the war. They threw open their arms and embraced, holding on for dear life. Within minutes, they made a plan to return home. First, however, there was business to take care of.

"We are going to burn those fuckers," Jack said, and he meant it.

Jack soon returned with two hulking giants, recommended to him by a local car dealer who used them as hired enforcers to collect bad debts. Jack thought it would be worth the $5,000 to send a message that messing with him was a bad idea. The plan was to administer a serious beating that would teach his former captors a lesson. Jack's two companions were massive enough and skilled enough to do that easily. As Jack rounded the corner to Diane's house, the entire holdup gang was pulling out of the driveway.

"Cut them fuckers off! Ram into them!" said the sumo-sized hired thug sitting in the front seat next to Jack.

Damn, this is a fucking rental car, Jack thought. Not wanting to look like the weak link in the retribution crew, Jack obligingly aimed the car directly at the perpetrators. What resembled a Hollywood car chase straight out of the Steve McQueen movie *Bullet* soon ensued but ended quickly on the streets of North Miami when several shots were fired from the car that Jack and his henchmen were pursuing. Jack's bullies may have been imposing, but they were no match for a gun. The only solace Jack garnered was the look of surprise and fear on the faces of his enemies when he tried to run them off the road—along with the good fortune of returning the rental car unscathed.

To this day, it is embarrassing for Jack to look back at the sociopathic behavior exhibited by a Catholic schoolboy who once believed in making the world a better place. He offers this poor explanation: he didn't see any of it coming.

CHAPTER THIRTY THREE

B y the time the 1980s rolled around, life was not getting much better for many of the guys from the Street. Now in their early thirties, their addictions required a lot of effort, most of which was illegal or at least counterproductive. They were either stealing from family, work, or life partners or engaged in some sort of activity that likely would land them in front of a judge. Do that often enough, and you most certainly end up in jail—and they often did. Most of the guys on the Street were transporting drugs, selling drugs, or both. Ship was a transporter. He would get into a truck, drive thousands of pounds of marijuana across the country, and then return home, faithfully carrying a few hundred thousand dollars in cash. He might have felt lucky, but his downward spiral had already begun.

After passing out in one too many pharmacies, Joey was in jail. Kid Paz already had a courtesy visit from the state police. Hank's bookmaking business staggered onward, but he now spent much of his time dope sick and desperate for his next big score. The parties, camaraderie, and fun had faded away.

The beginning of the end for Jack, Hank, and Eddie came on a cold night in January 1981. The temperature had dipped into single digits, and under cover of darkness, the three worked as quickly as they could to move over a thousand pounds of marijuana from the back of a truck into an upstairs bedroom of a huge Victorian duplex on Saint Elmo Street in Worcester's quiet West Side. The house had recently been purchased by Hank's current girlfriend, Elaine, and she had no idea it was being used as the drop zone for a major weed shipment—a small detail Hank failed to mention to her, even though she was in danger of losing her house or even going to jail if the plan fell through. At this point in his life, Hank didn't worry about telling her all the details. His goal in life was to be hammered every day, and he achieved that goal. He didn't care about his girlfriend's goals enough to warn her that there might be trouble.

For Jack and Hank, it was a return to their business relationship, which they resurrected from time to time as circumstances dictated. Jack, Hank, and Eddie waited at the Grass Roots Pub for the shipment to arrive in Worcester. They were completely wasted after three or four sleepless days and nights of snorting coke and swallowing methadone. Their condition wasn't ideal for any kind of business operation, let alone one that might end with them in jail. But as always, the drugs blurred the boundaries between fantasy and reality and reduced life to simple tasks, without thought of consequences. Jack received a cryptic phone call stating that the "stuff" had arrived and there was a U-Haul truck waiting at the Saint Elmo Street house that needed to be unloaded. Easy enough. What could possibly go wrong? They hopped into Jack's car and headed to the West Side.

Waiting in the truck was an amiable Georgian named Wylie, who had driven the load north and was clearly out of his element in the bitter cold of a Worcester winter. Shivering, he was anxious to get his cargo unloaded and head back to warmer climes.

He lifted the roll-up cargo door to reveal several bales of mari-juana, packed in heavy-duty plastic garbage bags. As quickly as they could, the men went to work carrying the bags up to the third floor bedroom where they would be safe. There was only one tiny glitch in the operation. As Hank carried one of the bags from the truck into the house, the bale split open, spilling pot all over the stairs and the outdoor porch.

"Yo, guys! I spilled some stuff," Hank hollered up the stairs. "We gotta clean this shit up." When no one responded, Hank tried to clean up the mess, but darkness and his wasted state made it hard to do a good job. He figured a more thorough cleanup could wait until morning. What he didn't know was that his voice had aroused the suspicion of a neighbor, who called the police to report a disturbance.

The crew had barely finished bringing the weed upstairs and had moved back down to the second floor when they heard a knock on the door. Looking out the window, Jack saw a Worcester police cruiser. Hank headed for the third floor, which, while closest to the weed, was farthest from the police. From his vantage point on the third floor, he watched in shock as a seemingly endless line of cruisers streamed up the hill toward the house. Wylie went upstairs with Hank to stay with the pot. Eddie mysteriously disappeared down a hallway, and unbeknownst to anyone, jumped out of a second-floor window. His only thought was to avoid being caught. And Jack, not thinking clearly in his doped-up state, went downstairs to try to talk himself out of another hot spot.

When Jack opened the door, a uniformed police officer stood on the porch, a clump of marijuana in hand.

"Can we come in?" the cop asked, glancing back over his shoulder.

"You're going to need a warrant." Jack replied, and quickly learned that such a response only worked for real in the movies.

"Get on the floor and stay there!" someone barked, as a team of cops swarmed into the living room.

Up in the attic with twelve hundred pounds of pot, Hank had other worries. He was carrying two ounces of coke and a couple hundred Percodan on his person. He quickly secreted the pills and most of the coke in the attic's drop ceiling, amid the insulation. Oddly enough, the police stayed downstairs, so for the next half hour, Hank and Wylie sat among the bales, snorting lines of coke, as one of the most promising nights of their life was turning into one of the worst.

Eventually, Hank and Wylie surrendered to the inevitable and headed downstairs, where the cops took them to the floor and put them in cuffs next to Jack. Always a storyteller, Hank began to threaten the cops with his connections, a state senator he knew and a lawyer who would have their asses. Nonplussed, the cops led the trio outside to the street, where the eerily flashing blue lights of over a dozen police cruisers made the night feel even colder.

Hank, Wylie, and Jack were loaded into the back of the paddy wagon, and after a few moments of looking at nothing but the floor, they began to commiserate. The great riddle was the absence of Eddie, who unbeknownst to them, had escaped, albeit with a painfully broken ankle.

At the police station, the three men were put into a holding cell and left to ponder their fate. Jack and Hank's thoughts soon turned to the bag full of Percodan that was hidden in the suspended ceiling above the room containing the thousand-plus pounds of marijuana. They needed those Percs; without them, withdrawal symptoms would soon arrive. The rest of their problems, including the trafficking charges, they could deal with later.

A couple of hours had passed when one of the cops came by and said, "The bail bondsman will be here shortly. Your bail is set at fifteen dollars." He might as well have said that they just hit the lottery, as they all breathed a collective sigh of relief. When the cop left, they began to hypothesize. A bail of fifteen dollars could mean only one thing: the cops had not found the pot. Maybe the police decided to honor Jack's request for a warrant after all and didn't search the entire house.

Based on this assumption, Jack and Hank thought they still might escape what would certainly be serious drug-trafficking charges. All they had to do was make the fifteen-dollar bail, go back to the house on Saint Elmo Street, and burn the yet-to-be-discovered marijuana in the fireplace before the police arrived with a warrant. It may have been magical thinking. It may have been a refusal to face facts, or a desperate attempt to grasp at their last ray of hope. But it was all they had.

It was two in the morning when Jack, Hank, and Wylie arrived at the house, only to have their plan dashed: the pot was gone. The police had definitely found the marijuana and confiscated it, and now the three men were in serious trouble, not to mention out quite a few bucks. At least, the cops didn't find the Percodan or the cocaine hidden in the ceiling. Thank God for small favors.

Dark times lay ahead, and it was the perfect time to fortify themselves against what was to come. Hank and Jack immediately downed a handful of pills, and together, the trio finished the cocaine. They would need the courage for their morning court appearance and even more courage to face their families' disappointment when the front-page headline of the *Worcester Telegram* read: "Biggest Drug Bust in City's History."

For Jack, that headline in some convoluted way became a "red badge of courage," a coming-of-age for him as a drug trafficker, some twisted measure of his significance in the world. For Hank, it meant utter humiliation. His parents worked hard every day. No one in his immediate family had ever been arrested. He was just twenty-nine years old, and he was in serious legal trouble. The headlines had an even more detrimental effect on Hank and Jack's loved ones. The two men's families, especially their innocent mothers, Phyllis and Toni, were mortified. The mothers bore their suffering quietly and continued to display their undying love and untiring sacrifice for their children. It was the kind of pain Hank and Jack had put their families through before, but this time, it was magnified a hundredfold.

Jack's girlfriend, Sandi, and her family felt the pain, too. Sandi's mother was a schoolteacher and her father, a court officer. As they read the newspaper headline, the shock and embarrassment overwhelmed them. Hank's girlfriend, Eileen, steadfast and nonjudgmental in her Christian beliefs, simply stated, "We have to pray."

But some imagined that her family was praying, too—only not for Hank but for Eileen to come to her senses and leave this embarrassing relationship behind. The families' pain is just a microcosm of the shame and humiliation that millions of families of drug addicts endure. Families are often ill equipped to deal with the distressful circumstances they find themselves or their loved ones in, and a solution to these predicaments can be elusive. An addict is often the last to know or care about the precariousness of his or her situation; but oftentimes the family has to deal with the collateral consequences long before.

Despite this serious interruption, the party continued. Hank sank so deeply into the morass of opioid addiction that he could barely function. He spent most of his time maintaining his habit on the couch, while watching soap operas. Jack continued to sell drugs and hoped he would hit the big time. Finally, after nine months, their trial date arrived. During the legal proceedings that followed, Hank could always be heard to say, "We are good kids," and "Conti would never send me to jail because my mother licked stamps for his campaign."

Jack's high-profile defense team from Boston had promised, "Give us fifty thousand dollars and you'll walk," and the three conspirators did walk—but not in the right direction. Fed up with the defense team's delay tactics, the judge offered a stark choice: take a plea bargain for a two-year sentence, or take your chances on a trial and a possible ten-year sentence. Hank and Wylie accepted the deal immediately. Jack didn't want to go to jail, not even for one day, but Hank eventually convinced Jack to agree to the plea. They would be eligible for parole in one year.

Nine months after the bust, Hank, Wylie, and Jack stood naked in the house of corrections receiving room. Humiliated. Embarrassed. Degraded. Jack could not adequately convey in words the sense of hopelessness they all felt at that moment. And if that despair was not sufficient, Jack and Hank both knew the pains of withdrawal were just around the corner.

There is a jailhouse celebrity that comes with having your name on the front page of the local paper, an unwarranted notoriety that arrives before you do. You are that headline or newspaper article, no matter how sensational or inaccurate it was. As you'd expect, people's opinions of you differ depending on what side of the bars they were on. Despite all the notoriety, the first few weeks of incarceration were a horrendous adventure in culture shock. The dankness of the small cement cell, the clanging of the steel doors, the utter absence of modern civility. Gone were the comforts of home: a soft bed, a friendly voice, intimate nights with a girlfriend, the accustomed privacy of going to the bathroom. Despite the infamy of the label "big-time pot dealers," their real crime was loving to get high, and compared to the violence in their new environment, they were rather low on the food chain. This hierarchy was highlighted by the occupant of an adjacent cell, a martial arts master awaiting trial for beheading his wife with a samurai sword.

Added to the standard torment of incarceration were the withdrawal pains of a hundred-plus-milligram-a-day methadone habit. Nausea. Chills. Vomiting. Diarrhea. It was the superfecta of dope sickness. Those early days passed by excruciatingly and painfully slowly and were followed by long, restless nights with not a single moment of sleep. It was like living a demented version of Bill Murray's *Groundhog Day*. Somehow, Jack and Hank made it through, and they promised themselves they would never use again. Nothing was worth that much aggravation.

As time passed, an ability to cope with life behind bars began to materialize, albeit ever so slowly. A couple of things eased their transition. For one, they did have some influence inside; whether it was a relative or a friend of a friend, Jack and Hank managed to get cells of their own. On occasion, they were invited off the cell block for a home-cooked meal, compliments of a well-connected deputy. For another, the withdrawal from the methadone ended in about a month, and sleep gradually returned. Having enough energy to go to the correction center gym was a welcome relief. Wylie was spared the withdrawal pains, but he suffered instead the ignominy of being the only southerner in a very northern population. A Macon, Georgia, native, his heavy southern drawl alienated him from most of the population, but his association with Hank and Jack helped to minimize the teasing. Soon, the trio settled into the monotony of life in jail.

Everything in jail is repetitive; you could set a watch to the opening and closing of the cell doors, the changing of the guards, and the trips to the chow hall. Each day blended into the next.

This monotony was definitely not the best way to spend one's time on earth, nor was getting high every day. This realization slowly started to sink in, and Jack and Hank promised each other that once set free, they would control their addictions.

During that year of incarceration, the two friends met quite a cast of characters. The most memorable and intimidating was Nicky Femia. Nicky was the alleged shooter in the Blackfriars Club massacre, a Boston bar shooting in 1978 that left seven people dead. Nicky never openly admitted to the shootings, but he reveled in the notoriety. His penetrating, cold, black eyes sparkled whenever he was in Jack and Hank's presence. The Blackfriars murders were drug related, and although it wasn't funny then, Jack always thought that Nicky saw dollar signs whenever he looked at them. Hank said Nicky gave him the chills.

The time passed by quickly, in large part due to the furlough program that was part of the reunification and reentry process. Jack and Hank were poster boys for the program, nonviolent pot dealers with Catholic-school backgrounds and good community ties. At first, they were given furloughs to go home for Thanksgiving and Christmas, three- and four-day reprieves from the confines of the jail. After the New Year, they received weekend passes every month. The furloughs never posed a problem to the authorities or a danger to the public, but they did allow Jack and Hank the necessary freedom to rekindle their appetite for opiates. They honestly believed they could control themselves. At first, they would do one pill, but only one and only on special occasions. Then they bumped up to two. Eventually, "special occasions" became whenever they could get their hands on the drugs.

In a time of liberal thinking at the jail, Hank and Jack also served as pioneers—they were the first two inmates at the Worcester County House of Correction (WCHC) to be allowed to attend college from jail. Hank chose Quinsigamond Community College, and Jack went to Central New England College of Technology to finish his engineering degree. Teaching was pretty much out of the question after the marijuana bust, and it likely was a good idea to give up on marijuana dealing as well. On Monday through Friday, Hank and Jack left the jail at 8:00 a.m. to go to classes. They had to return by 4:00 p.m. They were treated pretty well, but pretty well wasn't well enough; Jack had to push the limits. One day, after Jack arranged to have twenty pounds of deep-fried chicken wings brought into the jail by one of the guards, the administration drew the line. Jack was packed up and shipped to Western Massachusetts House of Correction. No more school. No more furloughs. Just a twenty-four-hour lockdown in a place where Jack knew no one and no one knew him.

After a few months, Jack was sent back to the WCHC, where he joined Hank on a work-release program. At the time, the work-release program consisted of working in nearby industries doing mostly menial tasks, but it gave short-timers an opportunity to earn some money and break up the monotony of prison while preparing for life on the outside. Hank and Jack spent their nights working the third shift in a plastics factory. Packaging toys and other sundry items was not the most exciting way to pass the time, so just like little kids, they found themselves hiding behind boxes and reciting the lines from every jailbird's favorite movie, *Cool Hand Luke*.

"Just shaking the bush, boss." Hank would call out from behind a pallet of cardboard boxes.

"What we have here is…a failure to communicate" Jack would reply in his best southern accent.

On Jack's last day of incarceration, he walked outside to find Eddie, his ankle now healed, waiting patiently outside the gate next to a white stretch limousine. Eddie was a good friend and meant well. What Jack failed to realize was that stepping into that limousine was a step right back into the life he wanted—and desperately needed—to leave behind.

CHAPTER THIRTY FOUR

I t didn't take long for Jack to become drug dependent again and leave the woman who had waited patiently and faithfully for his release. Sandi's father, now a humiliated chief superior court officer, and her uncle, a public figure in the area, constantly reminded Jack of his failures. Not that they had to say anything. They didn't; in fact, their capacity for forgiveness and understanding puzzled Jack. Sandi's mother had the patience of saint, as most mothers with addicted sons and daughters do. In short, they were two of the nicest prospective in-laws one could ask for, but Jack couldn't bear the shame of being an ex-convict and the look of disappointment on their faces whenever he saw them. It was the coward's way out, but breaking his promise to Sandi and her family made the shame go away. More importantly, it allowed him the freedom to use. He didn't have to lie anymore, at least not to Sandi.

In the months following their release, the relationship between Hank and Jack, which was strengthened during their shared ordeal in prison, once again began to deteriorate as the stark realities of addiction pushed aside their youthful ideologies and the Street's code of loyalty among friends. Jack's dependence on cocaine and opiates was worse than ever, and Hank's reliance on opiates continued to drive him downward. Of course, this was the normal pathway for addicts. Addiction slowly takes everything once held sacred, including friendship.

The reality check of a year in jail left little doubt that the life of drug dealer was not all Jack had imagined it to be. Any glamour or celebrity disappears when the steel doors close behind you. Once free, Jack discovered another sad truth: there were not many opportunities for a convicted drug dealer to make an honest living and support a drug habit. You didn't see many ads in the paper that read, "Wanted: nodding, out-of-touch individual for a rewarding and well-paid career. Must have prison experience."

Since employment proved elusive, Jack decided to start a legitimate business of his own. Fortunately, he still had a sizable war chest of cash; he had not spent all of the profits from his drug-dealing days on attorneys. Hank's cousin, Billy, was a retired professional football player, and he had a great job at a fledgling sneaker company called Nike, which, by the early 1980s, controlled a huge chunk of the domestic sports footwear market. Billy, whose territory included the entire Northeast, was one of a handful of Nike sales representatives who had access to discontinued sneaker models and manufactured overruns for pennies on the dollar. Luck is often described as preparation meeting opportunity. Jack had the funds, and Billy had the goods, so it was with this good fortune that Jack bought hundreds of pairs of Nike sneakers and began to wholesale them to discount stores. He also opened a discount-clothing store, Gina Marie's, named after his daughter, and started to dream of going completely legit. As a father with a drug habit, Jack's parenting skills fit perfectly with the polarity of the addictive personality. He was either overindulgent or absent. There was no middle ground. His now pubescent daughter had plenty of clothes but none of Jack's time.

The dream of going legit would take time to realize, as the demands of addiction would constantly require Jack's involvement in the drug trade. If Jack learned anything from the marijuana bust, it was that pot was too bulky, and since Jack now spent most of his nights awake snorting cocaine, he now found himself inextricably immersed in the more addictive and sometimes violent world of cocaine trafficking.

It was the antithesis of what Jack inwardly yearned for. He partied with rock-and-roll headliners courtesy of the backstage passes supplied by the Centrum's sound manager, a friend who shared Jack's affinity for cocaine, and masked his despair and hopelessness with fur coats, fast cars, and drug-seeking women. That was the dichotomy of his life. After a night of doing lines and partying with the rich and famous, Jack would find himself utterly alone, driving home in anguish, the pain of living so burdensome that thoughts of driving off a bridge or into a stone wall appeared to be the only solution to his agony.

Call it cowardice, call it fate, but ending his life was not in the cards for Jack. What continued was the roller-coaster ride of highs and lows with the BB King blues song "The Thrill Is Gone" constantly playing in the background.

According to statistics, most businesses fail within the first five years, and running a business while trying to support a drug habit assured that Jack's new ventures would fall into that "most" category. In an effort to keep the clothing business afloat, Jack joined forces with a degenerate Brooklyn gambler named Burt, who worked as a jobber or wholesaler of clothes.

The pairing of a drug addict and a gambling addict seemed extremely unlikely. Still, a close friendship developed. Burt soon became a father figure to Jack. And Jack, probably in large part because of his financial resources and/or his ability to generate money quickly, presented an opportunity for Burt to expand his business. Burt's obsession with money and gambling drove his business decisions; Jack's addiction to drugs influenced his. Jack willingly provided large sums of cash to fuel business expansion and keep alive his hope of leaving drug dealing behind.

In 1984, Jack's cash helped to finance the wedding of Burt's daughter at a Brooklyn temple. Burt may have had a serious gambling problem, but he was devoted to his daughter and would do anything to make her happy. The guest list included every notable organized crime figure in New York. The reception featured violinists playing at the tables and Smokey Robinson and the Miracles as the wedding band. The flowers alone (for which Jack footed the bill) cost a small fortune. It seemed to Jack that Burt must have watched *The Godfather* movies a number of times, as well. It was a fitting occasion for a young woman who, today, is a dedicated justice for upholding the law, an irony not lost on Jack.

In New York during the early eighties, Jack's access to money and Burt's connections enabled the two to grow their business rapidly. Burt's association with organized crime gave them direct access to the most fashionable manufacturers, and for a small arrangement fee, they soon became the primary buyer for Gloria Vanderbilt and Calvin Klein closeouts. They leased a warehouse in Staten Island, called themselves Progressive Distributors, and started shipping their cheaply bought clothing to secondary retail outlets across the East Coast. For a time, if you purchased a pair of designer jeans for less than twenty dollars anywhere on the East Coast, Progressive probably shipped them.

For Jack, this was a big step toward legitimacy. As vice president of Progressive, he finally put his education to use, implementing one of the early computerized inventory-control systems. He moved into a condominium on Amboy Road in Staten Island, stopped selling drugs, and tried to maintain a semblance of normalcy. Unfortunately, the one thing that hadn't changed was his reliance on drugs. Although Jack tried to stop or at least reduce his dependence on opiates, he still had seven hundred to eight hundred milligrams of methadone delivered every week by an addict from one of those opiate treatment clinics on Twenty-Third Street in New York. But soon, his addiction and criminal past would catch up with him.

In Progressive Distributors' heyday, they shipped over a million dollars of clothing a month. A business practice known as factoring made this possible. The clothing business operated on credit: everything was net thirty, net forty-five, or even net ninety days, a grace period for payment so to speak. In order to keep cash flowing, Progressive sold its accounts receivable to a lending company commonly known as a factor; in their case, it was Rosenthal and Rosenthal. R&R bought the receivables, paid Progressive the cash it needed to continue operations, and charged a fee for doing so.

In a few short months, Progressive had several million dollars of Rosenthal and Rosenthal money invested in both purchases and receivables. Business was booming. Burt was putting all the profits into expansion. He bought failing businesses, a risky endeavor to be sure, but Burt's obsession with gambling was fueled by the thrill of a risk and the potential of a big payoff. Jack's addiction and his desire to be done with drug dealing clouded his judgment, too. Drug addled and desperate for a big score that would render him legit, Jack foolishly invested in a gold mine in Africa (or, at least, the rights to it), falling victim to a simple con.

Success had gone to their heads, and their spendthrift behavior got the attention of others. At the zenith of Progressives' success, Rosenthal and Rosenthal abruptly and without warning pulled the plug on all financing and demanded the immediate return of all funds outstanding. Someone had leaked information relating to Burt and Jack's criminal histories to the executives at Rosenthal and Rosenthal. This information instantly damaged any trust that had been built and ended their business relationship.

With no money coming in, Progressive could not purchase the new merchandise necessary to sustain operations. Jack and Burt were stuck with several hundred thousand dollars in out-of-season clothing that no one wanted to buy, and their business came to a screeching halt. Their failure to save any money, an inconceivable thought for a degenerate gambler and a dope fiend, landed both of them in a familiar position. They owed money everywhere, including to people who did not recognize a bankruptcy filing or easily forgive a debt.

As if owing money to John Gotti and his crew was not trouble enough, a federal indictment for marijuana smuggling arrived on Jack's doorstep. Arnie Katz and Jack had moved some large loads of pot for mobster Salvatore Michael "Sonny" Caruana. With Arnie opting for the witness protection program instead of thirty years in federal prison, Jack found himself on a long list of coconspirators charged with bringing over sixty tons of marijuana into New England during the late seventies—an operation so audacious and sophisticated that a state trooper had been arrested for escorting the marijuana-laden tractor trailers on their interstate voyage from the loading dock.

Despite the indictment, Jack now needed money. In a short time, he found himself dealing once again, and the line from *The Godfather,* "Just when I thought I was out...they pull me back in," had new relevance in his life. The guys back home on Shrewsbury Street—or what was left of them—were happy to hear that Jack was back in business. This meant more opportunities to earn money and, more importantly, more opportunities to get high. With their lives increasingly defined by the lows, it was something they desperately needed.

Drugs had really taken a toll on the residents of the Street. The camaraderie had vanished, leaving pathetic desperation behind. Most were shooting dope, the Street term for injecting heroin intravenously. Some were using methadone, and a few had already experienced long stints behind bars. A few had put an end to their addictions forever with fatal overdoses.

Kid Paz had once again been admitted to Worcester State Hospital, the old nuthouse on the hill in the East Side, hoping that this time would be the last. Joey was in jail, probably for the fourth time, each stay longer than the last one. This time, he had OD'd and woke up behind bars; the cops had not bothered to take him to the hospital, figuring his death would cross one irritant off their list. Fudgy and Dumbo had stopped singing a cappella and were scrounging for money anywhere they could to score that next bag and keep the pangs of withdrawal at bay. Ship and Riley couldn't seem to maintain their drug supply and had turned to massive quantities of alcohol and street violence to take the edge off. The gang that hung around Paul Mac's, the little diner across the street from East Park, had disappeared, mostly into the alleys and the shadows of the city's drug spots, where hustle and predatory behavior were necessary for survival.

One player, however, had found his way out. Hank, now in his midthirties, a staunch holdout who had never before attempted treatment, had admitted himself to Dorchester Detoxification Unit. It was a new low, even for a Shrewsbury Street junkie. Simply put, he had run out of game. He'd spent way too many hours on the couch in his mother's house so dope sick that the restless leg syndrome that accompanied his opiate withdrawal had led him to scrape all the hair off his legs.

Located in an African American neighborhood in Boston, Dorchester Detox was definitely not for the rich and famous. Foremost on his mind was getting methadone to make the dope sickness go away. But Hank was never that lucky. Since he hadn't used for two days, the detox staff thought methadone would be a step in the wrong direction, and they declined to prescribe what he was looking for.

Psychologically, Hank was already headed toward the door but before he could figure out how to get home, an older street smart black man arrived on the scene.

"You can go if you want," said T-Baby who once pitched professionally during the twilight of Negro Major Leagues. "But before you do, can we talk for a minute?"

What followed was the conversation that saved Hank's life. Speaking honestly from the heart, with a nonjudgmental attitude, the man convinced Hank to commit to a new life, if only for one day. The day turned into two, then five, then a full week. After a couple of weeks, Hank finally listened to the advice his little Italian grandmother had often given him - to wash his brains the ocean.

The brain is so complicated that it boggles its own imagination.

—Charles Sherrington

Where do we begin trying to explain the damage that years of abuse do to an addict's brain? Drugs set off a chemical process in the brain in which the natural "feel-good" chemicals (neurotransmitters) that our bodies produce begin firing, making a person feel euphoric or high. Continuing this process depletes the supply of these chemicals and leaves the body unable to keep up with the demand. It also leaves the addict craving the intense feelings that these chemicals produce.

Recovery is a process of replenishing and resetting the brain chemistry after it has become accustomed to this unnatural pattern. This phase of recovery often includes examining sleep, diet, exercise, and other daily habits related to biological functions. It is important to note that this resetting does not happen quickly. It takes time for a person's system to get used to having these substances in it and longer still to get used to being without them.

Coping with the cravings that come as part of this resetting of the brain can be intolerable, which eventually drives many addicts to relapse. One of the benefits of having a support system in place for recovering addicts, where individuals honestly share their struggles and distress, is that, through their sharing, addicts can identify with others who are going through or have gone through the same experience. There is tremendous value in knowing that you are not the first person to go through this and that people do survive. It might not reduce the physical discomfort, but it helps to offset the psychological trauma with a powerful antidote: hope.

CHAPTER THIRTY FIVE

Progressive's financial difficulties in New York had landed Burt between a rock and a hard place, precipitating a slow descent into a hell that Jack, fortunately, was spared. Burt's debts compelled him to deal in marijuana and to engage in even dirtier work—hiring crooked New York police detectives to perform hits for the Luchese crime family, including one case of mistaken identity in which an innocent man was murdered. Sentenced to eighteen years for marijuana dealing, Burt agreed to testify against the detectives, but his testimony gained him little; he got his freedom in 2006 and died in 2009 of prostate cancer. You can read his story in one of the many Jimmy Breslin gangster books.

At thirty-six years old, Jack found himself on three years' special probation with the feds; the 1984 conviction for his involvement with the Caruana smuggling ring did not land him in jail, as the judge took into account the 1982 release from the WCHC and leniently gave him a second chance. Unfortunately for Jack, he failed to take advantage of this opportunity. Biweekly urine checks did nothing to deter him from continuing to get high. Even the threat of another incarceration couldn't compete with the obsession to use and the discomfort of withdrawal. Thinking it was his destiny to live and die as a drug addict, Jack spent considerable time and effort concocting devices and deceptions to avoid "dirty urine" detection. It worked for a while—or so he thought.

It was 1985 and in the East Side of Worcester, Jack's return did not go unnoticed. In his infinite wisdom or ignorance—take your pick—he had purchased a brand-new Jaguar XJS, which, while living in New York City, was no big deal. But on Shrewsbury Street, it stood out like a sore thumb. Years later, Ship would tell Jack the story about how the residents of Jack's old neighborhood viewed his return. Ship was standing on a corner in the neighborhood in which they both grew up when Jack drove by in his Jag. A little kid stared in awe as the car slid past. "Wow," he said. "There goes that drug dealer."

Despite the neon sign that was visible to everyone but him, Jack continued to believe that nobody knew he had a drug problem and, more importantly, that no one, especially the police, had any idea he was dealing drugs. Denial, it can be said, is a wonderful thing.

Jack inwardly wished for the day he could go straight, and he constantly worked toward that end. His next hope for salvation and respectability was the creation of a computerized athletic recruiting service. This great idea was spawned during a conversation with a former college coach on a plane trip. The coach explained the fierce competition and the need in college recruiting for large amounts of pertinent information.

In late 1985, with the help of some of the neighborhood guys, Jack started the National Collegiate Athletic Information Service, or NCAIS Inc. The business model was based on a new wrinkle in athletic recruiting prompted by an NCAA regulation called Prop 48, which stipulated that student-athletes must maintain a minimum high school grade point average and attain a minimum score on standardized tests in order to participate in freshman college athletic competition. This introduction of scholastic achievement to a system that had previously focused solely on athletic ability created a multifaceted demand for information. Before the Internet exploded in popularity, that information was extremely hard to come by. Imagine the advantages of being a college recruiter and having a list of all of the six foot five, 250-pound right tackles who run a 4.45 in the forty-yard dash and have a minimum 900 SAT score in the entire country at your fingertips. Pretty impressive, or at least that was Jack's theory. Unfortunately, as always, his addiction would be a serious obstacle to business success.

In an unusual moment of clarity, Jack used some good judgment in selecting his business partners. A few guys on the Street had managed to escape the ravages of drugs. They comprised the governing board of NCAIS Inc. The concept had great potential, but the business would be sidetracked by Jack's addiction and never reach its full potential. Jack's high profile and his deep need for drugs put him in the sights of local law enforcement, and it wasn't long before he found himself back in jail doing a thirty-day stint for possession of methadone.

Methadone was a perfect complement to cocaine, as its extended half-life enabled it to ameliorate unwanted cravings when the more ephemeral cocaine high abated.

By summer 1986, the drugs and the booze were proving to be too much a burden when combined with the cash flow required to employ eight people. This meant more drug dealing and more stupid decisions.

Jack's day always started with drugs. The drug du jour was a hundred milligrams of methadone and a few lines of cocaine. This daily routine was interrupted by a visit from Hank, who was now living in Rockport and had been clean for six months. It was good to see Hank when drugs were not in the way. There was a connection, a familiarity, that truly did make them brothers-in-arms. They had been through so much together. After some brief reminiscing about the good old days, Hank suggested that they visit his grandmother, who was in the hospital. Jack agreed, and the two set out in the Jag.

As they rolled through the streets of Worcester, Hank grew edgy. He didn't like what he saw turning the corner behind them.

"Jack," Hank said, "there's an unmarked cruiser following us."

High and blissfully unaware, Jack laughed it off. "Man, since you've got clean you are paranoid!"

Just then, the blue lights of the unmarked detective's car went on.

Hank's emotions immediately shot from worry to outright panic. He turned to Jack. "You got anything in the car?" he asked.

"No," Jack lied, trying to spare Hank additional alarm.

But Hank knew the truth. A drug addict always carried drugs, and this time was no exception.

Jack waited for the undercover cop to get out of his car. "What's wrong, officer?" Jack queried, as the cop approached the driver's side window, hand on his weapon.

"Get the fuck out of the car," the cop demanded unceremoniously.

This was going to be a drug bust, and the cop was hoping it would be a big one. An informant had tipped off the police that Jack had kilos of cocaine in his apartment, and the police were waiting for the right moment. The cops figured that the combination of Hank and Jack was the final piece to the puzzle. Two arrests would be even better than one.

To the cops' dismay, a search of the Jag turned up nothing illegal. Luckily for Hank, they failed to search thoroughly enough: Jack's small vial of cocaine was hidden well, or they would have found enough coke to implicate Hank. Jack, too, breathed a sigh of relief. He really didn't want Hank to suffer the consequences for his own foolishness.

After a few hours of questioning, the police realized that Hank was not a key player in Jack's dealing operation and released him. Hank was fortunate. He escaped charges and jail time. His only penance for his loyalty to an old friend was a few hours of detention and questioning about his association with Jack, who, by this time, had become a person of interest for nearly every branch of law enforcement. Upon his release from custody, Hank returned to Rockport and stayed there for several years, yet his support for Jack never slackened, nor did his yearning to return home. Hank's first clean visit to Shrewsbury Street was not his last, but his unusually good fortune that day doubly reinforced his determination to stay clean.

Jack was not so lucky. Continuing to act upon the information given to them, the police accompanied Jack back to his apartment, where they conducted a thorough search. Keeping drugs in your home was never a good idea, especially a quantity that could land you a fifteen- to thirty-year sentence. Jack had graduated from college, but he still wasn't smart enough to learn the life lessons required for a drug-free life. There is a section in the Narcotics Anonymous *Basic Text* that attempts to answer the question, "Who is an addict?" In part, it says, "Our whole life and thinking is centered on drugs in one form or another, the getting and using, and finding ways and means to get more." That describes the mind-set perfectly. If Jack was using—and he was—then he simply had to have drugs around at all times to avoid withdrawal.

After hours of ripping the place apart, the police were disappointed not to find several kilos of cocaine, but they did manage to charge Jack with possession of methadone with intent to distribute after finding a bottle of methadone in a bureau drawer.

This arrest prompted Jack's federal probation officer to suggest strongly that he go into treatment. He was courteous enough to arrange Jack's admission into Spectrum Primary Detox, which was housed on the grounds of the Worcester State Hospital Insane

Asylum, an appropriate setting. That stay lasted one day. Jack was thrown out for suspicion of using. The reality was that Jack loaded up on cocaine and methadone for three days prior to going, and it was a miracle that he didn't OD. Not wanting to send Jack back to jail for violating probation for drug use alone, the probation officer waited until Jack's charges were adjudicated before making a recommendation.

The resulting one-month sentence was long enough to thoroughly disrupt the collegiate recruiting business but not long enough to break Jack's addictive obsession for drugs. In fact, because Jack was housed in a low-security section of the jail, he arranged to have drugs smuggled in to him for most of his stay. This staved off the worst of the withdrawal symptoms until he was released, when he once again returned to the East Side, a place where drugs flowed freely and trouble was just around the corner.

The trouble around the corner came in the form of another violation of the special parole Jack had received in federal court. There is a moral to this story. With the divergent paths that Hank and Jack were on, the outcome should have been obvious. Hank, still clean, went back to Rockport to continue his recovery. But Jack, still using, went back to jail again.

CHAPTER THIRTY SIX

As JD and his girlfriend, Gail, pulled up to the drop-off zone for departing flights at McCarran Airport in Las Vegas in her little silver Toyota Corolla, JD rambled through his tired rap about having to go home to help his sister. Soon, he said, he would be back, and they could straighten out their relationship. But the air in the car that cloudy and cool afternoon was thick with unspoken feelings of loss, sadness, anger, and fear. Neither was able to face a truth they both recognized: it was clearly the end of the road for their relationship. The fatal blow had come months before, when JD had stumbled home drunk and high one night to discover Gail in bed with another guy. Not that their relationship was anything to write home about before the cheating, but things worsened afterward, spiraling into more drug- and alcohol-fueled episodes of madness and abuse as they struggled to repair the damage to their relationship.

In fact, the relationship couldn't be saved. It had arisen out of their mutual dependence on drugs. It resembled a business arrangement more than a romantic relationship, and it included little opportunity for mutual love and support. Gail made good money serving cocktails in a busy casino, and they both depended on it to survive. JD used that money to secure Percodans from Honest Fred and Roger, two reliable dealers. The men obtained the drugs from doctors due to their medical conditions and sold them for quite a profit to JD, who delivered them to Gail at work—after consuming his fair share, of course.

As Gail and JD sat at the airport, playing out their sick and twisted version of the farewell scene from *Casablanca*, they really had nothing left to say other than good-bye. Like any good addict in an emotional situation, JD focused on the most critical factor. Just how quickly, he wondered, would they be serving drinks on the plane? He desperately needed a Dewar's scotch—actually, many of them—to fortify the last of the Percodan he had ingested, which would wear off in a few short hours.

Aboard the plane and medicated with the drugs and liquor, JD lapsed in and out of a fitful sleep as he anxiously pondered what the next chapter of his life held in store. He felt failure and shame but also relief; he had finally escaped the madness he'd been living for nine years while working as a bartender and casino dealer in Vegas. The last few years had comprised a hellish, unstoppable descent.

Through the haze of the liquor and the remnants of the Percodan buzz, JD heard the flight attendant talking about preparing to land in Boston, where his family was waiting to take him home. As the 727 touched down at Logan Airport, he tried his best to pull himself together so they wouldn't see the shattered and empty being he had become. Putting on his best game face, he shambled into the arrivals area, looking around for someone he knew.

"Jimmy! Jimmy!"

From forty feet away, JD saw his mother, waving frantically, a broad smile on her face. In that moment, he needed nothing more than a soft place to land, and Mom had always provided that for him, regardless of what shape he was in or what her circumstances were. He walked toward her quickly and then broke into an unsteady run. As she threw her arms around him and squeezed, he felt a comfort and a hope that he hadn't experienced in what seemed like a lifetime. Though still at the airport, he was home.

Unfortunately, those feelings didn't last long. It was hard to keep the madness of addiction at bay. Homecoming or not, the beast must be fed. The novelty of being on the East Side again after nine years, of seeing friends and family, wore off quickly. Reality set in.

JD had escaped Vegas, but not his demons. He needed to move forward in his life, but doing so while managing his addiction wasn't easy. Shortly after his return, JD started to hang out with a group of guys next door, mostly married, working fathers who rewarded themselves at day's end with a few beers and a bong or two as they talked shop. But a beer and a bong didn't do the trick for an opiate addict. He found himself once again hanging out with the crowd using the more powerful and addictive substances. If he didn't get a change of scenery—and fast—he would be doomed forever.

JD's life choices had seriously narrowed his options, so he grabbed the easiest one available: working with his sister, Fran. She had just made a deal to take over the food concession at Scarborough Downs, a rundown horse track in the boondocks of Maine, and needed help with the operation. JD figured it was a good way to put some distance between himself and the drug scene on the East Side. It might even be a chance to get healthy.

Sadly, within hours of his arrival in Scarborough, JD knew that it would be a short-term gig. When he agreed to go to Maine, he had no idea what he was getting into. He had gone from the glitter and glitz of the Vegas lifestyle to bunking like a ranch hand in an outpost far from civilization. It was summertime, so it was detestably hot and humid, and the smelly horseshit from over-the-hill racehorses created a fly haven.

JD had been spoiled in Vegas, where everything was air-conditioned, even substandard apartments, so he struggled to adapt to the brutal New England heat and humidity. What made it even worse were the pains of withdrawal from the drugs he was running away from, and alcohol just couldn't take that sickness away. Each night, he went to sleep asking himself, "What the hell are you doing in this place?" Each morning, he woke up wrestling with his addiction, trying to figure a way out of the mess he was in.

Within days, JD was concocting schemes and stealing money to get the drugs he needed to cope. He even borrowed his sister's car while she was at work and made a four-hour round-trip to Worcester to score some heroin. Clearly, the geographical cure wasn't working.

Fran knew that her brother was stealing from her and in trouble again. When JD fabricated a story about wanting to return to Worcester to help their dad run his business, Fran didn't try to stop him. She even provided the money for his transportation home. Together, they just accepted that yet another attempt to salvage the train wreck that was JD's life had failed. Bolstered by alcohol and anything else he could find, he boarded a Greyhound bus and headed back to Worcester in defeat.

Back at his mom's house once again, JD quickly settled into a pattern: sleeping on the couch, consuming any alcohol he found in the house, borrowing the car to chase down drugs, and sinking deeper into despair and self-loathing. Belligerent and more miserable than ever, he needed increasing doses of heroin and alcohol to keep himself sane. The more his mom tried to help him become responsible, the more he behaved like a wounded animal, striking out or recoiling into isolation, pushing everything out of his life that required him to show up and be involved. He reduced himself to a short series of repeated actions: finding the means to get alcohol and drugs, ingesting them, and passing out.

For a while, JD worked at his dad's diner, washing dishes and slinging hash throughout breakfast and lunch. He worked from 6:00 a.m. to 3:00 p.m. through the summer, but the heat and humidity coupled with the smell of the place and exhausting drudgery made each shift feel like an eternity. Coming face-to-face with Muggsy was no picnic either, and JD dreaded the encounter each morning, but he knew he had to do the work he hated just to be able to afford the drugs he so desperately needed. The fact that this insane daily ritual was played out in front of his family and others who knew him only made the emotional burden heavier. In addition, his pay was too low to keep pace with his appetite for drugs, and inevitably, he resorted to stealing from his family.

Even loving parents' ability to tolerate bullshit reaches a limit, especially when they're watching a loved one self-destruct before their eyes. JD's parents hoped against all evidence to the contrary that they were witnessing a bad phase that their son would soon shake himself out of. When it became evident that it was more than a phase, they offered him help. But they couldn't get through his denial. Even when the evidence of his addiction and the stealing he did to support it was overwhelming, he refused to admit the truth. He fabricated unbelievable stories in an attempt to exonerate himself.

His father's breaking point came quickly. One afternoon, JD took advantage of some down time at the diner to visit a dealer's apartment across the street and score some drugs, which he immediately ingested. On his way back to work, he stopped at the convenience store run by Muggsy's friend Guy. While waiting in line to pay for his cigarettes, JD passed out and had to be rushed to the hospital by ambulance. Of course, Guy told Muggsy about JD's episode in the store. But when his dad confronted him, JD denied it.

"That wasn't me," JD said. "Guy must have confused me with someone else."

At that point, JD wasn't capable of being honest about anything, and after a number of similar incidents, Muggsy fired him.

Still, JD wasn't ready to give up his addiction. It got so bad that when JD walked into the restaurant, the staff would lock up all the money so he wouldn't have access to it. Everyone who knew him understood the truth: he was running on empty, and if he didn't get help soon, he would be dead.

Sinking fast and desperate, JD tried to con those he knew, because he knew their daily routines and counted on them being lenient with him when they found out. After being fired from the restaurant, JD picked up some work helping his cousin, Joe, install flooring. Tortured by withdrawal, JD would work a day, or as much of one as he could stand, and then haunt Joe's wife, Judy, to pay him immediately. He played the couple shamelessly, conjuring any kind of story he could think of to rouse their sympathies and get his cash. And when they wouldn't accommodate his desperation, he robbed them. His addiction never let him once consider how hard they worked for their money, how fair they were, or how much they cared about him. And they weren't the only caring people he screwed over.

Supporting an addiction takes creativity, spontaneity, lack of conscience, and money. Lots of money. By now, it was all a filthy blur.

One day while Joe was at work, JD took Joe's truck, along with his house keys, and drove to the house. He quickly ransacked it for valuables, including a coin collection that Joe and Judy had started for their son, Joe Jr. After bartering the stolen goods into drugs, JD returned to work alongside Joe as if nothing had happened. Joe and Judy knew it was JD who had robbed them, but they couldn't prove it, so they continued to hope that they were mistaken.

Eventually, when he was in recovery, JD would repay Joe and Judy and make amends for his behavior. But the shame and guilt of stealing the coin collection has never gone away.

The end was near for JD, and he knew it. He was like a caged animal, smashing against the bars in a futile attempt to escape. By then he was pawning anything and everything he could get his hands on, whether it was his or someone else's. His daily routine had narrowed down to scraping up enough cash to get drugs, and if he couldn't do that, guzzling as much cheap booze as he could afford. He would wake up at night in alcohol-withdrawal psychosis, having violent arguments with imaginary people, and unable to differentiate his mom's living room from the bathroom, scaring her tremendously. She watched helplessly as her baby, now thirty-one years old, sank into a tormented, twisted, and painful night-mare. She didn't want to give up on her son, but she could only take so much abuse. When she confronted him about his behavior, he threw a beer bottle at her, cursing wildly. Later, she discovered that he'd pawned a ring she'd had custom-made for him and that had deep sentimental value. After trying as hard as she could for as long as she could, she made the agonizing decision that many parents of addicted children have made.

"Jimmy," she said, "I got no choice. You can't stay here anymore. I want you out."

This represented the last straw for JD as well. He was now fully exposed, homeless, and broken, ready to run as he always had, but with absolutely no place left to go. He was utterly alone, full of shame and guilt about the person he had become and the things he had done. With no way left to soothe his pain, his only remaining option was surrender.

Self-awareness and empathy are (along with self-mastery and social skills) domains of human ability essential for success in life. Excellence in these capacities helps people flourish in relationships, family life, and marriage as well as in work and leadership.

—Daniel Goleman

As our story unfolds and our experience with recovery deepens, we see an undeniable value in belonging. Whether it is to a church group, a recovery community, a social vocation, or simply dedication to family, the neurologically hardwired drive for companionship plays a major role in stabilizing brain chemistry. However, this social nurturing can be a double-edged sword, since misguided influences can allow dysfunction to thrive.

Fortunately for the authors, those same influences helped to bring about change. They found ways to encourage and support one another through difficult times. They could always find something to laugh about (usually themselves) even in their despair, which proved to be quite therapeutic. There were times when they literally held one another up; they were truly brothers-in-arms. Love is powerful, and social bonds are vital to our mental health and well-being.

Again, the authors find themselves emphasizing the healing power of being connected to others. They were fortunate to have one another to lean on as they tried to understand and come to terms with their addictions and recoveries and worked to develop healthy lifestyle routines. They had each other. They were an active group. They enjoyed being together. They miss those days when life seemed simpler—or at least their lives weren't as busy and full as they are today.

CHAPTER THIRTY SEVEN

In 1985, at age thirty-three, JD finally entered treatment. After a short and hellish detox, he figured he was cured, and he intended to head back to Vegas or Florida, where the action was. The problem with that magical thinking was that he didn't have any action going on anywhere. He was played out and had nowhere to go. JD's counselor, Paul M., realized that his client wasn't ready to live on his own. He suggested that JD go to a halfway house called Project Cope in Lynn, Massachusetts, to start to rebuild his life. For once, JD listened.

Things got off to a rocky start at the halfway house. Discharged from detox a day before his scheduled interview at the halfway house, he spent the night at his mom's house. One condition of his acceptance into Project Cope for a one-year commitment was that he arrive "clean." At the start of his interview, one of the intake staff asked if he had used anything.

"Sure," he said. "I had a six-pack last night. That's it."

The intake worker wasn't happy with that response and let him know it.

"You said to be clean, and I didn't use any drugs," JD said in disbelief. For once, he wasn't trying to bullshit. He really didn't have a clue about addiction. He never considered drinking to be a problem, and at that time, he had no intention of stopping.

Despite the difficult interview, JD gained admission, and for the next ten and a half months, he made his home at Project Cope. There, he learned about addiction and recovery, immersed himself in a self-help support network, and managed to remain abstinent for the longest time since he began using drugs twenty years before.

JD's eyes began to open. He'd known that he was in trouble with drugs, but he denied the extent of it. It's hard to experience withdrawal and the insane cravings and not realize its power over you, but denial allows an addict to continue using in spite of the negative consequences. For a long time, JD had believed that if he could just shake his opiate habit, his life would be fine. He really didn't get it—but then, he had never been in any kind of treatment before.

One person who broadened JD's perspective was a fellow addict named Earle. Earle gave him a copy of the Alcoholics Anonymous *Big Book* to read. Having plenty of time, JD read it. Astonishingly, he identified with pretty much everything in the book.

One morning, he looked at Earle across the breakfast table.

"You know," JD said, "I think I might be an alcoholic, too."

Earle responded with a smile that said everything. For JD, that moment was huge. He had never seen his addiction so clearly. Now it was beginning to make sense. The veil of denial had been removed.

This awareness spurred a new determination to change once and for all. With the support of his counselors and fellow residents, JD even decided to quit smoking cigarettes, a habit he had acquired when he was about twelve. He managed to do so in part by acquiring a new but healthier habit—jogging. At first, his tar-damaged lungs rebelled vigorously against the new activity. He could barely sustain a slow jog for any distance. But after a few months of practice, he was able to run longer and with less difficulty breathing. He even competed in some short races. Cigarettes became one more element of his past.

For almost a full year, JD stayed drug and alcohol free. During that time, he learned a lot about himself, his addiction, and recovery while in the safe, well-monitored environment of a therapeutic community. But he hadn't surrendered completely, and just a month before his "graduation," his inability to curb his impulses once again got him into trouble. Intimate relationships between residents were against the rules, and when JD and a female resident became involved, he was terminated from the program. He couldn't see his behavior as being part of his addiction or his need to soothe his distress yet; that would come in the years ahead. Having nowhere to go and no means to get there, he ended up back at his mother's house, one of the few places he was welcome, and the only place he could stay for free.

Full of fear and as shaky as a newborn foal, JD tried to seek out self-help meetings to attend. He feared going to meetings close to home, where he would be recognized, and considered himself above the crowd that made its way to meetings on the East Side. So he found meetings out of town and went to them instead. After all, he thought, it was the twelve steps that mattered, not his connection to the people who sat beside him in the meetings. He slipped into meetings, made few connections, and headed back to Worcester as soon as they ended.

Given his lack of connection and support, JD soon found his old demons baying at the door. He had been clean for a year, but the bigger picture—his fears, his low self-esteem, his shame—hadn't changed as much as he'd thought. After a week, he headed into the old neighborhood to score a bag of dope.

Sitting in his mother's driveway, the car idling, and the dope cooked and ready, JD prepared himself for the sweetness of a long-delayed high. But when he pushed the plunger and the dope entered his veins, he felt the opposite: guilt, despair, shame, and self-hatred. Within minutes, it became simply unbearable. Perhaps it was the year of abstinence, the perceived freedom from his addiction, or all the recovery talk he had heard. He knew he needed to get help or die, and he could only think of one place to find it. Tossing the syringe aside, he put the car in gear.

Located just a couple of miles from his mother's house, Dinny's Tavern was the kind of neighborhood bar that JD had often patronized. This time, he wasn't in search of a buzz; he was looking for someone who might have an answer. His friend Eunice miraculously had been able to stop drinking and using drugs while working as a bartender. If she could do it, JD thought, maybe she could help him do it, too.

God works through people, and in this case, he worked through Eunice. She and JD had been friends since high school, and she listened without judgment as he cried his heart out. He told her about everything: his terrible feelings of inadequacy, his desperate need to make them go away, and the wrongs he had done. And when he was finished, she looked at him clearly and spoke without hesitation.

"Jimmy, there's only one thing you can do about this. Get your ass to a meeting."

At first, he begged God to offer him any solution besides dragging himself into a smoke-filled room full of people he viewed as inferior. The lack of an answer from above became his answer: there was no other choice left.

Not surprisingly, once JD surrendered completely to his addiction, things once again began to change for the better. The hometown AA and NA meetings not only served as a place for self-help and recovery but a place to forge connections with old friends who were walking the same road. Among the first people JD connected with was Kid Paz, who had just gotten out of treatment and was starting to attend meetings too. There were others, as well: Al R., Paul K., Dave B.—people he had known for years who were already actively involved in meetings in his area. Their presence did more than ease his anxiety about what he was experiencing. It gave him an example to live up to, which inspired and motivated him immensely. It was the first ray of hope he had felt in a long time.

For JD, one of the most empowering experiences of this period was hearing the Twelve Promises of Alcoholics Anonymous for the first time. Here is what JD (and all alcoholics) are promised, if only they are willing to trust and have faith in something greater than themselves:

> *If we are painstaking about this phase of our development, we will be amazed before we are halfway through. We are going to know a new freedom and a new happiness. We will not regret the past nor wish to shut the door on it. We will comprehend the word serenity and we will know peace. No matter how far down the scale we have gone, we will see how our experience can benefit others. That feeling of uselessness and self-pity will disappear. We will lose interest in selfish things and gain interest in our fellows. Self-seeking will slip away. Our whole attitude and outlook on life will change. Fear of people and economic insecurity will leave us. We will intuitively know how to handle situations which used to baffle us. We will suddenly realize that God is doing for us what we could not do for ourselves.* (AA *Big Book*, pages 83–84.)

Hearing these promises read aloud brought JD to tears, and at the same time, it gave him the hope he needed to push forward. The promises not only described his struggles but a way out of his madness too, if he could only believe in them. Thankfully, he did.

CHAPTER THIRTY EIGHT

S hortly after being convicted and serving his thirty-day sentence for possession of methadone, Jack, on the recommendation of his parole officer, was sentenced to report to the Federal Correctional Institute at Loretto, a minimum-security prison camp located in the hills of Pennsylvania overlooking the DuPont family mansion, for an eleven-month stay. It was late in the fall of 1986, and Jack prepared for his loss of freedom and involuntary confinement in the Pennsylvania countryside by flying to Atlantic City for one last weekend of nonstop partying. He then chartered a small private plane to deliver him to his "vacation destination."

Jack had planned ahead (insufficiently, as usual) for his stay at Loretto by packing the tongues of his sneakers with as many Dolophine as he could reasonably conceal, hoping they would minimize the excruciating discomfort that would accompany his involuntary withdrawal from a hundred-milligram-a-day methadone habit.

Jail or no jail, the concept of taking an opiate medication only as prescribed is an oxymoron for any addict. Once incarcerated, the Dolophine ran out with astonishing speed, and Jack found himself in front of a less than sympathetic Bureau of Prisons doctor, pleading for some relief from the sleepless agony of methadone withdrawal.

"Don't worry," the physician replied. "You are not a machine. You will fall asleep eventually."

Eventually, he did. After about a month, the obsessive cravings ceased, sleep mercifully returned, and his brain began to normalize.

The worst of the withdrawal over, Jack once again promised himself that he was going to put the drug life behind him. He also made that promise for the umpteenth time to his family, who made the ten-hour trek to Pennsylvania to visit.

Though he welcomed his family, the visits were painful. Jack simply couldn't look into his mother's eyes—mostly because they were always lowered. Her gaze directed at her feet, Phyllis, once the proud mother of a cute little boy, found it difficult to be pleased with her son any longer, especially in the visiting area of a correctional facility. When their eyes did meet, it was only for the briefest of moments before they both glanced away. Jack found it just as difficult to wrestle with the knowledge that he was the cause of the pain that was so evident in her tear-filled eyes. To add to his grief and guilt, Jack's daughter, now sixteen, dutifully accompanied her Grandma Phyllis to visit her estranged father, fueling her own feelings of loss and abandonment.

Jack was tired of his fragile existence and tired of a life with no meaning or purpose. With every incarceration, the receptions upon his release became smaller and smaller. There was no limousine waiting outside the prison gates, no Eddie, no Hankie, no one.

Jack returned home to his failing athletic-recruiting business, with no real hope for employment. His determination to stay drug-free ended just as quickly as his determination to get out of the drug-dealing life did. He immediately fell back into what he knew best, drug dealing. It was the only way he could support the drug habit that had come roaring back.

Still living the straight life on Boston's North Shore, Hank took pains to support Jack, even though he had been warned repeatedly that hanging out with old friends who were still using was a risk to his own sobriety. For Hank, loyalty and friendship trumped risk, even if things hadn't worked out so well the first time he came back to the East Side to hang with Jack.

Hank had now been sober for over two years and occasionally came back to town to meet with Ronnie, Kid Paz, and JD. JD and Kid Paz got clean only months after Hank. Ronnie, who had stopped using five years ago, was contemplating the priesthood.

During one of Hank's visits to Worcester, Jack invited him to the hotel that he was temporarily calling home to catch up and get acquainted with some "ladies of the night." Hank was single, and a little lonely, so this seemed like a good opportunity for female companionship. But when Hank arrived at Jack's hotel room, he found Jack and two hookers much more focused on a pile of cocaine than they were on any kind of companionship, purchased or otherwise.

"Well, Jackie boy," Hank said, "I don't think there's anything of any interest or good to me here."

Jack knew exactly what Hank meant. On a subconscious level, Jack realized there was nothing remotely good going on for any of the occupants of that hotel room that night.

"OK, Henry. Keep on the straight and narrow," Jack said as Hank walked out the door.

Hank left disappointed, not because his sexual appetite remained unsatisfied but because he had put himself in jeopardy once again. The only positive aspect of the evening was that his sobriety was still intact. Again, Hank had defied the odds. He had hit the lottery a second time.

Jack's troubles were far from over. In what seemed like the blink of an eye and with little recollection of the events that led to it, Jack again found himself in front of a judge. For Jack, it was nothing out of the ordinary. It was just the typical trouble that a drug addict creates for himself every day. This time, he was charged with possession with intent to distribute cocaine and marijuana. Truth be told, the amount Jack was carrying when he was arrested was no more than a couple of days' supply for a highly tolerant individual like himself.

From a global perspective, these were not the most serious of charges, and things could have been a lot worse. What did complicate matters, though, was the fact that Jack was still on special federal probation. This violation likely meant another stint in a federal correctional facility. It would not be the most severe punishment in the world, but it would mean a lengthy interruption in his drug use, complete with the terrors and pains of withdrawal in an extremely unsympathetic environment. It would not be fun, Jack knew from cold, hard experience. In his infinite wisdom, Jack decided to default on his scheduled court appearance. His new plan involved the woman he was seeing.

Jack's latest girlfriend was a former dancer for one of the original rappers—possibly LL Cool J, but that detail carried little importance. A crack pipe had put her dance career on the back burner, and this beautiful and extremely talented young woman was a victim of her desires, which brought her into Jack's orbit during one of his many visits to New York.

As smitten with his new love as he was desperate for a solution to his legal problems, Jack decided to move to the young woman's apartment in the Bronx under a new identity. There, as was always the case in his drug-skewed fantasies, Jack would live happily ever after.

That worked for a while, until Jack decided to visit a Massachusetts strip club one Sunday night and ended up in a mad chase through the woods, pursued and eventually captured by a contingent of state troopers. If it wasn't for the fact that somehow Jack had survived through all this misery, Jack's life could be a Shakespearean tragedy. But the most important part of his story is what came next.

CHAPTER THIRTY NINE

"Yo, asshole. You got a visitor."

In his first full day behind bars following the debacle in the woods with the state troopers, "asshole" was the most complimentary name Jack had been called. Led from the holding cell floor to the visitors' area, he expected to see his lawyer, or maybe if she wasn't still furious, his mother. Instead, his bleary vision registered the face and figure of one of his old partners in crime: Hank.

"Jesus, Jack. You look like shit."

Hank had a wicked sense of humor, and by nature was a hardcore ball buster. But it wasn't ball busting in this case; it was just an honest assessment.

Hank looked at his friend for a moment, his face registering pain.

"So what are you gonna do, Jack? Keep beating your head against the wall? I mean, you can do what you want, but I'm telling you, there's a different way to do this."

In the past, Jack wasn't able to hear any suggestion that involved giving up the life, let alone not getting high anymore. But this time, he was beat down flat. His whole being was in pain—and not just from the troopers' beating or the opiate withdrawal, which had already begun. He was exhausted and wounded, filthy and ashamed. He hated himself for sinking so low. He agonized over all of the people he'd betrayed, starting with his own mother. He'd tried everything he could think of to quiet his demons, except for the one thing he now knew he needed to do: stop using.

"You got to give it up," Hank said. "Go to a meeting. It works."

And eventually, Jack did, but it would be a while before his withdrawal symptoms eased and even longer before he was released.

Jack may have gone to college to be a "rocket scientist," but he definitely was not the first of the guys to learn that drugs are bad. Not even close. By this time Ronnie, Hankie, Kid Paz, Stevie, JD, Ship, and even Jack's oldest friend, Fudgy, had all stopped getting high and were starting to rebuild their lives. Hank had been clean for over five years now, and his life had begun to unfold in ways he never imagined possible. He had gone back to college, and this time he didn't wear a Worcester County House of Correction jumper. He took up jogging and soon found himself running in the Boston Marathon, an event he completed several times, often with Kid Paz, Ship, and JD, his old friends from the Street. Hank had once again reunited with his childhood sweetheart, Eileen— this time, without the drugs and alcohol.

Jack had always thought of himself as the smart one. His mother's refrain whenever Jack tried to rationalize his behavior, "You know what thought did," now made perfect sense. In fact, there is a saying in the rooms of recovery that alludes to the same misguided thought process. "Our best thinking got us to the seat where we are sitting in today."

Several of the other, less fortunate guys from the Street whose brains were held hostage to the allure of escapism never had the chance to grow up. They were dead before the age of thirty from drug overdoses. Miraculously, Jack and most of the crew had escaped that fate. Now it was Jack's turn to start down the path toward sobriety.

The first of those steps took place while Jack was still in jail. In a dingy meeting room at the Worcester County House of Correction, surrounded by fellow inmates, Jack raised his hand and in a quiet, hesitant voice, said, "My name is Jack, and I'm an addict."

Like that night in East Park so long ago, the stories began to pour out: the mistakes he'd made, the wrong paths he'd taken, his deep feelings of anger and inadequacy. This time, though, it wasn't as if Jack suddenly felt confident and comfortable. Instead, he felt unsteady, like an infant just rising to his feet for the first time. But along with the insecurity came a small, rising hope: the hope that if he could stay clean, he could have his life back again.

As the months added up, so did the twelve-step meetings. Eventually, Jack learned two important lessons. The first was that every time he'd found himself behind bars, getting high was the reason. The second and perhaps more important lesson was that the first place he needed to go when he got out of jail was not back to the old neighborhood and the people who used drugs but to a meeting. And then another.

During this long-overdue epiphany, Hank and Eileen were making plans to get married, and Hank wanted Jack to be part of that momentous occasion. There was just one small problem with that idea: Jack was still incarcerated. Not wanting to be left out of this significant event in Hank's life, Jack wrote the best man's speech from his jail cell. Hank was finally becoming that "good kid" he always believed himself to be, and Eileen was going to make sure of it.

Hank and Eileen were married on January 1, 1991, by the pastor of Mount Carmel Church and the onetime spiritual guardian of the recreation center where Hank once honed his basketball skills, Father Bafaro, who, having known Hank for a long time, didn't want to marry them. But despite his misgivings, he finally capitulated.

As fate and circumstances would dictate, however, it would not be long before Father Bafaro would find himself praying for them every day. Hank knew they needed it. Less than two years after their wedding, what should have been a cause for celebration, the joyous news of a pregnancy, was dampened by the shock of a breast cancer diagnosis. Eileen, who had been trying to have a child for years, learned that she was pregnant during a biopsy. It was like a blow to the head. An oncologist at Sloan Kettering suggested that Eileen might want to abort the fetus, which was less than two months old, but Hank and Eileen firmly told their doctor that was not going to happen. This decision would lead to an intimate patient-physician relationship with Dr. Robert M. Quinlan, as the unchartered journey of breast cancer treatment and pregnancy began.

Against all odds and nothing short of a miracle, their daughter, Ayla, was born on June 28, 1993. Two days later, when Hank and Eileen arrived at their Sewell Street home with their new baby girl, Hank asked Eileen, "What are we going to do with a baby?"

Both forty-two years old, they just looked at each other. Eileen shrugged her shoulders and gave Hank a comforting look. They had no idea.

After nearly three years, which included a second trip back to federal prison, Jack gained his freedom. When he left the Federal Correctional Institute in Danbury, Connecticut, there was no welcome party. No friends waited outside the gate. Jack had only the stark reality of heading back to the Street with a drug problem that wouldn't easily go away. The challenge of staying clean tested Jack constantly, but he realized that if his friends could do it, so could he.

Jack had a few more lessons to learn. A big one was the difference between abstinence and recovery. Abstinence means not using drugs or alcohol. Recovery means changing your life. You can have abstinence but without meaningful change; it is difficult to lead a meaningful new life. Substance Abuse and Mental Health Services Administration's new working definition of recovery, "a process of change through which individuals improve their health and wellness, live a self-directed life, and strive to reach their full potential," was relevant to the Shrewsbury Street crew.

Addiction runs deep, and it changes everything about a person—from the biological to the psychological and even the spiritual. Feelings of fear, shame, loneliness, boredom, and self-loathing fuel addiction. The guys from the Street needed to understand this and come to terms with it if they wanted to recover from addiction. In many cases, addicts and their families are lulled into thinking that since the addict has gone into treatment and been detoxified, life will get better and stay that way as long as the addict doesn't use. Unfortunately, recovery does not usually work that way.

The illness of addiction doesn't simply disappear when a person stops using. In fact, early recovery is often a time when the underlying issues really begin to flare up. And without drugs, those feelings can be extremely hard to manage. People don't become addicted or stay addicted because it's fun. Addictive substances work to numb pain, lubricate awkward and uncomfortable social situations, soothe bruised egos, and boost low self-esteem and self-confidence—and they do that job extremely well! To recover, an addict must learn to deal with all of those issues *without* misusing drugs.

In his book *Beautiful Boy*, which details his son's struggle with methamphetamine addiction, David Sheff talks about substance abuse as "what addicts do in response to their problem(s). If addicts fail to understand their problems, they might (and often times are) doomed to relapse." And there is a wonderful saying among recovering addicts that hits the target dead center: "If nothing changes, then nothing changes." This wisdom reveals a central truth of recovery, that abstaining from illicit drugs is where the process often *starts*. Abstinence can be very short-lived once the pressures and demands of everyday life (family, work, finances, and relationships) are back in the addict's face and he or she is forced to deal with them. In this situation, it's easy, and even common, to get knocked off the rails, to struggle until the discomfort becomes intolerable, and then reach for something to numb the pain. If addicts don't understand this process and don't do the work involved in treating their illness, the probability of relapse is much higher and the chance of recovery, much lower. Beating addiction isn't easy. In fact, it's probably the hardest thing an addict will ever have to do. But as Jack would discover, it's also the most worthwhile.

CHAPTER FORTY

I n an addict's recovery, a number of supportive people play criti- cal roles. One of those critical people was Jack's first sponsor, an old-time AA guy named Tommie. Early on in their relationship, Tommie gave Jack some simple words of advice.

"Jack, there are only two things you need to do to stay sober."

More than a little skeptical, Jack responded with sarcasm.

"Oh yeah, Tom? What's that?"

Tommie shot Jack his perpetual grin. "Don't drink, and get a job."

Jack was a drug addict, so the not drinking part was going to be easy. (Of course, not using drugs was another matter.) But getting a job? Tommie might as well have stabbed him in the heart. Jack had never really held a job in his entire life, unless he counted the summer job he had when he was sixteen, or bartending, which was now out of the question. Unfortunately, recovery from substance abuse often involves doing things that you think you don't want to do. And taking suggestions was not something Jack enjoyed. He had never been one who simply and easily did what he was told.

Jack had always been a talker, so he figured he could talk his way out of this predicament, too.

"Tommie, I'm going to meetings constantly. I'm working with you. That, I get. But how's a job supposed to keep me sober?"

Tommie's grin grew even broader. "Jack, my lad," he said, "at work, you will learn about a higher power, a power that will hold your life in his hands. A power can that feed you, starve you, and make it dark."

"You mean God? He's at work?"

"Not God, Jack. Your boss!"

After he finished laughing, Tommie explained. At work, Jack would get just what he needed: a chance to explore thoroughly his character defects. And if by chance he had trouble identifying them on his own, then his boss and his coworkers would eagerly and happily point them out. Jack would also learn to delay instant gratification, as he would have to wait for his paycheck to arrive.

It was hard to argue with Tom's logic, so Jack didn't. Instead, he went out to look for work. And soon enough, he found some.

Jack's first job, a part-time position at Adcare Hospital, was ideal. His task was a simple one—to drive a van full of patients to AA meetings. Jack had no one to supervise him; he actually was in charge of the patients, and that was fine with him. Work was not so bad after all; he was being paid to go to meetings that he needed to go to anyway. It seemed almost criminal, but then, he'd had no aversion to such behavior in the past.

The timing of the meetings—early evening—also proved to be a perfect fit. Jack had always used 6:00 p.m. as a psychological boundary. If he could hold off using drugs until then, he didn't have a problem. Therefore, 6:00 p.m. also served as the starting time for guilt-free intoxication. Of course, as the years progressed, that imaginary line moved earlier and earlier in the day until it disappeared completely. But evenings remained difficult, and driving patients to meetings helped Jack to stay focused during the most temptation-ridden time of the day.

Jack soon climbed the ladder at Adcare, one of New England's premier substance-abuse centers, moving from driving patients to meetings to admitting patients to the hospital, and then on to supervising the entire process. With the support and example of the Director of Admissions, Joanne, a spiritual centered Navy Nurse Practitioner; Jack flourished in the tension-filled environment of the admissions office, which, on many nights, resembled a packed hospital emergency room. The new position and its associated challenges played perfectly into Jack's strengths. His past association with many of the pharmacological aspects of substance abuse and his extensive personal history with addiction proved invaluable in the critical role of early assessment. In Jack's twenty-plus years of active using, he had encountered almost everything imaginable. He used his science and technology background to quickly analyze and solve problems that workers with more clinical skills and fewer technical ones found difficult to handle. In less than a year, Jack was named employee of the month and had his picture taken with the "higher power" that Tommie had talked about, in this case, the Adcare CEO.

Jack wasn't the only one who was making progress. In fact, he was one of the slower ones in the gang to get his life back together. By then, Hank had been clean and sober for over eight years. Ayla, the miracle baby girl, was now a mischievous three-year-old toddler and the center of Hank's life. Fearless, like her namesake from the Jean Auel's Earth's Children series, Hank taught Ayla how to dig in the mud and catch frogs in their backyard on Sewell Pond.

Fudgy got clean in Worcester's City Detox. Only a bit more upscale than the Dorchester Detox that Hank went to, it still featured delousing, paper pants, and slippers. Hank and Fudgy could easily have been Hazelden Betty Ford Foundation material clinically, but their socioeconomic status confined them to less comfortable surroundings. Still, despite the lack of opulence in their rehabs of choice, they survived.

Fudgy rebuilt his theatrical skills and once again hit the stage in Boston and beyond, this time with great success. He landed some cameo appearances on the big screen and had a small recurring role on the TV series *Law and Order*. Go figure. One of the habits that Fudgy did not give up was his penchant for marriage. During the time that Jack was in jail, Fudgy got hitched, fathered a beautiful baby girl, and, as rumor had it, had another future wife waiting in the wings.

Ship had given up the life, too. Somehow, he had made it into detox and recovery, due in large part, as he reluctantly admits, to shotguns and lacking the necessary permits to possess them.

Perhaps no one's transformation was greater than Ronnie D's. Ronnie was the first to give up the drugs, quit his rock-and-roll band and make plans to enter into the priesthood. Remarkably, those plans were interrupted by love and eventually marriage. Ronnie met and fell head over heels with an East Side woman whose quiet faith and inspiration truly created a match made in heaven.

One by one, all of the guys from the Street were on a path to turn their lives around, though some of the precipitants may have been different. Legal issues, forced abstinence, incarceration, and losing jobs, families, and children—whatever the reason, it was better than the alternative: death.

CHAPTER FORTY ONE

J D's relapse after nearly a year in formal treatment left him with few options beyond going it on his own. Determined to stay clean, he followed the advice of his friend Eunice and immersed himself in Narcotics Anonymous and Alcoholics Anonymous meetings. He went to meetings daily and often more than once a day and began the difficult journey of recovery. He learned important differences between sobriety, or merely abstaining from alcohol and drugs, and recovery, or life change. He began to understand his dependence on drugs and alcohol at a much deeper level and to process the pain he had been running from all of his life. He also came to appreciate the value of treatment and a support network.

Not surprisingly, the core of JD's support group included many old friends from the East Side who were also making their journey to recovery. Hank, Ship, Kid Paz, Ronnie, Jack, and Fudgy could always find something to laugh about, even in times of despair. This proved to be therapeutic—despite the fact that they were often laughing about their own foibles.

What these men discovered was the amazing power of friend-ships that had lasted for decades. They knew each other well, and it was hard to bullshit or fake it when they struggled. They "got it." They had all been through the hell of addiction, and they under-stood how hard it was to break free. Because of this, they were all willing to come at any time of day or night to listen, to be there, and to provide support in any way, from a cup of coffee and an open ear to a lift to and from meetings and everything in between. At times, they literally held one another up. They truly were brothers-in-arms.

For the guys from the Street, recovery often meant more than go-ing to meetings together. Exercise is one of the world's best mental-health drugs, and many of the guys got together for regular doses. Some, like JD and Hank, took up running. Some took their recovery to the field of dreams and joined a "sober softball" league. Some played tennis, hit the gym, or swam. It was a relaxed, no-pressure scenario—a phone call or a verbal agreement that they would meet at a certain time and place, and whoever showed up would join in. The benefits of physical activity, from reducing stress to generally improving physical health, helped them stay clean.

Of course, the boys had grown up eating a variety of great eth-nic foods and hanging at East Side restaurants like the La Scala and Paul Mac's. Given that, it was no surprise that eating played a role in their recovery, as well. They met on a regular basis for breakfast, lunch, or dinner (or all three meals on some days), fol-lowed by a morning, noon, or evening AA or NA meeting.

As JD's recovery progressed, his mind began to clear, and his work ethic and natural curiosity returned. Working in his family's restaurant business didn't interest or stimulate him—but helping other addicts did. He volunteered at Doctor's Hospital (later to become AdCare Hospital), a drug/alcohol treatment facility in Worcester, and at the Worcester Crisis Center to learn some clini-cal skills to fuse with his personal recovery experience. While vol-unteering at Doctor's Hospital, he met Dr. Patrice Muchowski, the facility's clinical vice president, who offered him his first real job in the field of drug rehabilitation treatment. For nearly thirty years since then, she has remained a mentor, supporter, and friend.

To enhance his clinical skills, JD also began taking college courses, which opened up the possibilities of a career in chemical dependency treatment. The college experience proved utterly revelatory. JD suddenly realized that he was intelligent and motivated, and for the first time in his formal schooling experience, he enjoyed learning. As his goal of helping others with chemical dependency became clearer, so did his academic objectives. He worked, studied, and lived within the world of chemical dependency treatment and recovery, which not only prepared him to help others, but strengthened his own support network and fortified his own recovery.

Eventually, after years of sobriety, JD's quest for knowledge and a respectable and meaningful career led him to Worcester State University for a bachelor of science degree in psychology, then to the University of Connecticut for an master's degree in social work, and ultimately to Boston University, where he earned a dual PhD in the disciplines of social work and sociology.

He worked at a variety of social service agencies and organizations as an advocate/educator, progressing from volunteer to clinician to supervisor to director. Along the way, he taught courses in human services at several local colleges with the ambition of teaching full-time while doing other addiction-related work as an adjunct. Eventually, after much hard work, he landed a full-time position as a faculty member at Anna Maria College, a small Catholic college in Paxton, Massachusetts. He continues to work with addicts in treatment programs and is in private practice.

JD's pursuit of a career in recovery changed his family life, as well. Early in his journey, he met and fell in love with his wife, Sherri, who was then working a summer job at Doctor's Hospital before attending graduate school at Rutgers University. Over the course of nearly three decades, they have been spouses, partners, and friends; they have raised their daughter, Gianna, and faced life's challenges together. Sherri, a successful self-employed therapist, is JD's main source of support and inspiration, the foundation of his achievements, and his greatest champion. She knows him better than anyone else and was instrumental in helping JD learn what it is truly to feel love. During their years together, Sherri has also come to know and love all of JD's friends. It was at Sherri's urging that JD decided to join forces with Hank and Jack to write this story. For her unwavering love and support, he is eternally grateful.

Throughout his thirty years in recovery, JD has been an advocate, a teacher, an administrator, and always a student in the world of chemical dependency treatment and education. As a result, he has gone from being a wounded and lost little boy in search of anything to numb his pain to a sober, confident, and respectable man. Through many years of therapy and hard work in recovery, guided by a belief and connection to a higher power, he has been able to develop a loving relationship first and foremost with himself, as well as with the family, friends, and supporters who have made his life rich and rewarding.

One of the most valuable lessons JD learned about chemical dependency treatment and recovery came from a great therapist, Dr. Brian Litzenberger, who said, "Love and compassion are what help people heal." JD's desire to learn and help educate others, especially those affected by chemical dependency, bolstered by his desire and commitment to give back what was so freely given to him, is what fuels and energizes him to be a part of the change he wishes to see and to help make the world a better place.

It's hard for JD to imagine going through the biological, psychological, and spiritual period of "coming to terms" with addiction alone, without the comfort, understanding, and support of his oldest friends, his colleagues, his wife, his family, and all of those he has met in the halls of recovery over the decades. Without the power of love, without the strength of numbers, he might not have won his battle. He will never forget those who lost theirs.

"A bug crawls across the paper, let it be, we need all the readers we can get."

Unknown

So what is the takeaway message from this story? Do people really just age out of dependency, as many of the large epidemiological studies suggest? Is addiction a chronic and progressive disease? Whatever the answer, the authors and the other people in this story present a compelling argument for the value of lifelong participation in recovery communities. The support and fellowship that such communities provide is an important element of long-term recovery. As Scott Peck stated in The Road Less Traveled, *"Life is difficult." The more people we have around us to help carry us through the complicated and trying times, the better our chances for positive outcomes.*

Is there evidence to support this belief? We think so. Recovery communities and support groups are motivational and celebratory of the intention to delay gratification (response flexibility). These groups remind their members not to pursue autonomy, achievement, acquisition, and authority apart from integrity or wholeness. Immersion in community and fellowship reinforces the brain's executive functions in the areas of morality, empathy, and insight.

Conditioned impulses woven into the fabric of experience and memory are difficult to eliminate. To do so requires a drastic remodeling of the environment, nourishment, and lifestyle that ushered those conditioned impulses into being. Repeated reinforcement and practice can help change new mental states into enduring personality traits and complete the integration process necessary for a successful recovery. Peer support unconsciously strengthens our fear modulation and gives us the ability to become vocationally mature. As Rachel Dawes, Bruce Wayne's childhood friend says in Batman Begins, *"It's not who you are underneath, it's what you do that defines you."*

CHAPTER FORTY TWO

It wasn't long before Ayla was playing in her first basketball game. When she made her first jump shot, Hank and Eileen both leaped for joy. Hank was so proud that he was already envisioning Ayla playing basketball for UConn—with a full scholarship to boot. After the game, Ayla told Hank that she did not plan to play next year; she wanted to be a cheerleader instead. So much for Hank's plan of calling Dee Rowe and exclaiming that his one-time "best camper" had a potential All-American daughter as a future recruit.

For Jack, the days, months, and years without using passed with far fewer trials and tribulations than his days of active addiction had. But even a life of sobriety comes with its share of troubles, and those troubles can be challenging to sobriety. Jack's first major obstacle to his recovery came when his first girlfriend since getting sober dumped him for another guy.

Breakups are always painful, but they are particularly dangerous to a recovering addict. And given the tenuous nature of early recovery, a time when people are struggling to find their place in the world, "quick fix" relationships—and the quick dissolution of them—are not uncommon. In the twelve-step fellowships of Al-Anon, AA, and its fledgling offshoot, NA, there have evolved a number of mnemonic devices to simplify or characterize ideals or obstacles commonly encountered during recovery. One such mnemonic device is RELATIONSHIP, which is an acronym for Really Exciting Love Affair Turns Into Outrageous Nightmare, Sobriety Hangs In Peril. Who had the time and perseverance to create these things, Jack had no idea, but he knew that he needed help.

As Jack paced the floor of his Chilmark Street apartment, his head overloaded with lyrics of Top 40 breakup songs, a web of inadequacy, abandonment, anger, jealousy, and shame hung over him. The elements were so tangled that he could not separate them into rational thought. It was as bad as any dope sickness, and the obsession, the unanswered questions, all heightened his misery. Since a return of the object of his affection wasn't likely, Jack became more than a little worried that he might turn to another, more deadly, source of relief.

It was in this darkness and despair that the unlikely discovery of the power of self-responsibility became apparent. Jack attended a twelve-step meeting that focused on step ten: Continued to take personal inventory, and when we were wrong, promptly admitted it.

For Jack, that simple sentence, delivered at a moment of struggle, proved unbelievably powerful. If he blamed the circumstances of his life on others—a girlfriend, a boss, a relative, or a colleague—he was helpless to change his situation. But if he accepted personal responsibility for the choices that had led him to that situation, he could make better choices in the future, and change was possible.

It was a remarkable epiphany: the sudden realization that Jack had placed himself in this predicament and he could get himself out of it. A feeling of relief washed over him and magically replaced the anxiety and obsession that had penetrated his every thought. It was not a blinding white light or a burning bush pronouncing the presence of God, but rather, it was a quiet understanding of the utility of integrating the principles of the twelve steps into his life. Jack firmly came to believe that practicing these guidelines equips one with the ability to navigate the ocean of unfortunate circumstances that life can present.

Outside the twelve-step program, Jack also discovered the value of alternative strategies, such as mindfulness meditation, Reiki, and the Buddhist philosophy that centers around the cultivation of loving-kindness. These centering exercises proved immensely helpful, as well. Jack's faith and adherence to integrating these universal principles slowly began to dominate his thinking. This, in turn, began to reshape his character.

Of course, not every addiction story has a happy ending. For nearly twenty years, Stevie the Sailor's life was a downward spiral of addiction, complete with all its by-products: jail, HIV, broken relationships, and unfulfilled dreams. It seemed like he could never catch a break and that he always fell short in life. Then a miracle happened, and he suddenly got clean and sober. No one but Stevie knew why he decided to change. He might have grown tired of the monotony of life behind bars. He might have experienced one devastating loss too many. Noticing the effect of a clean lifestyle on his friends might have prodded him in that direction. But what is known is that Stevie was able to see things differently, and he developed not only hope but a desire to change.

His opportunity came upon his release from a jail stint. The conditions of his release required that he attend self-help meetings, such as AA and NA. Now, anyone can attend a meeting, but attending them and working the program for all it's worth are two different things. But Stevie had something on his side: friendship.

At those meetings, he reconnected with friends from the East Side who welcomed him in as only old friends can. In their stories of recovery, he saw hope. He had been given another chance at life, and he grabbed on with all he had.

In the years that followed, Jack, JD, and the other friends from the Street watched Stevie develop into a strong, loving, and compassionate man who enjoyed everything that life had to offer. He formed a committed relationship with a woman he met in recovery, and they shared each day of their new lives. For the first time, Stevie discovered the joy of personal autonomy. He had his own apartment, a place to call home. He bought his first car and made a decent living at a job he enjoyed. All seemed right in his world. He ate, drank, and slept recovery, becoming a very active member of NA and AA and helping countless other lost individuals to find their way. He shared the principle of recovery with anyone willing to listen—and some who were not willing to listen, too. He was determined to help others who were struggling with addiction, and he used his own recovery as a teaching aid.

In the halls of recovery meetings, it is often remarked that it takes five years to get your marbles back, and ten years to learn how to use them. In Stevie's case, there wasn't enough time. For a recovering addict, coping with change can be deadly. When Stevie's girlfriend ended their long-term relationship, he collapsed. Lost, hurt, angry, and paralyzed by grief, he reached a point where the simple joys of life couldn't provide enough distraction from his pain. His East Side friends tried as hard as they could to support him, but eventually he succumbed to his addiction and began using opiates again.

As quick and impressive as his initial progress in recovery had been, the same was true of his rapid descent once he turned back to heroin. For six months or more, he holed up in his apartment, getting high in isolation, or from time to time joining up with other lost souls to scam cash and score drugs. As his isolation and loneliness increased, they only contributed to his need for intoxication. Eventually, Stevie cut off all contact with his friends in recovery, refusing to respond to any form of contact, from phone messages to knocks on the door.

The inevitable came in the form of a heroin overdose, a phenomenon all too common in the recovery community. But in Stevie's case, it resulted not in death but in serious brain damage, from which he never recovered. Stevie lived out his remaining two years in a paralyzed state, unable to function or communicate, at a rest home for the indigent. Finally, when even the machines could not keep him alive any longer, he passed away. Gone was that young boy with the bright gleam in his eyes and the win-you-over smile. Gone was the poster boy for recovery, who thrived on helping other lost souls. Gone was another one of the East Side brothers, a victim of his addiction, silenced in his pain.

CHAPTER FORTY THREE

After an hour of raucous tales and unrestrained laughter, the Passionist priest paused for a moment of solemn reflection. He leveled a serious gaze at what was once a murderers' row of miscreants and unreformed addicts. Hank, JD, Ronnie, Kid Paz, Jack, Joey S., Ship, Fudgy, and a host of other survivors from the Shrewsbury Street kids' battle with addiction had regaled the priests at a neighboring retreat center with their lurid tales of drugs and debauchery. In the quiet that followed, Father John spoke with sincerity and authority.

"You know, these stories about your mischievous youth are more than just that. Some of your friends died, but you survived. It truly is a miracle of transformation. Nothing less."

Suddenly, the room grew silent. Despite the stories and the laughter, the occasion was a solemn one, a prayer meeting for Hank's wife, Eileen, whose cancer, which had once been in remission, had now returned. Hank invited his closest friends, all in recovery and all from the Street, to join him in prayer for Eileen. He knew his friends weren't particularly religious. In fact, many of them were skeptics, to say the least. Some even described themselves as "recovering Catholics," but to Hank's surprise, they eagerly accepted his invitation and showed up.

For the boys from the Street, loyalty, once the victim of addiction, was now a call to arms for a friend. But that was not the only reason they were there. Within this group of friends, Eileen, or Ike as she was fondly known, was universally regarded as a miracle. Hank and Eileen had known each other since childhood. They had dated during the onset of his addiction and reunited after Hank "washed his brains out in salt water" in Rockport. Ike's kindness, compassion, faith, and empathy were legendary, and she provided Hank a strong foundation to build on. Her resiliency as a human being was exemplified not only by her persistence in building a successful and fashionable women's clothing store, but by her undying faith in overcoming the incredible odds of having her first child while undergoing intensive breast cancer treatment at the age of forty-two.

As the old friends gathered that evening, Ike was in their hearts. And with their prayers and support, she would eventually recover. Today, Hank is a dedicated father of an accomplished young woman, now in her third year of college, and husband to an amazing and courageous cancer survivor. Hank quietly and unassumingly steadies the household and supports the family business in the face of repeated medical obstacles, and he is a staunch recovery advocate.

Hank also owes much of his recovery to his late mother, Antoinette (Toni). She and Hank had a special relationship, one that years of addiction and heartache could not destroy. Constantly present—even when she was furious with her son—was the unconditional love that so often typifies the bond between a mother and her child, regardless of the obstacles or adversity. Always the optimist, Hank's wife looks at life through rose-colored glasses and regards Hank as her hero, despite his struggles.

In the gang's stories of recovery, an inescapable message reverberates, underscoring the importance of relationships in maintaining sobriety. While Stevie the Sailor's failed relationship may have been a significant factor in his losing battle against addiction, the support of strong women, such as Ike and Toni, helped many of the boys from the Street win their battles.

As human beings, we cherish our individuality, yet we live in constant relationship with other people, and they play a part in regulating our emotional and social behavior. Although this interdependence is a reality of our existence, scientists are just beginning to understand that we have evolved as social creatures with interwoven minds and bodies. The exploration of interpersonal neurobiology—how the brain develops through social interaction—offers exciting insights into mental health. Science is in the early stages of understanding brain development, how that development can become disordered, and how healing interaction can trigger changes in our brains that help them to grow in positive ways and heal suffering.

Sometimes the conditions for healing are not present. But when one door closes, another one opens—or at least that's how the saying goes in the halls of recovery. After the ending of Jack's first major sober relationship, the door that opened for him took the form of a state social worker named Barbara. Barbara was an Al-Anoner, one whose life had been dramatically impacted by an alcoholic relative.

There is an old riddle about the difference between AA and Al-Anon: How do you know if you are at an AA meeting or an Al-Anon meeting?

The answer: At an AA meeting, if someone spills a coffee, everyone gets up, points at the spilled coffee, and asks, "Who did that?"

At an Al-Anon meeting, if someone spills a coffee, everyone gets up, cleans it up, and says, "I'm sorry."

While at dysfunctional extremes, these anecdotes describe two types of people: the takers and the givers. Jack and Barbara were a prime example of the theory of magnetism: opposites attract. Jack was self-centered. Barbara was self-sacrificing. Jack was a drug addict. Barbara was a fledgling Mother Teresa in an overworked department of social services. It was a match that could only have been made by divine intervention. For Jack, Barbara was close to the second coming; she provided all of the attention and support he needed to move through the next phase of his recovery. Unlike many matches made in heaven, this match didn't last forever, which in retrospect is not surprising. But the support Jack received from Barbara helped him on his road to recovery, and for that he remains eternally grateful.

Later, Jack was lucky enough to hit the lottery a second time. This time, it was in the form of an Adcare Hospital human resource generalist, the mother of three wonderful young adults, a yoga instructor and Reiki master named Nina. Her kindness and understanding set the bar for excellence and was a constant example for Jack of just how rewarding it is to be of service to others. Their romance started accidentally at the tennis courts in Worcester's Lake Park on a summer Sunday morning. Jack and Nina were playing tennis on different courts, and Nina was learning the basics with the help of one of Jack's friends. Fortuitously for Jack, his friend was not a patient teacher, and he asked Jack to come over and help. The rest is history.

Kid Paz, another one of the guys from the Street, might minimize the influence his wife has had on his longevity in recovery, but he would never deny the importance of family. Fudgy was also an outlier—but only in the number of strong, supportive women he married. True to the Hollywood tradition of changing wives as often as one would change characters, Fudgy married six times, possibly seven; it was hard for even his close friends to keep track. Unbelievably, five or six of the aforementioned marriages took place after Fudgy got clean and sober. It is often said that many addicts exchange one addiction for another. For Fudgy, weddings replaced opiates.

Thankfully, Fudgy did have the good sense—or maybe the good fortune—to choose women who were either therapists or had been in recovery even longer than he had. The only inexplicable part was the mental status of those love-struck brides who, superficially at least, displayed all of the characteristics of highly functioning, rational human beings until that walk to the altar. This mysterious condition gives credence to an unknown author's definition of love as "a wildly misunderstood although highly desirable malfunction of the heart, which weakens the brain, causes the eyes to sparkle, cheeks to glow, blood pressure to rise, and the lips to pucker."

Completing the absurdity was the fact that Hank was the best man at several of these not-so-solemn occasions. Hank has always reveled in busting balls, one of his few bedrock traits that will likely never change. As he sat at the head table, Fudgy never knew what Hank was going to say when he gave the toast, and Hank was not above acting as a roast emcee as he detailed the trials and tribulations of each of Fudgy's previous peccadilloes, while hoisting a glass of sparkling white-grape juice. After twenty years, Fudgy eventually smartened up, marrying for the second and last time Shelia, a woman from the AA program who was thoroughly dedicated to him. Sheila remained faithfully by his side until he was taken prematurely by liver cancer. Fudgy became the second one of the gang to die from natural causes—if there is anything natural about liver cancer—and he joined Leo the Crusher to live on solely in our memories.

There was only one true exception to the strong woman theory, and that exception was Joey S, who found salvation in avian form. After getting sober, he began to raise racing pigeons, and his love for them has filled his heart with joy. Joey is now regarded as one of the premier pigeon racers on the East Coast, and his reputation in the pigeon-racing community is growing internationally, or at least that is how he tells it.

In addition to the luck of the draw that placed each of them with loving, understanding, dedicated, and loyal Al-Anon-worthy mates, the strength of simple (and rediscovered) values played a significant role in keeping the guys from the Street drug- and alcohol-free—and just as important, happy. The authors believe that the few secrets of happiness are simple ones, and that they are hidden within each of us, just waiting to be found. The real challenge, they think, is to come to that realization.

It is little coincidence that many of the old gang from the East Side have dedicated part of their lives to helping addicts recover, in both formal and informal settings. Jack, JD, Hank, and Ronnie spent many evenings in Hank's basement family room, contemplating the creation of a recovery community, and each in his own way has done just that. Hank and Ronnie selflessly poured their hearts into AA and NA, doing all they could to shepherd fellow addicts into recovery. Jack, with JD's help, worked to found a Recovery Center, located in a bucolic, rural area of central Massachusetts not far from the old Shrewsbury Street neighborhood.

It's interesting that, after years of abusing drugs, chronicling the sober life presents a challenge. Absent are the incidents of heightened tension, dangerous pursuits, devastating outcomes, and the front-page headlines that bring instant notoriety to the user and toxic shame to the family. Hustling for money, searching for drugs, waking up sick, begging for the next fix, and spending time in jail have been replaced by the more mundane activities of daily living: spending time with family, hanging out with friends, exercising, occasionally going on vacation, and, way too frequently, going to work. These everyday endeavors don't make the headlines or get passed on in oral lore, but they provide nourishment in a way that notoriety cannot.

In the end, the Passionist priest was right. This is a story of miracles. Why were Hank, Jack, JD, Kid Paz, Joey S., and others spared when Stevie the Sailor, JD's brother, Tom, Tony B., Dumbo, Leo, and many like them lost along the way? That question will likely go unanswered, but what the lucky ones from the Street do know is that they have been blessed with friends and family with whom to share the good, the bad, and the ugly for close to fifty years. Jack, JD, and Hank have no monopoly on the memories or experiences that are shared by many who have gone through life's struggles and triumphed. Together, they survived years of personal battles, and to their surprise, they emerged as the hardworking, law-abiding ham-and-eggers they once despised. That, they all agree, is a miracle.

WHERE THEY ARE NOW

At the time of this book's publication, **Hank** has been in recovery for over thirty years. An avid runner in his younger days, he ran in and finished several Boston Marathons, often with his recovery compatriots, JD, Fudgy, and Ship at his side. A regular at twelve-step meetings, Hank imparts a brutally honest message to anyone who will listen and has a group of disciples who espouse the traditional hard line that no medication is good medication. Despite that hard line, you will always find Hank in the forefront of trying to help anyone get clean. His approach may bring a few tears to the less than sturdy, but his willingness to give has helped many people on their roads to recovery. Hank still lives on Sewell Pond, not far from the old neighborhood, and enjoys frequent visits from his daughter, Ayla, who to this day remains Hank's pride and joy. His soul mate, Eileen, died peacefully in her sleep in May 2015, after her sixth bout with cancer. It was the inescapable ending of a love affair that really began in 1950. That year, two notable events took place. The first was on December 17, the day Eileen was born in Worcester City Hospital. The second was when Eileen came face-to-face with the person who would be her true love, Hank, born just one day before in the same hospital.

Over the years, Eileen gave of herself freely and worked tirelessly at several charity events, her favorite event was Hope Lodge.

At one such event, Eileen said, "As a five-time cancer survivor over a span of twenty-one years, I can honestly say that I know what got me here: God, my husband, my daughter, family and friends, incredible doctors, and a great support system. I also believe in the power of prayer. One must have a strong faith and a positive attitude. They can knock you down; don't let them knock you out."

These are wonderful words to remember and live by for everyone who struggles with life's inevitable obstacles, and they are especially relevant to this story and to those who suffer from the disease of addiction.

With the birth of his daughter, Isabella, **Ship** found his life's purpose. Isabella was born in Italy, where Ship and his wife, Mary Beth, who typified the strong, supportive woman mentioned earlier, were living as part of her work assignment with a large American retail company. Ship, to this day, remains an overly indulgent parent. Whether it's lacrosse, basketball, or softball, Ship is every coach's nightmare. Yet in the largest of ways, Ship's life has turned around. No longer a menace to society, he is now an expert on mold remediation—and if you can believe his patter, a new age guru on healthy eating, as well. His life resembles a replay of *Father Knows Best*, with a high-tech update. His Twitter feed and text messages consist of an endless stream of images depicting Isabella's adventures: hiking past a waterfall, shooting hoops, and clobbering an opponent over the head in lacrosse. Ship just celebrated his thirty years of sobriety this year.

Since earning a dual PhD in sociology and social work, **JD** has worked for several years as a college professor, helping students achieve academically and helping them manage their everyday challenges. He remains especially sensitive to those who struggle with self-doubt and appear to have a penchant for escaping through the use of drugs or alcohol. In conjunction with his work in academia, he has worked for his entire sober career in the field of addiction as a clinician, advocate, consultant, and educator, both teaching about addiction and sitting on boards and committees to help raise awareness around addiction. Recovery has afforded him the capacity to be a father to his sixteen-year-old daughter, Gianna, and a sober and loving husband to his partner and wife of nearly thirty years, Sherri. He is an active and involved member of the recovery community and takes every opportunity to share his experience, strength, and hope with others struggling with addiction. He also has a private clinical and consulting practice, helping individuals, families, and organizations affected by addiction to find their way to recovery. Like Hank, and Ship, JD has celebrated his thirty-year anniversary.

Fudgy, aka Michael, the East Side's most dynamic contribution to the entertainment world, never stopped trying to escape reality. After getting clean, he did so by bringing entertainment to audiences in Boston's theater district and in living rooms across America. Fudgy is no longer with us; he died of liver cancer before he could celebrate his twenty-fifth year of recovery, but his memory lives on at Michael's House, the main living area at the Recovery Center founded by his friends. Michael's House is a modern residence that offers comfort and hope to those afflicted with addiction and the precursor to Recovery Centers of America's Westminster facility, a recovery community designed to fundamentally transform addiction treatment and the lives of those that suffer from it. Memories of Michael still bring a smile to his old friends' faces.

Kid Paz, aka Robbie, is a regional school administrator, the father of two accomplished young men in college, and a political activist. Working with Jack and fellow activist Hector Reyes, Kid Paz played an instrumental role in establishing the Hector Reyes House, the first culturally sensitive residential facility for addicts in central Massachusetts. His continued efforts to "pay it forward," included behind-the-scenes work that secured a major grant to help Worcester reduce the high number of deaths of residents from opiate overdose and helped to overcome the initial skepticism among city officials. He recruited his old pals Jack and JD, which, to say the least, was a strange turn of events and a far cry from their mischievous days on Shrewsbury Street and created a Professionals in Recovery Board to help with the grant implementation and future initiatives. Among their accomplishments were; first time collaborations between police, treatment providers, and the substance misuse population, a conference that brought together emergency room providers to discuss the obstacles indigenous to treating the substance abuse population in the ER and the establishment of the city's first Recovery Walk. Kid Paz joined his cohorts Hank, JD, and Ship in celebrating thirty years of recovery this past year.

Joey S. is an OSHA-certified safety officer and a construction supervisor for a national bridging and shoring company. Still single, he has found love with his pigeons and a side career as an internationally renowned pigeon racer. He travels the country constantly, whether to oversee the safety of a million-dollar shoring project or to put his racing birds to the test in competition. Once a source of shame and embarrassment to his family, Joey now is a source of great joy. He dutifully provides comfort, companionship, and the occasional "pick up your clothes" or "when are you going to grow up" admonition from his mom in the wake of the recent loss of his father Freddie. Before his death, Joe's dad offered a broad smile whenever his prodigal son's name was mentioned. The camaraderie and closeness between father and son was evident in their jocular banter whenever they gathered with the guys from the Street.

Ronnie D. long ago gave up the rock-and-roll life for a career in the aerospace industry. He is the perfect illustration of the marriage between religion and spirituality, which many twelve-steppers consider mutually exclusive entities. Ronnie continues to lead prayer meetings and sing at local churches. To those who join him, his quiet, unassuming manner reflects the endless capacity of the human spirit to triumph. A talented craftsman, not only with a guitar but also with wood, Ronnie recently designed and built his own home. He still enjoys playing, writing, and producing music.

His performances and self-produced CDs are often spiritual in nature and capture the essence of his beliefs—not to mention that they are quite good. He shares a happy retirement with his wife, Bonnie, a woman of great faith and empathy. Ronnie recently celebrated his thirty-fourth year of sobriety.

After nearly twenty years of working at Adcare Hospital, the place where he was reborn, **Jack** realized a dream that had its genesis during hours of conversation with Ronnie, JD, and Hank. Jack founded a Recovery Center with the support from his colleague and good friend James M and his lifelong recovery friends. Now, with the opportunity to turn a onetime conference center and wedding destination into a recovery campus, Jack is collaborating with Recovery Centers of America to establish what he believes will be a life altering recovery community and place of refuge located the idyllic confines of Westminster, MA. Predicated on the belief that healing through Compassion, Understanding, Respect, and Empathy, represent a true CURE to lasting transformation.

Jack's goal is to be content with the comfort and importance of family and to assist others with their journey of discovery. He endeavors to appreciate the gift life has given him and to remember the simple joys of spending time with his daughter, Gina Marie, son-in-law, Tom, his four grandchildren, Brittany, Giana, Jake and Chase, and Nina's three young adults, Paola, Giovanni, and Andrea Daniela.

Jack is continually reminded of the meaning of selflessness from his soul mate, the yoga and Reiki practitioner, whose spiritual wisdom provides him a refuge from his occasional lapses in thinking; and the true meaning of unconditional love from their therapy dogs, Ollie, and the newest addition to the family, Samantha, a golden retriever puppy who constantly reminds the household of the joys of playfulness.

Once a dope fiend, a convicted felon, and an organized crime figure, Jack's biggest consternation now is the awkward feeling he gets when asking for the senior discount at the movie theater.